Study Guide

Biology
for CSEC®

Richard Fosbery
Charmaine Foster
Allison Peart

OXFORD
UNIVERSITY PRESS

Great Clarendon Street, Oxford, OX2 6DP, United Kingdom

Oxford University Press is a department of the University of Oxford. It furthers the University's objective of excellence in research, scholarship, and education by publishing worldwide. Oxford is a registered trade mark of Oxford University Press in the UK and in certain other countries

First published by Nelson Thornes Ltd in 2013
This edition published by Oxford University Press in 2014

British Library Cataloguing in Publication Data
Data available

978-1-4085-2242-4

12

Printed in Great Britain by CPI Group (UK) Ltd., Croydon CR0 4YY

Acknowledgements

Cover photograph: Mark Lyndersay, Lyndersay Digital, Trinidad
www.lyndersaydigital.com
Illustrations include artwork drawn by Barking Dog Art, GreenGate Publishing Services and Wearset
Page make-up: GreenGate Publishing Services

Thanks are due to Charmaine Foster and Allison Peart for their contributions in the development of this book.

Although we have made every effort to trace and contact all copyright holders before publication this has not been possible in all cases. If notified, the publisher will rectify any errors or omissions at the earliest opportunity.

The manufacturer's authorised representative in the EU for product safety is Oxford University Press España S.A. of El Parque Empresarial San Fernando de Henares, Avenida de Castilla, 2 – 28830 Madrid (www.oup.es/en or product.safety@oup.com).
OUP España S.A. also acts as importer into Spain of products made by the manufacturer.

Contents

Contents

This Study Guide has been developed exclusively with the Caribbean Examinations Council (CXC®) to be used as an additional resource by candidates, both in and out of school, following the Caribbean Secondary Education Certificate (CSEC®) programme.

It has been prepared by a team with expertise in the CSEC® syllabus, teaching and examination. The contents are designed to support learning by providing tools to help you achieve your best in Biology and the features included make it easier for you to master the key concepts and requirements of the syllabus. *Do remember to refer to your syllabus for full guidance on the course requirements and examination format!*

Inside this Study Guide is an interactive CD which includes electronic activities to assist you in developing good examination techniques:

- **On Your Marks** activities provide sample examination-style short answer and essay type questions, with example candidate answers and feedback from an examiner to show where answers could be improved. These activities will build your understanding, skill level and confidence in answering examination questions.

- **Test Yourself** activities are specifically designed to provide experience of multiple-choice examination questions and helpful feedback will refer you to sections inside the study guide so that you can revise problem areas.

This unique combination of focused syllabus content and interactive examination practice will provide you with invaluable support to help you reach your full potential in CSEC® Biology.

We have included lots of hints, explanations and suggestions in each of the sections. There are also two sections at the beginning that are designed to help you to use this book to best advantage and revise thoroughly and effectively. There are three sections at the back that give you advice on how to answer the questions in Paper 1 and Paper 2.

As you work through your CSEC® Biology course, read through any notes that you take during your lessons. While doing this you should read your textbook, this study guide and any other relevant information you can find. For example, when you study the sections on the human impact on the environment, disease, and variation and selection you may find that newspapers and leaflets from doctors and pharmacies have useful information. The internet is also a good source of up to date information.

When you finish a topic, answer the summary questions at the end of each section. You will notice that many of these start by asking for definitions of the terms relevant to each topic. This is to prompt you to use the glossary which is on the CD. Try all the exam-style questions that are at the end of each Unit. Use the answers, which are also on the CD, to check your answers. Do not look at the answers until you have tried all the questions for each section. The questions at the end of each unit only test the topics in that unit. In the examination you will find that each question may test more than one unit.

Try all of our suggestions about how to revise. These will help you to make your own revision notes that you can use in the weeks before the exams.

How to learn 1

On completion of this topic you should know how to:

- make learning and revision notes
- make and use a glossary of biological terms
- construct tables to compare structures and processes
- make biological diagrams.

STUDY FOCUS

Know your syllabus. It sounds very obvious but make sure that you know the syllabus so you can identify which part is being tested in each question. This will help you to recall the correct information.

STUDY FOCUS

Don't leave revision to the last minute. Each time you finish a section of the syllabus make sure you organise your notes and make some revision notes for yourself. You can come back to them later to improve them and make links to other parts of the syllabus.

Figure 0.1.1 This is when good revision notes are useful – the last few days and hours before you take the exam!

This study guide is designed to help you with your learning. Often we don't know how we learn or what are the most effective techniques for learning. There are plenty of people, books and websites that will give you ideas, but in the end you have to find what works best for you. The summary questions at the end of each topic in this book encourage you to use the following techniques to organise the information that you need to learn.

Make learning and revision notes

Learning notes

Divide the syllabus into sections and spend more time on the topics you find difficult. Make your own notes to help you learn. Some people find writing the same thing over and over again helps them to learn it. It may be a better use of your time to write the information in a variety of different ways using prose, bullet points, tables and graphic organisers. See the next section (How to learn 2) for ideas about how to do this.

Revision notes

These should be shorter than your learning notes and they should be easy to use in the days leading up to the exams. Make these for the topics that you find especially difficult. You could write them on cards and carry them around with you. You could put them on a computer or a mobile device, so it easier to edit them as you revise.

Draw diagrams

Find all the topics that require diagrams. Copy them from your textbook or this study guide. Add some labels. Turn over the diagram and try redrawing it from memory. Then check yourself. Do this several times until you have perfect diagrams. There are rules to follow when drawing diagrams. See the next section (How to learn 2) for these.

Make your own glossary

There are so many words to learn when studying Biology! You will find all of the terms that we think you should know in the glossary on the CD. Take the CD out of the folder now and look at the glossary. If you use other books, dictionaries or the internet you will find slightly different definitions of these terms. Start making a glossary of your own and incorporate links to your textbook and this study guide. Make yourself some vocabulary tests to make sure you know the meaning of the terms. There are two ways to use these tests: ask a friend to call out the term and you respond by giving the definition, or you give the term when your friend reads out the definition.

Tables

Comparison tables

You will see that throughout this study guide there are instructions to make tables to compare different structures or processes. When you make these tables, make sure that you always use an extra column for the features that you are comparing. Here is an example:

Features	Red blood cells	White blood cells	
		Phagocytes	**Lymphocytes**
Nucleus	✗	✓	✓
Contains haemoglobin	✓	✗	✗
Function	Transports oxygen	Engulfs bacteria	Secretes antibodies

Summary tables

There are many specialised cells, organs, diseases and processes listed in the syllabus. Get large sheets of paper and make up tables to summarise all that you need to know about these topics. You could put all the information on a spreadsheet so it is easy to update and sort. There are many other topics to organise in the same way.

Revise with others

Revision should not be a lonely experience. Find others to revise with and give yourselves tasks to do. For example, you can write tests for each other.

Use past papers

Paper 1

You cannot see past CSEC® multiple-choice papers, but there are plenty of multiple-choice questions in this book and on the CD. Work through these with your friends, always deciding why three of the answers to each question are not correct. You will see that we have done this for you in **Test yourself** on the CD.

Paper 2

You can obtain past question papers for Paper 2. Use these to help your revision by writing answers to the questions. You may do many of them in school. Keep the questions, your answers and any notes you made together in one folder.

Make your own list or glossary of the command terms that the examiners use in the question papers. All the words they can use are at the back of the syllabus.

Organise yourself with a folder to keep your learning and revision notes and/or start a folder on your computer.

SUMMARY QUESTIONS

1 Most questions begin with commands such as 'state', 'describe', 'explain', 'discuss'. Make a list of these words and find out how you should respond to these commands; add this information to your list.

2 Make a list of the seven characteristics of living organisms. Write down the key terms that are associated with each characteristic. Find out how many of the terms you have written down are in the glossary on the CD.

How to learn 2

On completion of this topic you should know how to:

- use the features of this study guide
- make some graphic organisers to help your learning
- use links between different topics in the Biology syllabus to help your learning.

STUDY FOCUS

Make sure you have plenty of writing paper and graph paper to use as you work your way through the book and the CD. It is also a good idea to have a copy of the syllabus to use during your course.

EXAM TIP

Spider diagrams are a good way to plan your answers to the essay questions in Paper 2.

STUDY FOCUS

As you work your way through this study guide try making many spider diagrams and flow chart diagrams.

You cannot do well in exams without putting in a lot of effort yourself. If you rely simply on listening to your teacher and reading your textbook you are unlikely to do as well as if you take more responsibility for your learning and write lots of resources for yourself.

This section is to help you prepare those resources. Throughout this book there are summary questions that ask you to make drawings, diagrams, tables, graphs and charts.

Graphic organisers make it easy to see how ideas fit together. Spider diagrams and flow chart diagrams are two examples.

Spider and flow chart diagrams

Here is an example of a spider diagram from topics in Unit 3. You can make diagrams like this for each of the topics throughout the book. They make good aids to revision as they link together all the points you need to remember.

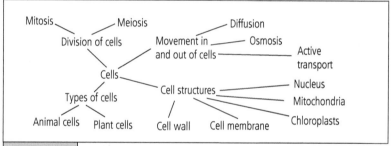

Figure 0.2.1 | A spider diagram showing different aspects of cells

Flow chart diagrams are a good way to show processes that occur as a sequence or as a cycle; showing the procedure to follow in a practical investigation; showing how aspects of the body are controlled and the stages involved in complex processes, such as digestion. You often see them drawn with boxes and arrows.

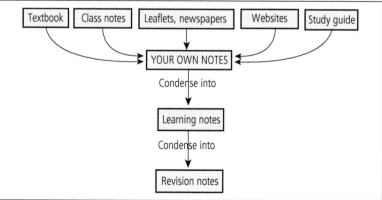

Figure 0.2.2 | A flow chart diagram about revision. See Summary question 2.

You can mix graphic organisers with diagrams, sequences and links. For example here is a diagram drawn by a student to show how the body supports respiration – a key process that provides the energy for muscle contraction.

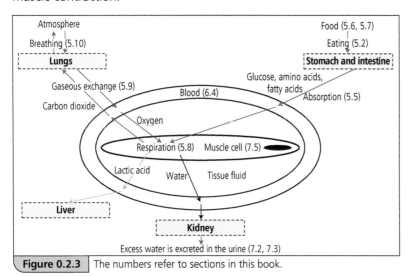

Figure 0.2.3	The numbers refer to sections in this book.

The thinking involved in making graphic organisers is good for revision. The final product is always worth keeping even if it doesn't look very good. It will help you remember how you made it.

Diagrams

A diagram is a simplified view of a structure, often with arrows to indicate direction of movement. As you may be asked to draw diagrams in the exam, so it is a good idea to practise making them. Follow these simple rules:

• use plenty of space

• draw clearly with bold, sharp lines

• do not shade

• use colour only if necessary, e.g. to show oxygenated and deoxygenated blood

• use a ruler to put label lines on your diagram; write labels.

In this guide you are asked to annotate the diagrams. An *annotation* is a note that gives further information about an aspect of your diagram.

Here are some examples of diagrams you should practise:

• vertical sections of the heart (6.3) and a villus (5.5)

• generalised plant and animal cells and some specialised cells (3.1 and 3.3)

• food chains (1.4)

Presenting and analysing data

You need practice at analysing, presenting and interpreting data. Use the exam-style structured questions in this book to help you develop these important skills.

LINK

You could convert this diagram into a poster and put much more information on it. Use the links in the book to make connections between different topics.

KEY POINTS

• Spider diagrams are good for organising your knowledge and showing the links between topics.

• Flow chart diagrams are a good way to summarise information about sequences and cycles.

• More complex diagrams can include diagrams, labels and annotations (notes).

• Diagrams and drawings should be made using sharp lines; they should be labelled using straight lines made with a ruler.

SUMMARY QUESTIONS

1 Draw a spider diagram to show what you already know about topics in Biology and how they link together.

2 Make a flow chart diagram for something simple, such as writing an e-mail, frying an egg or making a cake.

3 Make an outline drawing of the human body and show the positions of the following organs: heart, brain, eye, lungs, stomach, kidneys, pancreas, liver. Annotate your diagram with one function of each organ.

4 Make a simple diagram of a flowering plant. Label the following structures: roots, stem, leaves, flowers and fruits. Annotate your diagram with one function of each structure.

1 Biodiversity

1.1

The world around you

LEARNING OUTCOMES

At the end of this topic you should be able to:

- group organisms together based on their shared features
- classify organisms into groups based on the physical similarities and differences between them.

Figure 1.1.1 The Andromeda Botanical Gardens in Barbados

STUDY FOCUS

You should study plant diversity by looking at different species. You do not have to go to botanical gardens to do this; any vacant plot will have enough diversity for you to study.

DID YOU KNOW?

A key that has only two answers for each question is called a *dichotomous* key. Try question 2 to see if you can make one.

A group of students went on a visit to a botanical garden (Figure 1.1.1). They were equipped with cameras, rulers and notebooks. They took photographs of some of the plants that they found and made lists of the features they could see. Figure 1.1.2 shows some of their results.

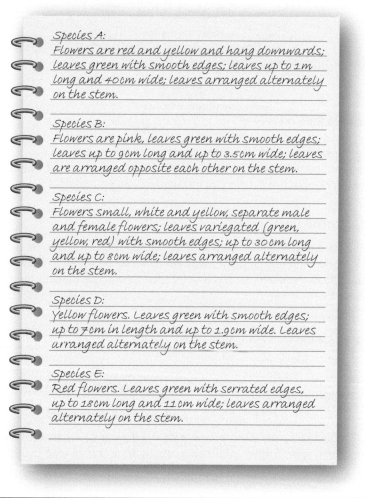

Species A:
Flowers are red and yellow and hang downwards; leaves green with smooth edges; leaves up to 1 m long and 40 cm wide; leaves arranged alternately on the stem.

Species B:
Flowers are pink, leaves green with smooth edges; leaves up to 9 cm long and up to 3.5 cm wide; leaves are arranged opposite each other on the stem.

Species C:
Flowers small, white and yellow, separate male and female flowers; leaves variegated (green, yellow, red) with smooth edges; up to 30 cm long and up to 8 cm wide; leaves arranged alternately on the stem.

Species D:
Yellow flowers. Leaves green with smooth edges; up to 7 cm in length and up to 1.9 cm wide. Leaves arranged alternately on the stem.

Species E:
Red flowers. Leaves green with serrated edges, up to 18 cm long and 11 cm wide; leaves arranged alternately on the stem.

Figure 1.1.2 Part of the students' notebook

Another group of students collected some small invertebrate animals and looked for features that the animals had in common and features that distinguished between them.

Using the information that they collected the students devised a flow chart **key** that other students could use to identify the organisms (Figure 1.1.3).

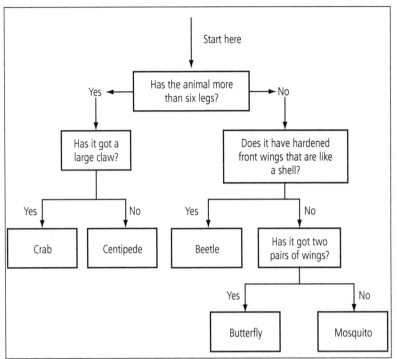

| Figure 1.1.3 | A flow chart key to identify some invertebrate animals |

Flow chart:

Start here → Has the animal more than six legs?
- Yes → Has it got a large claw?
  - Yes → Crab
  - No → Centipede
- No → Does it have hardened front wings that are like a shell?
  - Yes → Beetle
  - No → Has it got two pairs of wings?
    - Yes → Butterfly
    - No → Mosquito

Biologists **classify** organisms into groups, for example plants, animals and microorganisms (microbes). The students next visited a zoo where they saw examples of different animal groups and wrote down the features that they could see. They made this table of similarities and differences.

Table 1.1.1

Name of animal	Features			
	Legs	Wings	Feathers / fur	Scales
Owl butterfly (insect)	✓ (6)	✓ (4)	✗	✓ (minute)
Angelfish	✗	✗	✗	✓
Tree frog (amphibian)	✓ (4)	✗	✗	✗
Iguana (reptile)	✓ (4)	✗	✗	✓
Blue and yellow macaw (bird)	✓ (2)	✓ (2)	✓ (feathers)	✓ (on legs)
Red howler monkey (mammal)	✓ (4)	✗	✓ (fur)	✗

STUDY FOCUS

Search your local environment for different animal species. Make a species list; classify the species that you find into groups, e.g. insects, reptiles, birds, mammals, etc.

LINK

Biologists used to classify organisms using external and internal features that they could see. Now they also use information gained by studying molecules, such as proteins and DNA. You can read more about this in 11.1.

SUMMARY QUESTIONS

1 Make a table to compare the features of the five different plants described by the students.

2 a Make a flow chart key to identify the plants from the features given in your table.

   b Make a similar key to identify the animals in Table 1.1.1. You need one less question than the number of organisms.

3 Make a collection of local plants and write a table summarising the similarities and differences between them.

KEY POINTS

1 Organisms can be grouped using observable similarities and differences.

2 Biologists classify organisms into groups, such as plants, animals and microorganisms.

3 Keys are used to identify organisms.

Figure 1.2.1 These students are using a quadrat to estimate species density.

A pond is an example of a **habitat** – a place where organisms live. The habitat provides all the resources that an organism needs to survive. Some animals live in more than one habitat, e.g. migratory birds and fish. One of the first things you might do when studying a habitat is to make a species list. This gives you an idea of which plants and animals are present, but gives you no idea about where they live within the habitat or how many there are. To do this you need some apparatus to help you take samples within the habitat.

Quadrats

A **quadrat** is a frame made of wire or wood that encloses a known area, such as $0.25\,m^2$ or $1\,m^2$. It makes it easy to sample the vegetation and sometimes the animal life within a known area. If samples are taken at various places within a habitat, then the results can be used to make estimates of the total numbers (Figure 1.2.1).

Table 1.2.1 shows some results taken by some students to show how to calculate the species density – the number of organisms of each species within $1\,m^2$.

Table 1.2.1

Species	Number in each 1 m² quadrat (Q)					Mean density/ number in 1 m²
	Q 1	Q 2	Q 3	Q 4	Q 5	
Heart seed	5	6	4	3	7	$\frac{25}{5} = 5$
Mexican poppy	11	8	6	8	2	$\frac{35}{5} = 7$
Wild cress	11	9	10	13	7	$\frac{50}{5} = 10$
Wild dolly	4	3	6	5	2	$\frac{20}{5} = 4$
Grass	15	25	17	18	10	$\frac{85}{5} = 17$

Transects

Quadrats placed randomly over an area are good for estimating the numbers of individuals and their density. However, in some habitats species are not distributed randomly. For example, at a beach, the species change as you move away from the sea. You can record this simply by putting down a tape and recording the vegetation at intervals. This is a **line transect**.

A line transect does not tell us how many organisms are present at each sampling point along the line. To find out the abundance of organisms along the line, quadrats are put down at intervals and the density of each species recorded. This is a **belt transect**. The results can be plotted as graphs to show how species are distributed along the transect and how abundant they are.

Sometimes it is impossible to use quadrats to gain results about animals. Some other techniques are:

- **Beating tray** – this can be a large white sheet placed on the ground or supported by struts and held below a tree. The tree is shaken to dislodge the animals. Very small animals can be collected from the beating tray with a small paintbrush.
- **Pooter** – by sucking on the tube small animals are drawn into the glass or plastic tube (Figure 1.2.2).
- **Sweep nets** – these large nets are used to catch flying insects.
- Pond nets – these are stronger nets that can lift volumes of water from ponds or rivers; the water drains through the net to leave vegetation and animals behind.
- Sieves – the contents of nets can be emptied into white trays for sorting; sieves are useful for removing the animals and putting them into smaller containers of water for identification and study.
- **Pitfall traps** – cans or jars buried in the ground, filled with paper or cardboard to provide shelter and covered with a lid or stone to keep out the rain; these are useful for collecting ground dwelling insects that are often nocturnal.

To improve our estimates of population sizes of animal species we can use the method known as **mark–release–recapture**. Some animals are collected from a habitat, marked carefully with a non-toxic substance in such a way that they are not obvious to their predators and then released back to their habitat. Some time later, the animals are collected again and the numbers of marked and unmarked individuals are counted. This formula is used to calculate an estimate of the total population in the habitat.

$$\text{total numbers in the population} = \frac{\text{number captured and marked} \times \text{number recaptured}}{\text{number recaptured that were marked}}$$

When you study the organisms in a habitat, make sure you record features of the habitat and ways in which plants and animals are adapted to survive there (see Figure 1.2.3 for an example).

Figure 1.2.2 This scientist is using a pooter to collect tiny insects from an epiphyte high in a forest in Argentina.

Figure 1.2.3 Adaptations for floating on water: water lilies have air-filled leaves; the smaller water lettuce has non-wettable leaves.

SUMMARY QUESTIONS

1 Explain how you would sample the following habitats:

   a   a small pond

   b   an area of grassland

   c   the branches of trees.

2 Some students caught 36 crabs, marked them and released them. Two days later they caught 45 crabs of which 6 were marked. Calculate the numbers of crabs in the area sampled by the students.

3 List the assumptions that must be made **a** when sampling with a quadrat, and **b** when using the mark–release–recapture technique.

KEY POINTS

1   A habitat is a place where an organism lives.

2   Apparatus and techniques for sampling habitats depend on the nature of the habitat and the organisms that live there.

3   A quadrat is a frame made of wire or wood that encloses a known area, e.g. 1 m². It is used to estimate species density.

1.3   Ecology

At the end of this topic you should be able to:

* define the terms *environment, ecology, ecosystem, biotic, abiotic, niche, population, community* and *species*
* list some major abiotic and biotic factors
* discuss the impact of abiotic factors on organisms.

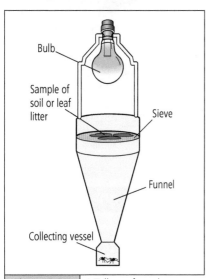

Figure 1.3.1   A Tullgren funnel

Labels in figure: Bulb; Sample of soil or leaf litter; Sieve; Funnel; Collecting vessel

EXAM TIP

'Dry to constant mass' is a useful phrase to use if you have to describe a way to determine dry mass of soil or plant material.

A habitat supports many different species of organisms. A **species** is a group of organisms that can breed together to produce fertile offspring. Within the habitat there are **populations** of each species.

Ecology is the study of organisms and their surroundings or **environment**. The organisms that live in a particular place form a **community**. An **ecosystem** comprises the community and all the factors that influence the organisms. A **niche** is the role fulfilled by a species in an ecosystem including its trophic level and the relationships it has with other species (see 1.6).

Many aspects of the surroundings influence organisms. We can divide these influences into two groups of factors: **abiotic factors** and **biotic factors** (see Table 1.3.1).

Table 1.3.1

Abiotic factors	Biotic factors
All the non-living features of an ecosystem that influence the organisms in the community	All the influences that organisms in the community have on each other
Latitude, altitude, climate, temperature, water, oxygen concentration, carbon dioxide concentration, light intensity, light duration (hours of daylight), rainfall, soil depth, soil pH, soil water content, mineral ion content	Food, water, disease, predation, competition for food, water and living space with members of the same species and with other species

Soil as a habitat

The soil provides a habitat for many organisms. You can collect samples of soil and the leaf litter from the surface of the soil. Spread out your samples in trays or on newspaper and sift through looking for animals. This method depends on eyesight as many of the animals are very small. Another way to sample soil for animals is to set up a funnel like that shown in Figure 1.3.1. The light dries out the soil; soil animals prefer damp, dark conditions so they move away from the lamp, fall through the sieve in the funnel and are collected for study.

The physical features of soil can be analysed easily in the laboratory:

* Water content – Take a sample of soil, weigh it and leave it to dry. Every day weigh the soil sample until the mass stays the same. The difference between the original mass and the dried mass gives the water content.
* Water holding capacity – Take a known mass of dry soil and place it into a flower pot or filter funnel with filter paper at the bottom.

Pour a known volume of water from a measuring cylinder onto the soil. Collect the water that drains through and measure. The volume of water remaining in the soil is the water holding capacity.

- Organic and mineral matter – Take a known mass of dry soil. Place it into a crucible and heat strongly with a Bunsen burner. Stir the soil frequently. Allow the crucible to cool and then weigh. Keep heating, cooling and weighing until the mass stays the same. The mass that is lost is the organic matter; the mineral matter is what remains (Figure 1.3.2).

- Air content – Push the open end of an empty tin can of known volume into the soil so that it fills up and then dig it up. Scrape off the soil from the top of the can. Tip out the soil into a large beaker containing a known volume of water and stir to break up the soil pieces and allow the air to leave. The volume of air in the sample is calculated by subtracting the new volume in the beaker (water + soil) from the expected volume (water + volume of tin can).

- **pH** – Take a small sample of soil and add some water. Shake or stir. Take a small sample of the water and put it on a tile. Add a pH indicator such as universal indicator.

- **Salinity** – This is measured with a conductivity meter. Take 20 g of dry soil and add 100 cm³ distilled water. Shake well and pour off the water. Put the probe into the water and take a reading. The higher the reading the more salt there is in the soil.

Important components of the air in the soil and in the atmosphere are:

- Oxygen – required for respiration of plant roots and all organisms. See 5.8 for details of respiration.

- Carbon dioxide – required as a raw material for photosynthesis; there are microscopic plants and algae that live in the upper regions of the soil where light reaches them. See 4.2 for details of photosynthesis.

- Nitrogen – an inert gas, but some microorganisms are able to use the nitrogen to make into organic forms, such as **amino acids**.

Two other important abiotic factors that influence the distribution and abundance of organisms are light and temperature. Light is needed as a source of energy for green plants and other photosynthetic organisms, such as algae and some bacteria. Temperature influences the rate at which chemical reactions occur in the bodies of organisms. There are many aspects of both of these factors that influence the distribution and behaviour of organisms, for example light duration and light wavelength, and maximum and minimum temperatures.

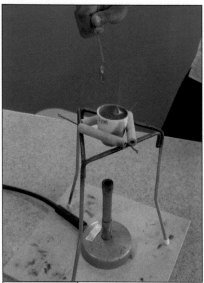

Figure 1.3.2 | As dry soil is heated the organic matter is burnt off leaving the mineral matter to be weighed.

KEY POINTS

1 Ecology is the study of living organisms in their environment.

2 Biotic and abiotic factors affect the distribution and abundance of organisms in ecosystems.

3 Abiotic factors are all the non-living features of an ecosystem; biotic factors are all the influences that organisms have on each other.

SUMMARY QUESTIONS

1 Explain the differences between the following pairs of terms:
   a *abiotic* and *biotic*
   b *habitat* and *niche*
   c *population* and *community*
   d *species* and *population*.

2 a Discuss the importance of abiotic factors for animals that live in the soil.
   b Explain how these factors influence the plants that grow in soil.
   c Discuss the abiotic factors that influence plants that live in ponds.

3 Write a set of practical instructions for an analysis of soil for the following features:
   a water   b air
   c organic content
   d water holding capacity.

   You could use flow chart diagrams (see page 8).

Food chains and energy flow

Food chains

A **food chain** shows the feeding relationships between some of the organisms in an ecosystem.

In the food chain in Figure 1.4.1, the arrows show the direction in which food and energy flows. Arrows always point away from the food and towards the organism doing the feeding. In this food chain the grasshopper is a **herbivore** and the lizard and the broad-winged hawk are **carnivores**.

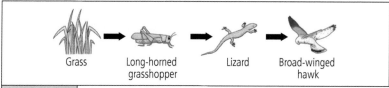

| Grass | Long-horned grasshopper | Lizard | Broad-winged hawk |

Figure 1.4.1 A food chain with organisms at four trophic levels

Many birds, such as mockingbirds, are **omnivores** as they feed on plants (especially the fruits and seeds) and animals.

The different feeding levels in a food chain are called **trophic levels**. Plants are **producers**, animals are **consumers**. Herbivores are **primary consumers** and carnivores are **secondary consumers**. Omnivores feed at two, or more, trophic levels. If you eat fish, then it is likely that you are eating animals that are carnivores. An animal, such as the broad-winged hawk, that feeds at the top of a food chain is a **tertiary consumer**.

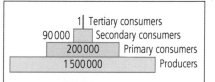

1	Tertiary consumers
90 000	Secondary consumers
200 000	Primary consumers
1 500 000	Producers

Figure 1.4.2 A pyramid of numbers

Pyramids

After estimating the populations of organisms at each trophic level, the data can be used to draw **pyramids of numbers** (Figure 1.4.2).

The actual shape of a pyramid of numbers depends on the community. In many communities there are many producers with far fewer consumers.

There are two reasons for this:

• Organisms at higher trophic levels tend to be larger.

• Habitats cannot support large numbers of large organisms. As energy flows up a food chain it is lost, so there is not much energy left to support large carnivores.

Biomass is the quantity of biological material. Weighing representative samples and multiplying up by the estimated numbers present in a habitat estimates the biomass of the organisms at different trophic levels. The data is presented in a **pyramid of biomass** (Figure 1.4.3).

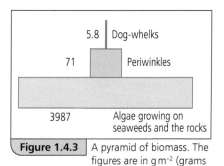

5.8	Dog-whelks
71	Periwinkles
3987	Algae growing on seaweeds and the rocks

Figure 1.4.3 A pyramid of biomass. The figures are in $g\,m^{-2}$ (grams per metre squared).

Much of the biomass in trees and animals is not available to the next trophic level. As a result, biologists estimate the energy that flows from one trophic level to the next and this is shown in a **pyramid of energy**.

At the top of the pyramid there is too little energy to support another trophic level (Figure 1.4.4).

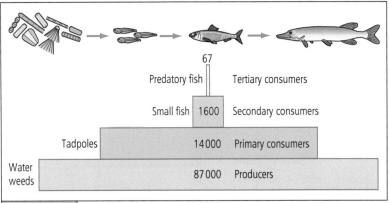

| **Figure 1.4.4** | A pyramid of energy. The figures are in kJ m^{-2} y^{-1} (kilojoules per metre squared per year). |

The flow of energy through a habitat shows that much of the energy absorbed by plants is lost as a result of respiration and heat loss to the environment (Figure 1.4.5). Much is also lost in dead leaves and animal waste (faeces and urine) to decomposers.

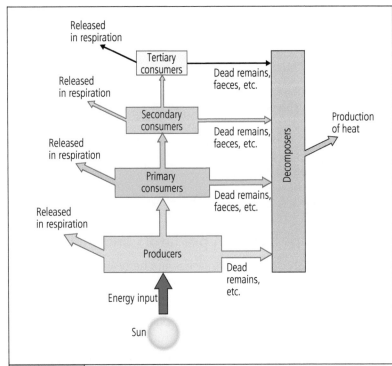

| **Figure 1.4.5** | Energy flow in a habitat; about 10% of the energy that enters a trophic level is available for the next. |

SUMMARY QUESTIONS

1 Draw a food chain using the following information: small beetles feed on orange leaves; bananaquits eat small beetles.

2 Use the food chain you have drawn to identify the following: *producer*, *herbivore*, *primary consumer*, *carnivore*, *secondary consumer*.

3 Bananaquits also feed on oranges. Redraw your food chain to show this extra information. Why are bananaquits described as *omnivores*?

Food webs

Figure 1.5.2 | Anolis lizards are an important part of food webs in the Caribbean.

STUDY FOCUS

In most habitats, each predator has many prey species to feed on, so their numbers do not rise and fall in such a regular pattern.

DID YOU KNOW?

The mongoose is thought to be responsible for the extinction of several Caribbean birds including the Jamaican night hawk and the Antiguan owl.

A terrestrial food web

Figure 1.5.1 shows a **food web** for a terrestrial habitat. Food webs show that there are many more feeding relationships than shown in simple food chains.

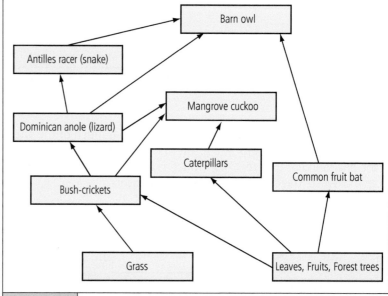

Figure 1.5.1 | This food web shows some of the feeding relationships between organisms in a forest in Dominica.

If you are given information about the feeding relationships in an area, then you can draw a food web. Remember that each type of plant may be eaten by different species of herbivore, each species of herbivore may have more than one predator and omnivores eat both plant and animal species.

Relationships between predators and their prey

The food web shows that the success of a herbivore in its habitat depends on at least two biotic factors:

- **Quantity of plant food available** – If the number and biomass of plants decrease then the herbivore population will probably decrease as there is not enough food and some animals may die of starvation.
- **Number of predators and the prey species that they feed on** – If there are many predators and they have few prey species then the effect of the predators on any one species of herbivore will be much greater than if there were few predators with many different prey species for them to eat.

The relationship between the numbers of predators and prey species has been studied in different habitats. Figure 1.5.3 shows the changes in numbers of a prey species that has only one predator and that predator only feeds on one prey species.

As the population of the prey species increases, there is more food for the predator species so its numbers also increase because more offspring survive to reproduce. As the number of predators increases, they eat more of the prey species so numbers of prey decrease. The lack of food for predators means that fewer offspring survive to reproduce, as many do not gain enough food and starve to death. The number of predators decreases and the cycle starts again.

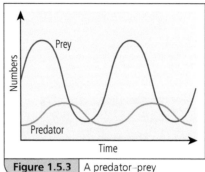

Figure 1.5.3 A predator–prey relationship

Biological control

Predators can be used to control pest species, this is called **biological control**. It avoids the use of chemical pesticides that may be harmful to the environment. The small Indian mongoose was introduced to Jamaica from India in 1872 to control rats that were eating much of the sugar cane crop. They were so successful that they were introduced to other parts of the Caribbean. However, as with many such introductions, the mongoose fed on other prey species too.

Armyworms are serious pests of many vegetable crops in the Caribbean. The larvae (caterpillars) of the moths eat large quantities of leaves destroying crops of callaloo, onions, soya beans and maize. Pesticides are often ineffective as caterpillars become resistant to them. Alternative methods of pest control are to release viruses that cause disease in armyworms and wasps that lay their eggs inside pest species (Figure 1.5.3).

Figure 1.5.4 A highly effective biological control – this wasp lays its eggs inside caterpillars. When the eggs hatch the larvae eat the caterpillar from the inside out.

Decomposers

Decomposers are microorganisms that feed on dead and decaying matter. Bacteria and fungi are decomposers that secrete enzymes onto dead material and digest it. They break down huge quantities of material releasing much of it into the atmosphere as carbon dioxide, therefore playing an important role in the recycling of carbon.

SUMMARY QUESTIONS

1 Define the terms *food web*, *biological control* and *decomposer*.

2 Use this information to draw a food web for a pond.

   The algae that grow in water and on the leaves of water weeds are eaten by small crustaceans; dead leaves from overhanging trees are decomposed by bacteria and fungi. Dead leaves and decomposers are eaten by water boatmen and water lice. Dragonfly larvae and diving beetles feed on the primary consumers. Small fish feed on algae, small crustaceans and water boatmen. Herons feed on fish and dragonfly larvae.

3 a Sketch a graph to show the fluctuations of predator and prey over time.

   b Explain the changes you have drawn in part **a**.

4 Explain why careful research is needed before a new biological agent is released to control a pest species.

KEY POINTS

1 A food web shows the links between food chains in a community.

2 Numbers of predator and prey species are dependent on each other. An increase in a prey species often leads to an increase in numbers of its predator.

3 Predators and parasites of pest species are used as a means of biological control rather than using pesticides.

4 Decomposers are bacteria and fungi that feed on dead and decaying matter.

Living together

LEARNING OUTCOMES

At the end of this topic you should be able to:

- define the following terms: *symbiosis, parasitism, commensalism* and *mutualism*
- give examples of each of these relationships.

Figure 1.6.1 This coconut tree is covered in epiphytes.

Figure 1.6.2 Egrets gain a good source of food by living with large herbivores, such as cattle, buffalo and hippos.

Eat and be eaten

Food chains and food webs show the feeding relationships within communities. But these are not the only relationships that exist between species. Many species 'live together' with different degrees of closeness and with different degrees of harm or benefit to each other.

Symbiosis

The term **symbiosis** means any form of close relationship between two species. In many tropical forests the canopy of leaves is so dense that there is little light reaching the forest floor. Many of the trees are covered in plants, known as **epiphytes** (Figure 1.6.1). These plants, such as bromeliads and air plants, gain sufficient light for their photosynthesis. These plants do not take anything from the trees and do not harm the trees; they just use them as a place to grow.

Commensalism

Commensalism is a form of symbiosis in which one species benefits from the relationship but the other, usually the larger, is unaffected. Egrets are white birds that have a close relationship with cattle. They feed on the insects that are disturbed from the ground as the cattle move about (Figure 1.6.2).

Parasitism

Parasitism is a form of nutrition where one organism, the parasite, gains at the expense of the other, the host. Lice and ticks are external parasites of many species of mammal and bird (Figure 1.6.3).

Animals also have internal parasites, such as tapeworms. These parasites live inside the gut and absorb digested food. Much of the energy is used in reproduction to produce millions of eggs to maximise the chances that the larvae from some of them will invade new hosts.

Yellow dodder is a plant that parasitises other plants. Dodder twines around stems and uses suckers to penetrate the host's transport tissues to absorb water, mineral ions, sugars and other molecules (Figure 1.6.4).

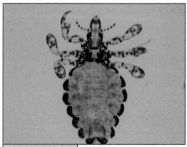

Figure 1.6.3 A human body louse

Figure 1.6.4 Yellow dodder, a parasitic plant

Mutualism

Not all relationships are harmful to one of the participants. There are many examples of two or more species existing in relationships in which both partners benefit; this is called **mutualism**. Many plants have flowers that are pollinated by animals, such as insects, birds and bats. This ensures that the plants are pollinated and can reproduce sexually. The plants produce nectar, which is a sugary solution, to reward the animals with a supply of energy-rich food (Figure 1.6.5). Similarly, many tropical trees produce edible fruits that are eaten by monkeys and birds. These animals disperse the seeds and this ensures that the trees are spread to avoid competition. See 9.5 and 9.6 for more about this.

Legumes are flowering plants with distinctive flowers and pod-like fruits. Many of the tree species that live in the Caribbean are legumes. The roots of legumes have swellings, known as nodules that contain bacteria. These bacteria convert atmospheric nitrogen (N_2) into organic forms of nitrogen, such as amino acids, that the host plants use to make their protein. This is mutualism, because the plant gains a supply of nitrogen in organic form and the bacteria gain protection within the nodules, and a supply of energy in the form of sugar (produced by the plant) (Figure 1.6.6).

Figure 1.6.5 This Pallas's long-tongued bat is pollinating a banana flower.

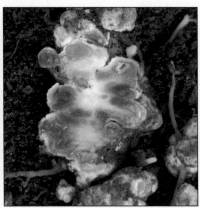

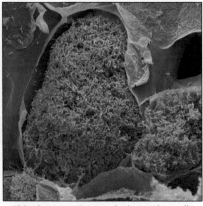

Figure 1.6.6 **a** The swellings on the root of this legume are root nodules.

b These root nodules have been sectioned vertically to show the pink areas inside where nitrogen-fixing bacteria are most active.

c This electron micrograph shows that cells inside root nodules are full of bacteria ($\times 300$).

KEY POINTS

1 Any form of close relationship between two or more species is symbiosis.

2 In commensalism species live together to the benefit of one of the species (usually the smaller).

3 A parasite lives in or on a host species, obtaining its food from the host and causing it harm.

4 In mutualism both species benefit from the relationship.

SUMMARY QUESTIONS

1 a Define the following: *symbiosis*, *commensalism*, *parasitism* and *mutualism*.

b Give an example of each of these relationships, explaining the benefit or harm to each of the species involved.

2 Make learning notes on the different relationships described here. See page 6 to help you.

SECTION 1: Multiple-choice questions

1 The most common reptile in a mangrove community is a species of Anolis lizard. It feeds on insects including moth caterpillars and is prey to the pearly-eyed thrasher, a type of bird. Moth caterpillars feed on the leaves of mangrove trees.

Which of the following correctly identifies the trophic level of these four organisms in this food chain?

	Producer	Primary consumer	Secondary consumer	Tertiary consumer
A	Anolis lizard	pearly-eyed thrasher	mangrove tree	moth caterpillar
B	pearly-eyed thrasher	Anolis lizard	moth caterpillar	mangrove tree
C	mangrove tree	moth caterpillar	Anolis lizard	pearly-eyed thrasher
D	moth caterpillar	mangrove tree	pearly-eyed thrasher	Anolis lizard

2 Nitrogen-fixing bacteria live inside the root nodules of legumes. This is an example of

  A   commensalism

  B   decomposition

  C   mutualism

  D   parasitism

3 Which one of the following is *not* an abiotic factor?

  A   oxygen concentration of river water

  B   mineral content of the soil

  C   salinity of the soil in a wetland ecosystem

  D   the numbers of bacteria in a soil sample

4 A student used a quadrat to find the density of a plant species. The results for five $1\,m^2$ quadrats were: 14, 6, 12, 8, 10. The mean density per m^2 of the species was:

  A   8

  B   10

  C   12

  D   15

5 Using predators and parasites of pest species to reduce the damage to crop plants is known as

  A   biological control

  B   community control

  C   ecological control

  D   population control

6 Fungi and bacteria are important in recycling carbon and nitrogen in ecosystems because they are:

  A   decomposers

  B   herbivores

  C   parasites

  D   producers

7 Some students collected a soil sample in a tin can with a volume of $400\,cm^3$. They added the soil to $300\,cm^3$ of water in a beaker and stirred to remove all the air from the soil. They found that the volume of water and the solid soil particles was $500\,cm^3$. The percentage by volume of air in the soil sample was:

  A   25%

  B   40%

  C   50%

  D   71%

8 Herbivores are

  A   primary consumers

  B   producers

  C   secondary consumers

  D   tertiary consumers

9 Some students began a study of a coastal area by drawing a line transect from the shallow water, across the beach to a group of acacia trees 50 m from the beach as shown in Figure 1.

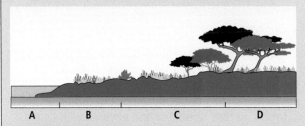

Figure 1

a Describe the procedure to follow when collecting data for a line transect. *(4)*

b The students divided the area into four regions, **A** to **D** as shown in Figure 1.

 i State two abiotic factors that influence the plants that live in region **B**. *(2)*

 ii Explain how you would determine the density of trees, shrubs and smaller plants in region **D** of the area. *(4)*

c Nocturnal ground beetles were found living in regions **C** and **D**. The students used pitfall traps and the mark–release–recapture method to estimate the number of ground beetles in the study area.

 i Explain why pitfall traps are suitable for sampling the numbers of ground beetles. *(2)*

 ii The students caught and marked 33 ground beetles on the first day. Two days later they caught 16 beetles of which 7 were marked.

  Use the formula given in 1.2 to calculate the total number of beetles. Show all your working. *(3)*

d A marine ecologist working in the area talked to the students about the ecology of seagrass communities in the Caribbean. One of the students noted the feeding relationships that were mentioned:

'Sea grass provides food for sea urchins and turtles. Many organisms live on the sea grass including photosynthetic algae, which are grazed by parrotfish. Sea urchins are eaten by puffer fish. Groupers are predators of parrotfish. Humans catch and eat turtles, parrotfish and groupers.'

 i Define the term *ecology*. *(1)*

 ii Draw a food chain showing the feeding relationships between four organisms given in the passage. *(2)*

 iii Identify the trophic levels of the four organisms you have given in the food chain. *(4)*

 iv Use the information provided in this question to explain the meaning of the term *community*. *(3)*

Total 25 marks

10 Some students investigated the small invertebrates living in leaf litter in a forest ecosystem.

a Explain what is meant by the term *ecosystem*. *(3)*

Figure 2 is a diagram of a pooter

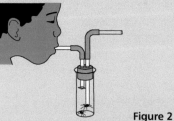

Figure 2

a Describe:

 i how students would use a pooter to collect small invertebrates *(3)*

 ii two other ways in which the students could collect these animals. *(4)*

b Many of the invertebrates found in the leaf litter also live in the soil.

Explain how the soil provides a suitable environment for small invertebrates. *(5)*

Total 15 marks

Further practice questions and examples can be found on the accompanying CD.

23

2 The impact of humans on the environment

2.1

Waste management and recycling

Figure 2.1.1 Non-biodegradable waste collected from a beach. Huge quantities of rubbish like this endanger marine wildlife.

Have you ever wondered how much waste you produce each year?

Human body wastes (urine, faeces and carbon dioxide in breath) and discarded food are **biodegradable wastes**. They can be broken down by decomposers (bacteria and fungi). Decomposers cannot break down many manufactured products and these **non-biodegradable wastes** remain in the environment often indefinitely. Both types of waste can be hazardous to the health of the environment and us.

In places with good **sanitation**, human body wastes enter sewers and are treated in sewage works.

Similarly, household rubbish is collected regularly by garbage collectors and taken to designated dumps for proper disposal.

Many areas in the world do not have good sanitation and human wastes contaminate aquatic habitats, drinking water and some foods. These places often have no organised rubbish collection and garbage is dumped close to human habitation. Household garbage is a mix of biodegradable and non-biodegradable waste.

Often the biodegradable material is not sorted and removed from the garbage to reduce the total volume. Decomposers need a good supply of oxygen, warmth and damp conditions. Warmth and water are not a problem in the Caribbean. However, garbage is usually compressed so much that there is not enough air for fungi and bacteria to respire efficiently, so biodegradation is rarely complete. Few places have the facilities for composting wastes (see 2.6).

Plastic forms one of the largest components of non-biodegradable waste. It is used for packaging because it does not decay easily. However, this is a problem when we want to dispose of plastics. Most plastic waste goes into rubbish dumps or landfill sites where it takes up a lot of space. Plastic waste causes special problems in the sea (Figure 2.1.1):

- Turtles eat plastic containers and plastic bags mistaking them for jellyfish.

- Marine mammals and many fish get trapped in discarded plastic wire and netting and suffocate.

- Plastic may break up into tiny pieces that are ingested by small animals and build-up in food chains.

- Plastics absorb toxic substances, such as PCBs (polychlorinated biphenyls) and DDT (dichlorodiphenyltrichloroethane); these chemicals persist and build up in food chains.

Difficulties in waste management

The quantity of solid waste in the Caribbean has doubled over the past 30 years. Over time the wastes have become more non-biodegradable and hazardous. In Jamaica, 1.2 million tonnes of waste is generated each year. Approximately 828 000 tonnes are taken to legal disposal sites. None of these are properly managed landfill sites that take precautions not to harm the local area. Almost 300 000 tonnes of waste is illegally dumped causing severe environmental problems (Figure 2.1.2). There are problems with poor waste disposal:

- Toxic liquids leak from the sites into surrounding land, water courses and ultimately the sea.
- The partial decomposition of organic matter produces methane. Methane is a greenhouse gas (see 2.4).
- Diseases spread from waste dumps. Houseflies transmit diseases, e.g. diarrhoeal diseases like typhoid.

Waste management solutions

Integrated waste management system in St Lucia

This comprises one sanitary landfill site at Deglos in the north of the island and an upgraded disposal site at Vieux Fort in the south. The Deglos sanitary landfill is a nine-hectare purpose engineered facility with clay lining, piping and two ponds that prevent toxic substances leaching from the site and contaminating the groundwater. The site also has an industrial autoclave and a tyre shredder. Waste collection services are provided for both kerb and communal bins, and are organised into eleven collection zones, which are run by private contractors, thereby providing garbage collection to 100% of the island.

Figure 2.1.2 | Illegal dumping of unsorted waste causes all sorts of environmental problems, as shown here in Belize.

SUMMARY QUESTIONS

1 Explain the difference between biodegradable waste and non-biodegradable waste.

2 Why has the volume of waste in the Caribbean increased so much over the past 30 years?

3 The table shows the quantities of waste taken to the two sites in St Lucia.

Year	Waste quantity (tonnes)		
	Deglos sanitary landfill	Veux Fort waste disposal facility	Total
2004–5	49 885	23 130	73 015
2005–6	59 426	22 191	81 617
2006–7	58 663	20 173	78 836
2007–8	64 691	19 836	84 527

Calculate the percentage increase in the total quantity of waste collected in St Lucia between 2004–5 and 2007–8.

4 Outline the environmental problems of the illegal dumping of rubbish.

KEY POINTS

1 Decomposers (bacteria and fungi) break down biodegradable waste into carbon dioxide, ammonia and other simple compounds.

2 Non-biodegradable waste cannot be broken down and persists in the environment indefinitely.

3 The Caribbean has seen a huge increase in solid wastes and rarely has the facilities to reduce this quantity and bury it safely in sanitary landfill sites.

4 St Lucia has an integrated waste management system which is a model that other countries could follow.

The impact of human activities

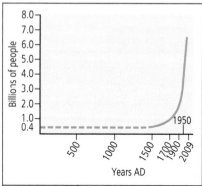

Figure 2.2.1 The human population has increased exponentially since about 1850.

LINK

There is more about population growth in 2.6; the practice exam questions on the CD have some data about populations in the Caribbean.

Population growth

The world's population has increased significantly since the middle of the 19th century. During the 20th century, populations in the Caribbean increased on average by 1–2% per year. This was because the death rate fell steeply from the 1930s onwards while the birth rate remained high until the 1960s. After this the birth rate too started to decrease. Populations increased even though large numbers of people migrated to Panama, North America and Europe during the 20th century. Rates of increase now vary throughout the region with some countries having rates as low as or lower than countries in Europe (Figure 2.2.1).

Resources

As the population of the world increases, more raw materials are being used up. Raw materials fall into two main categories: **renewable resources** and **non-renewable resources**.

- **Renewable resources** can be replaced by plants and animals. Examples are timber for building and making paper, and fish, molluscs and crustaceans harvested from the sea and from lakes. The term 'renewable' is also applied to forms of energy, such as solar power, wind energy, hydroelectricity and ethanol-based fuels.

- **Non-renewable resources** include energy sources, such as the fossil fuels, and minerals, such as copper, nickel, zinc and lead. When we have used these resources, they are gone forever.

Fossil fuels

Most of our energy comes from the combustion of fossil fuels, which will run out eventually. Caribbean countries import most of their energy as oil and natural gas. Only Trinidad and Cuba have reserves of oil. Oil spills occur when oil tankers run aground or there is a leak from a drilling platform, as in the Gulf of Mexico in 2010. They have devastating effects on the marine environment.

Fisheries

Catches from coastal stocks increased until the late 1980s, but since then have declined because of overfishing and habitat destruction. Reefs are the habitat of coastal fish. Coral reefs have been blown up with dynamite to help catch fish. Reefs have also been damaged by hurricanes and other storms. Much of the region's deep sea fish stocks are taken by foreign fleets dominated by those from South Korea, Japan, Venezuela and Taiwan.

Minerals

The major industry is bauxite extraction, which is concentrated in Jamaica, Guyana and Suriname. In Jamaica the industry has had severe effects on the environment, such as the red lake at Mount Rosser which is heavily polluted with alkali. Nickel is extracted in Cuba and the Dominican Republic. Nickel mining has led to environmental degradation in Cuba, where toxic mining waste has entered the Cabañas River and a huge area of coastal water. Deposits have destroyed 275 hectares of coastal vegetation. Large companies carry out most mining. They have largely ignored the welfare of the local environment in the past.

Forest resources

Humans have cleared forests for over 10 000 years to grow food, provide land for settlements and provide transport links. Most forests in temperate regions have been affected. Tropical forests in South-East Asia and Latin America have been cut down over the past 100 years. Many of these are rainforests.

There has been large-scale deforestation to provide the following:

- timber for building materials
- paper for newsprint and other forms of paper and cardboard
- land for farms, cattle ranches and plantations of oil palms, sugar cane and soya beans
- land for roads, towns and factories
- firewood and charcoal as fuels.

Deforestation has caused environmental problems (Figure 2.2.2):

- Layers of soils in tropical rainforests are very thin. When the vegetation is removed the soil is washed away, causing soil erosion, formation of gullies and loss of plant nutrients. The land is rapidly degraded after all the trees are cut down.
- Flooding is more frequent and rapid as water runs off the land. The water is not absorbed by plants and transpired into the atmosphere. Forests act as 'stores' of water, their leaves slow down the rate of evaporation from the soil and the rate at which water reaches the soil. Diego Martin in Trinidad is an example of a place affected by flooding because of deforestation.
- Many habitats are destroyed and some species face extinction when tropical forests are destroyed. Many species in rainforests have not yet even been studied and classified.
- When vegetation is burnt, carbon dioxide is added to the atmosphere. There is increased decomposition of plant material, such as roots, that also releases more carbon dioxide. This carbon dioxide is not absorbed by plants as they have been cut down.

Figure 2.2.2 Deforestation in Belize (see question 10 on page 37)

(see question 10 on page 37)

EXAM TIP

It is very important to know the correct terms when answering examination questions. The term resources is a good word to use in several contexts. As you revise, see how many times it appears in this book.

KEY POINTS

1. The human population has increased exponentially since about the 1850s. Caribbean populations increased significantly in the 20th century often by 1–2% a year.

2. Increasing population puts pressure on resources – energy, minerals, forests and fisheries.

3. Fish stocks in the Caribbean are under threat from overfishing and habitat destruction.

4. Deforestation has environmental consequences, such as flooding.

SUMMARY QUESTIONS

1 Outline the human population growth over the past 500 years.

2 Describe the effects on the environment of energy provision in the Caribbean.

3 Explain the effects of overfishing on marine environments in the Caribbean.

4 Describe the impact of population growth in the Caribbean on the region's forests.

Pollution

At the end of this topic you should be able to:

- define the term *pollution*
- describe pollution by agricultural practices and the products of industrialisation
- discuss the effects of improper garbage disposal
- describe the pollution of aquatic environments
- discuss the impact of pollution on ecotourism.

Figure 2.3.1 Do we have the right to pollute this egret's habitat?

Figure 2.3.2 Coral reefs like this one off the coast of St Kitts attract divers keen to see the diverse ecosystem with riches like this purple tube sponge.

Anything released into the environment as a result of human activity that has the potential to cause harm is a **pollutant**. We think of most pollutants as being chemical substances, such as fertilisers, oil and carbon monoxide or as biological material, such as human body wastes. However, heat released from power stations and noise from industrial and domestic sources are also pollutants. **Pollution** is the release of substances from human activities that are harmful to the environment.

Pollution from agriculture

Fertilisers drain from the land into rivers and lakes. Fertilisers are applied to crops to increase their yield. Farmers need to know the best type of fertiliser to use for their particular soil and crop and how much to add. Problems can occur if a farmer uses too much fertiliser or if the fertiliser is added before a period of heavy rain.

Excess fertiliser can cause water pollution. This causes **eutrophication**, which means that waters are enriched with plant nutrients, mainly nitrate ions and phosphate ions. In the Caribbean, rivers are short, so much of this pollution ends up in the sea where it causes growth of algae, such as seaweeds. Coral polyps build the reef and contain microalgae as **symbionts**. The microalgae photosynthesise and provide energy to the polyps. The seaweed grows faster than herbivores can eat them so they overshadow the reef, preventing the microalgae photosynthesising, so the reef dies.

Pollution from industry

Industrial processes produce large quantities of waste. Some of these are fairly harmless, like hot water. Others are taken up by organisms and not excreted, so build up in food chains. Examples are:

- lead from car batteries
- mercury, which is used in gold mining
- cadmium, which is used in industrial paints
- PCBs, used in making products such as electrical insulation.

Pollution from improper garbage disposal

Household rubbish and other wastes such as building rubble should be disposed properly, not thrown anywhere such as into rivers, streams and gullies. The Riverton disposal site near Kingston receives 60% of the waste produced in Jamaica. It is 119 hectares in area and is next to mangroves and the Duhaney River. As the site is not managed correctly it has a huge environmental impact on the surrounding area and to the health of local people (Figure 2.3.1). A wide range of air pollutants are produced when the dump burns; amongst these are particulates, such as dust, carbon monoxide, hydrogen cyanide, nitrogen oxides (NOx), sulfur dioxide and dioxins.

The public health risks from Riverton are:

- water pollution into the Duhaney River (used for drinking and bathing)
- pollution of Hunts Bay, which scientists call 'The Dead Zone'
- heavy metal contamination from cadmium, manganese and lead
- pesticides for use in eliminating disease vectors and plant pests.

Pollution and the marine environment

There are three important marine ecosystems in the Caribbean:

- coastal ecosystems dominated by mangrove trees
- ecosystems in shallow water where sea grasses are the dominant vegetation
- coral reefs.

Mangrove trees protect coastlines and estuaries throughout the tropics; shrimp fishing, pollution, deforestation, storms and coastal building development have damaged them. Sea-grass ecosystems found in shallow waters throughout the region are important feeding and breeding sites for many species. They too are at high risk of destruction from pollution and development.

Coral reefs are one of the most biodiverse places in the World with over a million different species; they provide fish for human consumption, protection for coastlines and are a tourist attraction (Figure 2.3.2). In the Caribbean it is estimated that over 23% of coral reefs have been destroyed and many are considered at high risk. Some scientists have predicted that coral reefs will disappear by the end of the 21st century. Reefs, such as the famous Buccoo reef off the coast of Tobago, have been severely degraded. Pollution from land run-off, poorly treated sewage, domestic grey water, agricultural run-off, fertilisers, herbicides, pesticides, chemicals and oil spills have had devastating effects. Overfishing has also contributed, by removing too many herbivorous fish, such as parrotfish and surgeonfish, so that seaweeds have grown and starved the symbiotic algae in corals of sunlight. Disease has also wiped out sea urchins, which graze algae on coral reefs.

Another threat to reefs is sea water becoming more acidic. The pH of sea water has decreased making it more difficult for organisms, such as clams, to make shells of calcium carbonate. The same applies to coral polyps that secrete the calcium carbonate that makes up the skeleton of the coral. With global carbon dioxide concentrations increasing, this is likely to get worse.

Many countries in the Caribbean have realised the benefits of conserving areas like these for the aesthetic and economic benefits they bring. Ecotourism has become important as visitors from abroad wish to see the spectacular wildlife associated with coral reefs and tropical forests. Pollution has a negative effect on such areas and can cause countries like Belize, Dominica and Costa Rica, which rely on ecotourism, to lose some important sources of revenue and income.

KEY POINTS

1 Pollution is the release of substances harmful to the environment from human activities or their presence in the environment.

2 Agriculture and industry release wastes that pollute the environment.

3 The improper disposal of garbage poses health and environmental hazards.

4 Aquatic ecosystems throughout the Caribbean have been damaged by pollution, development, overfishing and climate change.

5 Ecotourism is an important source of income for many Caribbean countries. It is at risk from pollution.

SUMMARY QUESTIONS

1 Make a table to show pollutants of land, air and water. In your table state the sources of each pollutant and the effects that it has on the environment.

2 State some industrial pollutants, and describe their sources and the effects that they have on the environment and on humans.

3 a Explain the term *ecotourism*.

b Outline why ecotourism is important in the Caribbean.

c Explain the threats to this form of tourism.

The effects of climate change

Life in the greenhouse

The atmosphere is like a blanket surrounding the Earth keeping it warm. Some of the gases in the atmosphere act like a greenhouse. They keep heat inside the atmosphere that otherwise would be radiated into space. These are carbon dioxide, water vapour and methane, which are **greenhouse gases**.

These gases allow solar energy to pass through to the Earth's surface and warm it. Some of this energy enters food chains and is eventually lost to the atmosphere as heat. This radiates away from the Earth's surface. Some of this energy escapes into space, but much is absorbed and emitted towards the Earth as infra-red radiation (heat). Greenhouse gases keep our atmosphere at the temperatures that allow life to exist.

The **greenhouse effect** is a natural process and without it the average temperature on the Earth would be about −17 °C. However, over the last 100 years, there has been a build-up of greenhouse gases from human processes (Figure 2.4.1).

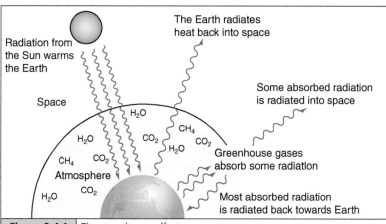

Figure 2.4.1	The greenhouse effect

Power stations, factories, domestic heating and transport use fossil fuels and release huge amounts of carbon dioxide into the atmosphere. As we have seen, deforestation has resulted in large areas of forest being removed. In Latin America the trees are cleared for farming, releasing carbon dioxide into the atmosphere when they are burnt. Microbes in the soil decompose roots and other remaining tree parts, producing even more carbon dioxide.

There has also been a significant increase in methane (another greenhouse gas) due to the expansion of rice cultivation and cattle rearing. Cattle excrete methane and bacteria also release it in the anaerobic conditions found in flooded rice fields and natural wetlands. Rotting material in landfill sites and rubbish tips and the extraction of oil and natural gas are other sources of methane.

Of all the greenhouse gases, the largest increase has been in carbon dioxide, which has risen by 10% in the last 30 years. However, molecules of methane and CFCs have a much greater impact on the greenhouse effect than molecules of carbon dioxide.

The presence of greenhouse gases in the atmosphere causes the air to warm up. Without carbon dioxide and water vapour the heat energy would pass straight back out into space. Human activity is causing a large increase in the atmosphere of carbon dioxide and other greenhouse gases, such as methane, which has a greater impact than carbon dioxide (see question 9 on the CD).

Climate change

Human activities are causing an increase in the concentration of greenhouse gases so the atmosphere is getting warmer. This is causing the **enhanced greenhouse effect**. The surface of the Earth has warmed by 0.7 °C over the past century. Global climate models suggest that average temperatures in the Caribbean will rise by 0.5–1.0 °C by 2039, 0.8–2.5 °C from 2040 to 2069, and 0.94–4.8 °C between 2070 and 2099.

If the temperature of the Arctic and Antarctic were to rise above 0 °C, the polar ice would start to melt. This would cause a rise in sea level and flooding of many low-lying areas. These would include most of the capital cities of the Caribbean and much of the region's farmland (Figure 2.4.2).

There could also be a change in wind patterns and the distribution of rainfall, leading to more extreme weather. Some parts of the world are expected to become very dry. Some of these are important agricultural areas, such as parts of the USA and Asia. Warming of the climate could mean a massive reduction in the grain crops of Central Asia and North America. The pattern of the world's food distribution could be affected with economic and political consequences.

Measures to reduce the effects of global warming involve reducing carbon emissions. Strategies to do this include using energy more efficiently and using renewable sources of energy such as solar, wind and wave power and ethanol-based fuels.

The Caribbean is at high risk of storm damage. The severity of tropical storms has been increasing, with eight Category 5 hurricanes between the years 2001 and 2010, compared with a total of 23 between 1928 and 2000. Storms are also reaching high intensity more quickly. More severe storms will increase damage to the mangroves. If the coastal protection provided by mangroves is lost, erosion happens more quickly.

Figure 2.4.2 If sea levels rise, low-lying areas that provide most of the tourism facilities in the Caribbean, as here in St Lucia, could be lost.

SUMMARY QUESTIONS

1 a Define the term *greenhouse gas*.
  b Name two greenhouse gases.

2 Explain what is meant by the *enhanced greenhouse effect*.

3 Describe the steps that can be taken to reduce carbon emissions.

4 Use specific examples to outline the likely effects of global climate change on island states.

KEY POINTS

1 Carbon dioxide, methane and CFCs are greenhouse gases that absorb infra-red radiation from the Earth and emit it back to heat up the atmosphere.

2 The greenhouse effect maintains the temperature of the Earth so life can exist. The enhanced greenhouse effect is the result of an increase in the concentration of greenhouse gases.

3 Global climate change involves increased air and sea temperatures and more unpredictable weather, such as more frequent hurricanes and storms and rises in sea level.

Conservation

At the end of this topic you should be able to:

- describe ways in which the impact of agriculture on the environment can be reduced
- outline methods for conserving the natural environment
- outline methods for restoring degraded land and damaged aquatic (marine and freshwater) environments.

Reducing the environmental impact of agriculture

Farmers can reduce the effect that fertilisers have on the environment by controlling the use of chemicals, such as fertilisers, pesticides and herbicides. They should only apply the chemicals when necessary and not use them as insurance 'just in case'. Some farmers are turning to organic agriculture, which does not use chemicals. Organic farmers use natural methods of fertilising crops. Animal and plant wastes are added to the soil to decay naturally. Farmers can also reduce the use of pesticides by using biological control (see 1.5).

Conservation methods

As we have seen the natural world provides many of our renewable resources. Our very existence depends on the activity of organisms in producing our food and decomposing our wastes. It is important that we conserve the environment for our benefit as well as the benefit of future generations. We have a duty of care to maintain the **biodiversity** and protect **endangered species**. Biodiversity is a catalogue of all the species in an area, a country or even the whole world. But it also includes the different habitats in an area and the genetic diversity within each species.

We should conserve ecosystems, habitats and species for the following reasons:

- Ecosystems provide us with services, such as treating waste, providing food and fuels and giving us areas for recreation. They provide us with useful substances such as medicines.
- Ecosystems help to maintain the balance of life on the planet, e.g. nutrient cycles.
- Habitats support a wide variety of organisms that interact in ways we do not fully understand, but are vital for continuing life on this planet, for example by keeping pests and diseases in check.
- Other species have as much right to live on this planet as we do. We have a role as guardians of the planet (Figure 2.5.1).

No species lives in isolation, so we have a duty to conserve ecosystems and habitats. Here are some ways in which this is done:

- National Parks – large tracts of land set aside for wildlife and patrolled by wardens. Parks may also be occupied by people.
- Protecting areas of the sea from damage from fishing and pollution by establishing marine parks.
- Rescuing endangered animals, breeding them in captivity and then returning them to the wild.
- Growing endangered plants in botanical gardens and re-establishing them in the wild.

Figure 2.5.1 The conservation of species like this ocelot requires large areas of land to be set aside and protected from deforestation and development.

- Reducing habitat destruction, e.g. issuing licences for logging in forests or preventing it altogether.
- Encouraging sustainable management of ecosystems. In forests, allowing natural replacement or replanting when trees are removed but not destroying habitats by clearing large areas.
- Storing seeds of endangered or valuable species at very low temperatures. Seed banks around the world hope to collect and store seeds from many species in case they become extinct in the wild. Their genes may be useful for crop improvement in the future or to produce valuable products, such as drugs.
- Removing alien species, such as dodder (see 1.6), lionfish and bottle brush.

Restoration methods

Restoring habitats that have been degraded or destroyed by human activities and natural catastrophes is an important part of conservation. The following are examples:

- Re-establishing ecosystems where land has become degraded, for example establishing dry forest in Guanacaste National Park in Costa Rica, which may take up to 300 years to achieve!
- Tree planting day in Jamaica and schemes in Haiti to reforest degraded land to reduce the severe effects of heavy rain (Figure 2.5.2).
- Restoring land degraded by mining and waste disposal, for example the soda lake at Mount Rosser in Jamaica.
- Restoring mangrove to protect coasts that are at risk of storm damage.

Education and public awareness campaigns are an important part of conservation work. Much can be achieved by people in their own locality in habitat restoration and conservation. Governments can also legislate to protect habitats at risk from development and destruction.

Resources need to be conserved as well. We have already discussed how using energy efficiently may conserve fossil fuels. Recycling materials, such as aluminium, glass and paper reduces energy consumption, damage to the environment (by creating less waste) and saves raw materials. Water consumption globally has increased considerably and many sources of water are becoming exhausted or polluted. Water must not be wasted and must be used sensibly so that everyone may have some.

Figure 2.5.2 | No-one is too young to plant a tree like this mango, which will provide fruit and habitats for other organisms and will help to reduce soil erosion.

SUMMARY QUESTIONS

1 Outline how the effects of agriculture on the environment can be reduced.

2 Suggest how individuals can promote conservation of resources and energy.

3 Explain how damaged environments can be restored.

4 Discuss the benefits of tree planting.

5 Suggest ways in which the success of conservation and habitat restoration can be monitored.

KEY POINTS

1 Taking steps to reduce the use of fertilisers and pesticides by integrating their use with biological control can reduce the impact of agriculture on the environment.

2 Conservation is the protection and management of ecosystems to maintain biodiversity, control depletion and prevent extinction.

3 Tree planting helps to reduce soil erosion, provides habitats for other organisms and restores degraded habitats.

What will the future bring?

Figure 2.6.1 The lionfish

DID YOU KNOW?

The Fisheries Department in Jamaica is encouraging people to eat lionfish flesh as one approach to controlling numbers.

LINK

Go back to 2.2 to remind yourself about population growth.

Population growth

Populations of animals, plants and microbes increase if there are plenty of resources and space available. However, there are certain factors that limit the maximum numbers in a population. These are:

- availability of food and water
- competition for space, food, water and mating sites (e.g. nesting sites for birds)
- disease – as populations increase in number, diseases spread more rapidly and have a greater effect on large populations than on small ones
- predators that also have a greater effect on larger populations than they do on smaller populations.

When a species invades a new environment, there may be no competitors, no predators and no disease. There are many examples of species that have been introduced, or have invaded, a new environment. The effects of the small Indian mongoose in the Caribbean were described in 1.5. The lionfish (Figure 2.6.1) comes from South-East Asia and escaped from aquaria in the USA. It has colonised much of the Caribbean and feeds on other species of fish. It has no natural predator in its new environment and has increased in numbers.

Human populations

Since the 1850s, human populations began to grow exponentially because the checks on our numbers have been reduced. Food production has increased and there are better facilities for storage and transporting foods. Many infectious diseases have been controlled. We do not have any predators. More people demand higher standards of living which lead to overconsumption of resources.

The HIV/AIDS pandemic shows us that we are not completely free of checks to population increase. With antibiotic resistance on the increase, there may come a time when antibiotics are no longer effective and other diseases that are currently curable become incurable. There is more about this in 12.2.

Scientists are also concerned that our main crop plants are too genetically identical. This makes it highly likely that diseases of crops like wheat, maize and rice, will wipe out all the different varieties that exist, as those varieties are genetically very similar. The collection of seeds from wild varieties of our crops and from local varieties is important. They may have genes that we can use to give our crop plants resistance to diseases.

An example of what might happen is the banana. Farmers propagate new banana plants by taking stem cuttings. As this is a form of asexual reproduction, all the plants are genetically identical. The Cavendish variety of banana is grown across huge areas of land and it is susceptible to two diseases: Panama disease and black sigatoka (Figure 2.6.2). If the fungi that cause these diseases become resistant to fungicides and cannot be controlled in any other way, the Cavendish will be wiped out by disease, like the Gros Michel variety was in the 20th century.

Projections for global and local populations

The global human population has just reached 7 billion. It is still increasing at a fast rate, but not everywhere. In some countries the birth rate has dropped remarkably over the past few decades. The fall in the birth rate in some Caribbean countries means that in the near future there will be an ageing population with a higher proportion of elderly people than in the past.

Challenges and solutions

If our species is to survive, we must find some way to reduce population growth and provide resources to support everyone with a reasonable standard of living. We need to make better use of non-renewable resources and develop renewable sources of energy (Figure 2.6.3). Sugar cane is grown in Brazil to provide sugar for fermentation to make ethanol, which is mixed with petrol to make gasohol. Nuclear power is used in a number of industrialised countries like France.

We are in danger of ruining our environment totally by pollution. We should apply technology to solve the problems caused by improper waste disposal. Biodegradable waste can be composted to provide a valuable resource for agriculture and horticulture. This needs organisation to collect, separate and store household waste, while the biodegradable waste decomposes into compost. The waste that cannot be composted or recycled could be incinerated to provide energy or, as a last resort, buried in sanitary landfill sites where the threats to the environment are minimised.

But every solution brings its problems. Plastics produce toxic gases when they burn and in some places there is no market for compost.

Fishing is a form of hunting. Fish farming, or aquaculture, is practised widely in many parts of the world, notably in South-East Asia. Few Caribbean countries have invested in aquaculture, although there are some farms that rear the fast growing tilapia fish. Perhaps it is time we started to farm fish as we did cattle, sheep and goats many millennia ago.

Figure 2.6.2 | A banana plant infected with the fungus that causes black sigatoka.

Figure 2.6.3 | Fossil fuels will not last forever. We can make use of solar energy by fitting panels like these to houses and commercial buildings.

KEY POINTS

1 Factors that influence population growth are: availability of food and water, competition for resources, disease and predation.

2 Human populations are not affected by these factors to the same extent. The HIV/AIDS pandemic is an example of a factor that is limiting human population growth.

3 Human populations are growing at a high rate and this presents problems for the environment and human health.

4 Population growth is slowing in many countries in the Caribbean; the impact if this will be an increasing proportion of elderly people.

SUMMARY QUESTIONS

1 Explain why a population of organisms does not increase indefinitely.

2 Outline the problems facing a world population in excess of 7 billion people.

3 Summarise the environmental problems facing your country.

4 Suggest ways in which new technology may solve some of the problems you have identified in question 3.

SECTION 1: Multiple-choice questions

1 The concentration of carbon dioxide in the Earth's atmosphere has increased significantly. Which of the following is the most likely cause of this increase?

  A   increase in sea levels

  B   less photosynthesis

  C   more combustion of fossil fuels

  D   melting of the ice caps

2 Which human activity causes eutrophication of coastal waters in the Caribbean?

  A   drainage of toxic compounds from rubbish tips

  B   overuse of fertilisers in adjacent farmland

  C   overuse of pesticides

  D   pollution by oil

3 Different pest control chemicals were tested to see how poisonous they were to freshwater fish. The concentration of pesticide that kills 50% of the fish within four days is known as the lethal dose 50 (LD50). The table shows the results.

	Pest control chemical	LD50/parts per million
A	DDT	0.03
B	dieldrin	0.01
C	malathion	12.20
D	parathion	2.11

Which chemical, A, B, C or D, will have the most serious effect on freshwater fish if allowed to contaminate a river?

4 The quantity of solid wastes collected in Caribbean countries can be reduced by:

  A   burying it all in sanitary landfill sites

  B   composting the biodegradable wastes

  C   incinerating the non-biodegradable wastes

  D   introducing recycling schemes

5 Species that successfully colonise a new habitat are known as invasive species. These species are more likely to become established in their new habitat if they have

  A   competitors

  B   limited resources

  C   no predators

  D   parasites

6 Tree planting is an example of

  A   conservation

  B   environmental monitoring

  C   organic farming

  C   recycling

7 In 1900 the population of Guyana was 287 000. By 2010 this had increased to 769 000. The percentage increase in the population of Guyana between 1900 and 2010 was:

  A   32%

  B   37%

  C   63%

  D   168%

8 Which of the following does *not* directly influence the growth of an animal population?

  A   competition for food

  B   diseases

  C   light intensity

  D   predators

9 Which is the best definition of the biodiversity of an island state?

  A   all the species living within the country

  B   the genetic diversity of all the species

  C   all the different ecosystems within the island and offshore

  D   all of the above

10 a 'Tropical forests have great biodiversity.' Explain this statement. *(3)*

Scientists have used satellite imaging techniques to follow the loss of forests all over the world.

b List four reasons for deforestation in countries in the Caribbean. *(4)*

Tables 1 and 2 show the loss of forest cover in Belize between 1980 and 2010.

Table 1

Year	Forest cover/km²
1980	16 834
1989	16 443
1994	15 452
2000	14 652
2004	14 153
2010	13 900

Table 2

Years	Area deforested each year/km²	Percentage loss per year
1980–89	12	−0.3
1989–94	207	−1.4
1994–2000	71	−0.9
2000–04	291	−0.9
2004–10	61	−0.3

Data adapted from SERVIR: Forest Cover and Deforestation in Belize 1980–2010

c The total land mass of Belize is 22 167 km²
Use the data in the tables to calculate

  i the percentage of the total land mass of Belize that was forested in 1980 and that which was forested in 2010, showing your working. *(4)*

  ii the mean annual area of Belize that was deforested between 1980 and 2010

  iii the mean percentage loss per year. *(2)*

d Outline the environmental consequences of continued deforestation in Belize. *(6)*

e Explain, using examples, the distinction between renewable and non-renewable resources. *(4)*

f Fish are an important resource. Suggest two ways in which fish stocks can be conserved for the future. *(2)*

Total 25 marks

11 a i Define the term *pollutant*. *(1)*

  ii Distinguish between biodegradable and non-biodegradable waste. *(2)*

b Make a table to show the sources and effects of three named pollutants that have significant effects on the environment in the Caribbean region. *(3)*

c The quantity of solid waste in the Caribbean has increased considerably over recent years. Suggest ways in which regional governments can reduce the quantity of such waste. *(4)*

d Outline the environmental and economic reasons for conserving natural habitats in the region. *(5)*

Total 15 marks

12 Coral reefs are polluted by water draining from farmland. As a result they often receive fertiliser and sewage.

a Describe the effect of this pollution on coral reefs. *(5)*

b Describe two other threats to coral reefs. *(4)*

c i State three reasons why organisms become extinct. *(3)*

  ii Scientists have suggested that some animals that have become extinct in recent times be 'brought back' using modern techniques including isolation of DNA from museum specimens and cloning. One such animal is the Cuban macaw.

Discuss the rights and wrongs of such a programme. *(3)*

Total 15 marks

Further practice questions and examples can be found on the accompanying CD.

3 Cells

3.1

Plant and animal cells

Cell structure

Cells are sometimes called the 'units of life', as all organisms are made of cells. All cells share features in common, although there are significant differences between the different types. Cells from animals, plants, fungi and bacteria are all surrounded by a **cell membrane** and contain **cytoplasm**, but the rest of the cell structure is quite different. Figure 3.1.1 shows plant cells seen through a light microscope. Even with very powerful light microscopes there are cell structures that are not visible and we need an electron microscope to see them. Figures 3.1.2 and 3.1.3 have been drawn from photographs taken with electron microscopes that allow us to see these structures, called **organelles**, found within cells.

Animal and plant cell structure

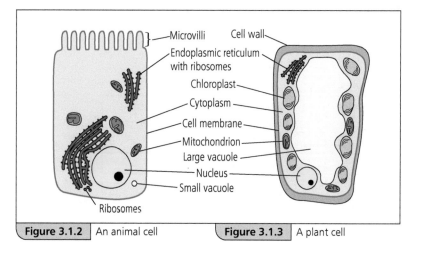

Microvilli
Endoplasmic reticulum with ribosomes
Chloroplast
Cytoplasm
Cell membrane
Mitochondrion
Large vacuole
Nucleus
Small vacuole
Ribosomes
Cell wall

Figure 3.1.2	An animal cell

Figure 3.1.3	A plant cell

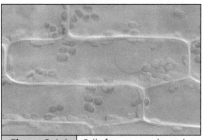

Figure 3.1.1	Cells from a pond weed have a fixed shape because they are surrounded by cell walls. These leaf cells are full of green organelles called chloroplasts (× 1000).

Functions of cell structures

Table 3.1.1   Cell structures and their functions

Cell structure	Functions
Cell wall (plants only)	• made from cellulose; stops cells from bursting when they are full of water • gives fixed shapes to cells • allows water and dissolved substances to pass through freely (often described as freely permeable – see 3.4)
Cell membrane	• forms a barrier between cells and their surroundings • keeps contents of cells inside • allows simple substances to enter and leave cells, e.g. oxygen, carbon dioxide and water • controls movement of other substances into and out of cells, e.g. glucose and ions • often described as differentially permeable (see 3.4)
Nucleus	• holds the chromosomes, which carry genetic information in the form of DNA (see 11.3) • controls all activities inside cells • controls how cells develop
Cytoplasm	• place where many chemical reactions take place, e.g. respiration and making proteins for cells
Mitochondrion	• carries out aerobic respiration (Figure 3.1.5)
Chloroplast (plants only)	• carries out photosynthesis (Figure 3.1.4) • stores starch
Vacuole	• *plants* – large and full of water to maintain shape and 'firmness' of cells • *animals* – small and stores enzymes for digestion within cells

Figure 3.1.4 | A chloroplast, the organelle that carries out photosynthesis ($\times$ 10 000)

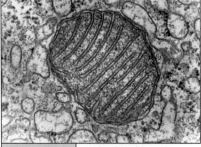

Figure 3.1.5 | A mitochondrion, the organelle where aerobic respiration occurs ($\times$ 40 000)

KEY POINTS

1   Some cell structures can be seen with the light microscope; details of these structures and some very small structures can only be seen with an electron microscope.

2   Animal and plant cells have cell membranes, nuclei, cytoplasm and mitochondria.

3   Plant cells have cell walls, chloroplasts and large, central vacuoles. Animal cells do not have these.

SUMMARY QUESTIONS

1   State *four* structures that are found in both plant and animal cells.

2   Make a table to compare the structure of plant and animal cells.

3   Distinguish between each of the following pairs: chloroplast and mitochondrion; cell wall and cell membrane; chromosome and nucleus. You could use tables for this question and add more information about these structures as you work through the rest of this unit.

Microbes

At the end of this topic you should be able to:

• state that bacteria, fungi, viruses and protists are microbes

• describe the structure of each of these groups of microbes

• state the similarities and differences between the different groups of microbes.

Microbes

Bacteria, fungi, viruses and protists are often known as **microorganisms** or just **microbes** for short. Fungi have a cell structure that is similar to the structure of plant cells except that they do not have chloroplasts. Bacteria do not have nuclei and are much smaller than plant and animal cells. Viruses are quite different as they do not have cells at all. Protists have more in common with plant and animal cells.

Bacteria

Each bacterium is made of one cell and is described as **unicellular**. You can see that the cell has a cell wall and a cell membrane, but there are only a few of the cell structures you can see in the animal and plant cells. Their genetic material is in the cytoplasm as there is no nucleus; the cytoplasm contains ribosomes to make proteins but there are no other structures (Figure 3.2.1).

Fungi

Yeast is a fungus that is also unicellular, but unlike bacteria each yeast cell has a nucleus, mitochondria and a large vacuole. In many ways yeasts are like plant cells except that they have no chloroplasts. Figure 3.2.2 shows a mould fungus. Many of these do not have separate cells at all but long thin threads, known as hyphae which are not sub-divided into cells but contain all the structures in one long 'tube'.

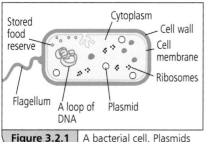

Figure 3.2.1 | A bacterial cell. Plasmids are small loops of DNA.

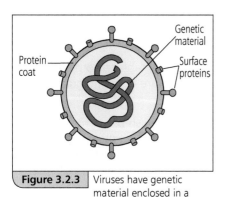

Figure 3.2.3 | Viruses have genetic material enclosed in a protein capsule.

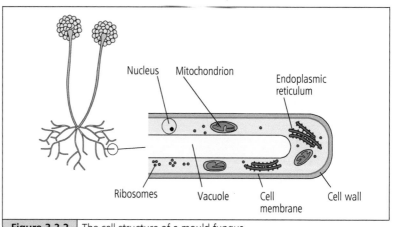

Figure 3.2.2 | The cell structure of a mould fungus

Viruses

All viruses are parasites of cells of organisms. They are thought to have developed from cells, but now all they have is a central core composed of genetic material (DNA or RNA) surrounded by a protein coat or capsule. Some of them are enveloped in cell membrane from their host cell (Figure 3.2.3).

Protists

Unlike the other microbes, protists have a cell structure, which is similar to that of plants and animals; for example, their cells have nuclei. Some protists are more animal-like, such as *Amoeba* (Figure 3.2.4); others, such as *Euglena* (Figure 3.2.5), are more plant-like. Not all protists are small unicellular organisms; some are large multicellular organisms. Seaweeds, including the large kelps, which may grow up to 50 metres long, are classified as protists.

EXAM TIP

It is difficult to remember the similarities and differences between bacteria, fungi, protists (such as *Amoeba* and *Euglena*) and viruses. Make a table to show all the features that they have and then complete it with ticks and crosses – see question 1.

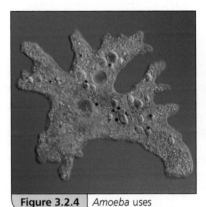

| **Figure 3.2.4** | *Amoeba* uses extensions called pseudopodia for movement and feeding. Note the green algae trapped inside food vacuoles where they are digested (× 60). |

| **Figure 3.2.5** | *Euglena* uses its flagellum to reach places where there is light for photosynthesis (× 400). |

DID YOU KNOW?

Biologists classify organisms into five different kingdoms: bacteria, fungi, animals, plants and the protists. The protists contain organisms that are either unicellular, e.g. *Amoeba* and *Euglena*, or have simple bodies made of many cells.

KEY POINTS

1 Bacteria are unicellular with cell walls and cytoplasm but without organelles, such as nuclei.

2 Fungal cells have cell walls, nuclei, large vacuoles and mitochondria, but no chloroplasts.

3 Viruses do not have cells. They are made of genetic material enclosed in a protein coat.

4 Some protists, such as *Amoeba* and *Euglena*, are unicellular; others, such as seaweeds, are multicellular and can be very large.

SUMMARY QUESTIONS

1 Make a table to compare the structure of bacteria, fungi and viruses.

2 Distinguish between each of the following pairs: bacteria and viruses; yeasts and mould fungi; bacteria and protists.

Cells make bodies

At the end of this topic you should be able to:

- define the terms *tissue*, *organ* and *organ system*
- explain what is meant by *cell specialisation*
- list some examples of specialised cells in animals and plants
- explain the advantages of being multicellular.

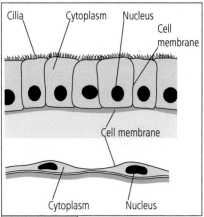

Fig 3.3.1 Ciliated cells from the human windpipe and squamous cells from the alveoli

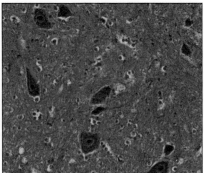

Figure 3.3.2 Nerve cells in the spinal cord are specialised animal cells. The nuclei are visible in four of these cells (× 70).

Animals and plants are **multicellular** with bodies made of many cells that work together. Most multicellular organisms develop from a single cell – a fertilised egg. This cell divides to produce a two-celled embryo. The cells continue to grow and divide to form a much larger structure. Some cells retain the ability to carry on dividing throughout life: these are the stem cells (see 11.2). Other cells lose the ability to divide and change in structure to become specialised for certain functions.

Specialised cells

To function efficiently we have cells that are **specialised** to carry out certain functions. This means that the functions of the body are divided between different groups of cells.

Animal cells

Epithelial cells are found on the surfaces of organisms, for example forming the outer layer of our skin. They also line internal structures, such as the windpipe and lungs. Two are described here: ciliated epithelial cells and squamous epithelial cells.

Ciliated epithelial cells are found in the air passages in the lungs (windpipe and bronchi) and in the fallopian tubes in the female reproductive system (Figure 3.3.1). These cells have tiny hair-like **cilia** on their surfaces. Cilia beat back and forth to create a current in the fluid next to the cell surfaces.

In the lungs, cilia move the mucus that traps dust and pathogens up to the nose and throat. In the fallopian tubes, cilia move the egg from the ovary to the uterus.

Squamous epithelial cells are very thin cells. They form the outer layer of the skin and line the tiny air pockets in the lungs. Squamous cells form the lining of blood vessels.

Most **neurones** (nerve cells) have very long processes that transmit nerve impulses over great distances in the body. Some nerve cells, like the one in Figure 3.3.2, have short processes that connect nerves together. There are many of these in the brain and the spinal cord (Figure 3.3.3).

The **muscle cells** in the gut and other places in the body are long thin cells which each have a single nucleus (Figure 3.3.4). The 'cells' in the muscles that move our skeleton are different. They each have many nuclei and are often called muscle *fibres* rather than muscle *cells*.

Plant cells

There are far fewer types of specialised cells in plants than in animals. Epidermal cells form the tissue that surrounds leaves. The **guard cells** that open and close the stomata are specialised epidermal cells. Root hair cells that absorb water and mineral ions are also epidermal cells.

Some cells become specialised for transport. **Xylem** cells gain a thick cell wall as they develop; they also lose their cell contents to make it easy to transport water from roots to leaves (see 6.6). **Phloem** cells do not develop thick cell walls and retain some of their contents. They are used for the transport of a solution rich in sucrose, amino acids and other solutes. This fluid moves from leaves to roots, flowers and fruits (Figure 3.3.5).

Organisation of cells

Most specialised cells are organised into **tissues**. A tissue is a group of similar cells that work together to carry out one major function. Ciliated cells are arranged into thin sheets that line the trachea. Their function is to move mucus away from the lungs carrying any bacteria, dirt or dust that we breathe in.

Ciliated epithelial tissue is just one of several that make up the whole of the trachea. For example, there is cartilage, muscle tissue, some nervous tissue, blood tissue and glands that secrete mucus. The trachea is an example of an **organ**. An organ is a group of tissues that perform one or more functions for the body. Plants have three organs: root, stem and leaf. Any other structure in a plant is a modification of one of these three organs.

The trachea and the lungs make up the gas exchange system. An **organ system** comprises several organs that work together for one or more major functions of the body. In animals, there are systems for digestion, movement, coordination, excretion, transport and reproduction; in plants, there are systems for the transport of water through the plant leading to **transpiration** (see 6.6) and the **translocation** of compounds such as sucrose (see 6.8).

The idea that cells specialise in certain functions is known as **division of labour**. Cells work together for the efficient functioning of the body. Most specialised cells carry out one function in the body and rely on other cells and tissues to provide the substances that they need and take away their waste products. The body maintains conditions, such as temperature and pH, constant so that the cells can work efficiently (see Figure 0.2.3 on page 9).

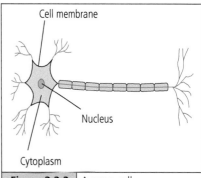

Figure 3.3.3 | A nerve cell

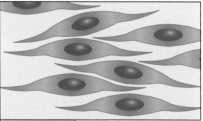

Figure 3.3.4 | Muscle cells from the wall of the human gut. Cells like this are also found in the reproductive system, the trachea and in the walls of arteries and veins.

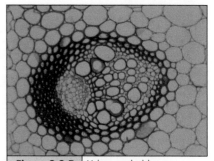

Figure 3.3.5 | Xylem and phloem

SUMMARY QUESTIONS

1 Define the following terms: *multicellular*, *specialised*, *tissue*, *organ*, *organ system* and *division of labour*.

2 Name the specialised cells, tissues and organs that make up the human gas exchange system.

3 Make some learning notes on the specialised cells in this section. See How to Learn 1 on page 6 to help you make these notes.

KEY POINTS

1 Cells in multicellular organisms are specialised for one major function or several related functions.

2 Epithelial cells, nerve cells, muscle cells, xylem cells and phloem cells are examples of specialised cells.

3 Cells are organised into tissues; tissues are organised into organs; organs are organised into organ systems.

Transport across cell membranes

LEARNING OUTCOMES

At the end of this topic you should be able to:

- define the terms *diffusion*, *osmosis* and *active transport* and explain why they are important for cells
- explain that osmosis is a special type of diffusion
- explain how active transport differs from diffusion.

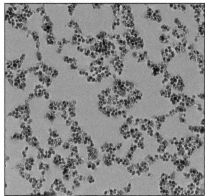

Figure 3.4.1 These yeast cells have been placed in blue dye which has diffused into them.

STUDY FOCUS

Cellulose cell walls are described as fully or freely permeable as all substances can pass through them. *Impermeable* means that *no* substances can pass through. *Differentially permeable* means *some* substances can pass through, but others cannot. You will find these terms used throughout this study guide. Make sure you know what they mean and can use them correctly.

Cells cannot exist in total isolation from their surroundings, they have to take in substances that they need and get rid of their wastes. Cell membranes surround the cytoplasm and keep everything inside the cell, but they are a *partial* barrier to movement. Some useful substances are kept in; others are exchanged with the surroundings. Membranes allow some substances to enter but not others; this is why they are described as **differentially permeable membranes**.

Diffusion

Oxygen is needed by mitochondria for aerobic respiration. The concentration of oxygen within our cells is very low as it is used up all the time. The concentration outside the cell in the tissue fluid is much higher. Molecules of oxygen move about randomly and, over time, more pass through the membrane into the cell than pass out. This movement is **diffusion** and the molecules are said to move down their **concentration gradient**, from high to low concentration.

Unicellular organisms, such as *Amoeba*, rely on the diffusion of oxygen and carbon dioxide across the cell membrane that forms their body surface. In contrast, large animals have specialised gas exchange surfaces like the alveoli in our lungs (see 5.9).

Osmosis

The diffusion of water through membranes is known as **osmosis**. The movement of water is influenced by the concentration of the solutions on either side of the membrane (Figure 3.4.1). Osmosis is the diffusion of water from a place with a low concentration of solutes (dilute solution) to a place with a higher concentration of solutes (more concentrated solution) across a differentially permeable membrane.

Blood consists of cells suspended in a solution of salts, glucose and proteins called **plasma**. Figure 3.4.2 shows what happens to red blood cells when drops of blood are put into three different solutions.

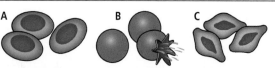

A Red blood cells in a salt solution that has about the same concentration as blood plasma
B Red blood cells in tap water
C Red blood cells in a solution with a concentration of salt greater than the concentration of blood plasma

Figure 3.4.2

In **A**, the liquid becomes cloudy red. If a small drop of this liquid is examined under a microscope the red blood cells have their usual shape. In **B**, there is a sudden change. The water goes red, but is not cloudy. There are no red blood cells when some of the water is put under a microscope. This is because water has moved by osmosis through the differentially permeable membrane around each red blood cell into the cell. So much water has entered that the volume has increased and burst the membrane. In **C**, water moves out of the cells by osmosis and the cells decrease in volume and become crinkly.

Plant cells behave differently to animal cells because they have a cell wall. When plant cells are put into water, they absorb water by osmosis. The vacuole fills with water and pushes against the cell wall making the cell **turgid**. When placed into a solution with a high concentration of solutes, water leaves the cell by osmosis and the vacuole shrinks pulling the cytoplasm and the cell membrane away from the cell wall. This is called **plasmolysis** (Figure 3.4.3); cells in this state are described as **flaccid**. Water can move from cell to cell by osmosis when they have cell contents with different concentrations.

Active transport

Active transport is the movement of ions or molecules in or out of a cell through the cell membrane *against* a concentration gradient, using energy released during respiration. Cell membranes have **carrier proteins**. These carrier proteins span the cell membrane and work to move ions and molecules into or out of cells by active transport.

Active transport occurs in almost all cells, but as we will see it is important in nerve and kidney cells and also the cells that line the villi in the small intestine (see 5.5). Root hair cells absorb mineral ions from the soil by active uptake.

LINK

Amoeba is a unicellular protist – see 3.2.

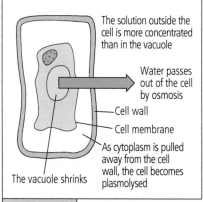

The solution outside the cell is more concentrated than in the vacuole

Water passes out of the cell by osmosis

Cell wall

Cell membrane

As cytoplasm is pulled away from the cell wall, the cell becomes plasmolysed

The vacuole shrinks

Figure 3.4.3 When put into a solution with a high concentration of solutes, plant cells become plasmolysed like this.

KEY POINTS

1 Substances move into and out of cells by diffusion, osmosis and active transport.

2 Diffusion is the movement of molecules down a concentration gradient.

3 Osmosis is the diffusion of water molecules from a solution with a low concentration of solutes (dilute solution) to a solution with a high concentration of solutes (concentrated solution) across a differentially permeable membrane.

4 Active transport is the movement of molecules and ions across a cell membrane against a concentration gradient using energy from respiration.

SUMMARY QUESTIONS

1 Write definitions of the following terms: *diffusion*, *concentration gradient*, *differentially permeable membrane*, *osmosis* and *active transport*.

2 Make a table to show the similarities and differences between diffusion, osmosis and active transport. Remember to include a column to show the features that you are comparing.

3 Explain why it is important that the concentration of the blood plasma does not become too low or too high.

4 Describe how active transport occurs to move a molecule *out of* a cell.

5 Make a spider diagram to summarise movement across cell membranes. (See How to Learn 2, on page 8 to remind yourself about how to do this.)

SECTION 1: Multiple-choice questions

1 Chloroplasts in a palisade mesophyll cell are in the
  A cytoplasm
  B nucleus
  C sap vacuole
  D space between the cell wall and the cell membrane

2 Which structures must be present for osmosis to occur between a cell and its surroundings?
  A cell wall and cell membrane
  B cell wall and cytoplasm
  C cytoplasm and cell membrane
  D vacuole and cell wall

3 The table shows the components of four groups of microbes. Which of the following, A, B, C or D, indicates the components found in bacteria?

	Cell membrane	Cell wall	Nucleus	Chloroplast	Mitochondrion
A	✓	✗	✓	✗	✓
B	✓	✓	✓	✓	✓
C	✓	✓	✗	✗	✗
D	✓	✓	✓	✗	✓

4 Substances cross cell membranes by active transport, diffusion and osmosis. Which shows the correct examples of each of these three processes?

	Active transport	Diffusion	Osmosis
A	Glucose by epithelium of small intestine	Mineral ions by root hair cells	Carbon dioxide by red blood cell
B	Mineral ions by root hair cells	Oxygen by epithelium of alveolus	Water by *Amoeba* in pond water
C	Oxygen by red blood cells	Carbon dioxide by red blood cells	Glucose by epithelium of small intestine
D	Water by *Amoeba* in pond water	Mineral ions by root hair cells	Oxygen by red blood cells

5 Which of the following is an organ?
  A blood
  B epidermis
  C kidney
  D xylem

6 Which of the following is a protist?
  A a bacterium
  B *Amoeba*
  C a mould fungus
  D yeast

7 Visking tubing is similar to cell surface membrane in that it is differentially permeable. Some students followed this procedure.

- Six pieces of Visking tubing measuring 140 mm in length were tied at one end to make a bag. Five bags were filled with different concentrations of a sugar solution until they weighed 10.0 g. The sixth bag was filled with distilled water of the same mass.

- The bags were tied with cotton thread and suspended in a large beaker of distilled water.

- After 6 hours, the bags were removed, blotted dry with paper towels and reweighed. The results are shown in Figure 1.

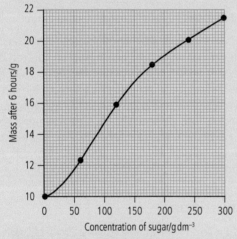

Figure 1

a Explain why the students

   i   included a bag that contained distilled water   *(2)*

   ii surface-dried the bags before weighing them.   *(1)*

b Make a table to record the data shown in Figure 1.   *(4)*

c Explain the results of the students' investigation.   *(5)*

d One student criticised the results saying that they were not reliable.

   State how the procedure should be changed to make the results more reliable.   *(1)*

e Predict what will happen to the mass of the bags if left for another 18 hours. Explain your prediction.   *(3)*

The students continued their investigation by peeling 50 small onions. They divided the peeled onions into five batches of 10 onions and weighed them. Each batch was placed into a solution of different concentrations of salt (sodium chloride). After immersion for two hours each batch was surface dried and reweighed. The students calculated the percentage change in mass. The table shows their results.

Concentration of salt / g dm⁻³	Mean mass of onions/g		Percentage change in mass
	before immersion	after 2 hours immersion	
0	147	173	+18.0
25	153	165	+8.0
50	176	172	−2.0
100	154	149	
150	149	142	−4.5
200	183	175	−4.5

Information and data used to compile the table from Practical osmosis in vegetable pickling, Ray W James. Journal of Biological Education (1993) 27 (2), pages 90–91

f i Calculate the percentage change in mass for the onions kept in the 100 g dm⁻³ salt solution. Show your working.   *(2)*

   ii State why the students calculated the percentage change in mass.   *(1)*

   iii Draw a graph of percentage change in mass against concentration of salt solution.   *(5)*

   iv Use your graph to find the salt solution in which there is no change in mass. *(1)*

Total 25 marks

Further practice questions and examples can be found on the accompanying CD.

4 Nutrition

4.1 Types of nutrition

Figure 4.1.1 Mangrove trees, like all green plants, are autotrophic.

Figure 4.1.2 In the open ocean, the main autotrophs are microscopic planktonic algae like these.

Producers and consumers

You will remember from 1.4 and 1.5 that we can write food chains and food webs to show feeding relationships. Producers, such as green plants and phytoplankton (Figure 4.1.2), are at the base of almost all these food chains and webs. They convert light energy from the Sun into chemical energy. These organisms also absorb simple inorganic compounds (carbon dioxide and water) and use them to make complex organic compounds. The type of nutrition used by producers is **autotrophic nutrition** and the organisms that feed this way are called **autotrophs**. Consumers are not able to utilise simple inorganic compounds or absorb and make use of light energy. Instead they feed on other organisms. This type of nutrition is **heterotrophic nutrition** and organisms that feed in this way are called **heterotrophs**.

Autotrophic nutrition

Autotrophic means 'self feeding'. Autotrophic organisms need only simple inorganic substances from their environment. Carbon dioxide and water are the raw materials that provide the elements carbon, hydrogen and oxygen; in addition autotrophs need other elements to make a range of substances. These other elements are absorbed from the surroundings as ions. The three major elements required by green plants are nitrogen, potassium and phosphorus. These are required in larger quantities compared with elements, such as magnesium, sulfur, iron and calcium. There is more about these elements in 4.5.

Heterotrophic nutrition

Heterotrophs gain their food in a variety of way. Protists, such as *Amoeba*, engulf food particles into food vacuoles. This process is called **phagocytosis** (see 3.2 and 6.4). Multicellular animals that eat solid food bite into their food using jaws and teeth. Fluid feeders pierce the surface of the body and suck body fluids. Aphids feed from the phloem of plants like this (see 6.8) and mosquitoes feed on blood in the same way (see 10.2).

Fungi are all heterotrophic. The fruiting bodies of mushrooms in Figure 4.1.5 are supported by an extensive network of hyphae that spreads through the dead wood. These hyphae release enzymes onto the food where it is digested. The hyphae then absorb the products of digestion.

Parasites feed in a variety of ways. Some parasitic animals live on the surface of their hosts. Lice, ticks and fleas hold onto the body of their host and use piercing mouthparts to suck blood. Many parasitic animals live inside the bodies of their hosts feeding on digested food in the gut or on nutrients that are transported in the blood. There are some parasitic fungi that live on human skin; ringworm is an example. There are many species of bacteria that are parasites of animals; examples that affect us are the bacteria that cause cholera, typhoid and tuberculosis (TB) (see 10.1).

Saprophytic nutrition

Many bacteria and fungi feed on dead and decaying matter rather than on living organisms. Earlier we considered these organisms as decomposers because they break down the dead remains of plants and animals and help to recycle elements, such as carbon and nitrogen. This is a form of heterotrophic nutrition because they obtain the carbon compounds by secreting enzymes onto their food source and then absorbing the soluble products. Many decomposers, such as fungi that grow on dead wood, can digest cellulose. Without them, the world would be full of dead but not decomposed trees.

Table 4.1.1 summarises the differences between these three types of nutrition.

Table 4.1.1   Types of nutrition

Feature	Types of nutrition		
	Autotrophic	**Heterotrophic**	**Saprophytic (saprotrophic)**
Source of energy	Light	Complex carbon compounds of carbon, e.g. starch, fat, protein, cellulose	
Source of carbon	Carbon dioxide	Complex compounds of carbon (as above)	
Types of organism	All green plants; algae; some bacteria	Animals; parasitic fungi and bacteria; parasitic plants, e.g. dodder (see 1.6)	Decomposers – many species of bacteria and fungi

Figure 4.1.3   Animals such as sheep, cattle, horses and termites have guts that contain many microbes that help digest their food.

Figure 4.1.4   This boy has ringworm of the scalp.

Figure 4.1.5   These mushrooms in a Costa Rican forest release millions of tiny spores.

DID YOU KNOW?

Scientists have found communities of organisms at depths of over 4000 m in the Cayman Trench between Jamaica and Cuba. No light penetrates to these depths, so the autotrophic bacteria at the base of the food webs obtain their energy from simple chemical reactions using sulfur and hydrogen sulfide released from holes in the sea floor known as *hydrothermal vents*.

KEY POINTS

1 Autotrophic nutrition involves the conversion of simple inorganic compounds (carbon dioxide and water) to complex organic compounds. The energy for this comes from light.

2 Heterotrophic nutrition involves feeding on organic compounds.

3 Saprophytic nutrition is a form of heterotrophic nutrition that involves feeding on organic material from dead and decaying matter.

SUMMARY QUESTIONS

1 Draw a spider diagram to show the different types of nutrition; include named organisms that show each type of nutrition.

2 Make a table to show the different trophic levels and assign each to a type of nutrition. Give examples of each trophic level from the wildlife in your locality.

3 Name the type of special relationship between sheep and the bacteria that live in their stomachs (see 1.6 for a hint).

4 Suggest why saprophytic fungi produce many spores.

Figure 4.2.1 In bright sunshine the freshwater plant, *Elodea*, releases bubbles of gas rich in oxygen.

Water weeds oxygenate the water in fish tanks, ponds, lakes and rivers. During daylight hours they release bubbles of gas that are rich in oxygen – the waste product of photosynthesis (Figure 4.2.1).

Photosynthesis is a process that uses light energy to drive chemical reactions in which carbon dioxide and water are changed to glucose and oxygen.

Light is absorbed by **chlorophyll**, a green pigment which is found only in chloroplasts.

The process is summarised in this word equation:

$$\text{carbon dioxide} + \text{water} \xrightarrow[\text{chlorophyll}]{\text{light energy}} \text{glucose} + \text{oxygen}$$

The chemical equation for photosynthesis is:

$$6CO_2 + 6H_2O \xrightarrow[\text{chlorophyll}]{\text{light energy}} C_6H_{12}O_6 + 6O_2$$

In the process of photosynthesis, carbon dioxide and water diffuse into chloroplasts. Chlorophyll absorbs light to split water to form hydrogen ions, electrons and oxygen. These ions and electrons are used to reduce carbon dioxide to a simple sugar.

The simple sugar produced in photosynthesis is used to produce a wide range of substances for the plant. Some is respired immediately by cells as it provides the energy needed to keep the cells alive.

The fate of glucose

The plants use the glucose they produce to make:

- sucrose – this is transported around the plant in the phloem. It is used in nectar and fleshy fruits to attract animals for pollination and seed dispersal (see 6.8, 9.5 and 9.6)
- starch in storage organs, such as seeds, swollen roots (e.g. yams), swollen stems (e.g. Irish potatoes), as a long-term energy store
- starch in leaves to store energy for use in respiration at night
- cellulose to make cell walls, also used to make fibres in cotton bolls to help seeds disperse in the wind
- lipids to make cell membranes and for energy storage, e.g. in seeds.

By combining sugars with nitrogen from nitrate ions, plants can make amino acids and then use them to make proteins, such as enzymes (see 5.3) and carrier proteins in cell membranes (see 3.4).

Gas exchange in plants

Plants use the oxygen they make for their own aerobic respiration (see 5.8). However, they cannot use all of it and much diffuses out of leaves into the atmosphere for other organisms, like us, to use. So during the day carbon dioxide diffuses into leaves through stomata and oxygen diffuses out. At night, photosynthesis cannot occur as there is no light. Most stomata tend to close at night to conserve water, but some remain partially open to allow some oxygen to diffuse into leaves and some carbon dioxide to diffuse out. Much more carbon dioxide is absorbed during the day than is produced at night (Figure 4.2.2).

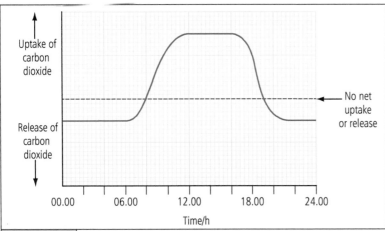

Figure 4.2.2 The uptake and release of carbon dioxide from a plant during 24 hours on a very bright sunny day.

The graph shows that at night, the plant releases carbon dioxide because it is respiring and not photosynthesising. The sun rises at 07.00; over the next hour the light intensity increases and so does the rate of photosynthesis. At 08.00, the plant uses all the carbon dioxide produced in respiration for its photosynthesis and does not absorb any from the air. Between 09.00 and 11.00 the rate of photosynthesis becomes higher than the rate of respiration so the plant absorbs more carbon dioxide from the air.

KEY POINTS

1 Photosynthesis is the conversion of carbon dioxide and water to sugars using light as a source of energy.

2 Photosynthesis occurs in chloroplasts.

3 Chlorophyll is the green pigment in chloroplasts that absorbs light energy.

4 The sugar produced in photosynthesis is converted to starch for storage, sucrose for transport and cellulose for cell walls. Some is combined with nitrogen to make amino acids which are used to make proteins.

5 During the day carbon dioxide diffuses into leaves through stomata and oxygen diffuses out; at night the reverse happens.

SUMMARY QUESTIONS

1 a Write out the balanced chemical equation for photosynthesis.

   b Annotate the equation by identifying the raw materials, the source of energy and the products on the equation.

2 Explain the role of chlorophyll in photosynthesis.

3 Make a spider diagram to show what happens to the glucose produced in photosynthesis.

4 Make a diagram to show the exchanges of substances that occur between mitochondria and chloroplasts during the day.

5 Describe the gas exchange that occurs between leaves and the atmosphere **a** during the day, and **b** at night. Explain your answers by reference to photosynthesis and respiration.

6 Discuss the importance of photosynthesis for life on Earth.

At the end of this topic you should be able to:

- describe the external structure of a typical leaf
- describe the internal structure of a typical leaf as seen in cross-section
- explain how leaves are adapted for photosynthesis.

| **Figure 4.3.1** | The blade and petiole of a hibiscus leaf. |

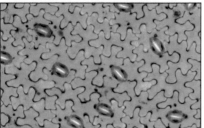

| **Figure 4.3.2** | Carbon dioxide and oxygen diffuse through these stomata (× 200). |

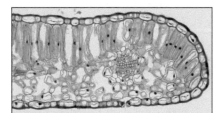

| **Figure 4.3.3** | A cross-section of the edge of a leaf blade. You can see large intercellular air spaces, a stoma and a vein (× 100). |

Leaves are plant organs adapted for photosynthesis. A typical leaf, like that of hibiscus, is green with a large flat surface. The petiole or leaf stalk attaches the leaf to the stem. Extending from the petiole is the midrib which contains the main vein. Minor veins branch from the main vein all over the thin part of the leaf known as the blade (Figure 4.3.1).

Some of the external features are adaptations for photosynthesis:

- green to absorb light – the green colour is chlorophyll
- large surface area – to absorb as much light as possible
- veins – to carry water and ions throughout the leaf and carry sucrose out of the leaf
- thin – so there is are short diffusion distances for carbon dioxide and oxygen

If you tear the blade of some leaves it is possible to peel off the lower epidermis. Figure 4.3.2 shows the lower epidermis of a leaf as viewed with a light microscope. You can see that there are many **stomata** scattered throughout the epidermis. Each stoma consists of two guard cells that control the width of the hole in between them. Stomata allow gases to diffuse in and out of the air spaces inside the leaf. They are another adaptation for photosynthesis.

When typical leaves are cut in cross-section and studied under a microscope, they have the appearance of the leaf in Figure 4.3.3. Figure 4.3.4 is drawn from a section through another leaf from the same plant.

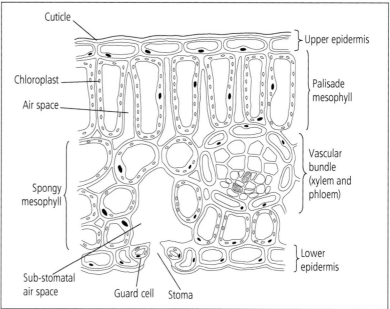

| **Figure 4.3.4** | This drawing shows the tissues inside the blade of a leaf. |

Table 4.3.1 summarises the functions of the tissues that you can see in Figures 4.3.3 and 4.3.4.

Table 4.3.1 Functions of the tissues in a leaf

Tissue	Function
Upper epidermis	Cells make a waxy cuticle that reduces the loss of water vapour to the air (see 6.7); cuticle and epidermal cells are transparent to allow light to pass through to the mesophyll; may have stomata (see lower epidermis below)
Palisade mesophyll	Cells contain many chloroplasts to absorb much light; the cells are packed together to allow the chloroplasts to capture as much light as possible; large vacuole pushes chloroplasts to the edge of each cell
Spongy mesophyll	Cells separated by larger air spaces than in palisade mesophyll to allow diffusion of carbon dioxide throughout the leaf
Xylem	Supplies water and ions
Phloem	Phloem transports sucrose away from the leaf to other parts of the plant
Lower epidermis	Cells are like those of the upper epidermis; some are specialised as pairs of guard cells that control the aperture of stomata through which carbon dioxide and oxygen diffuse in and out and water vapour diffuses out.

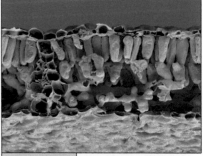

Figure 4.3.5 This electron micrograph of the inside of a leaf shows that palisade cells are cylindrical in shape and that there is a very extensive system of air spaces inside the leaf ($\times$ 200).

Some of the internal features are adaptations for photosynthesis:

- close packed palisade mesophyll cells near the upper surface of the leaf – to maximise absorption of light where its intensity is highest
- stomata (usually in lower epidermis) to allow carbon dioxide to diffuse into the leaf (and oxygen to diffuse out)
- thin – short distance for diffusion of carbon dioxide from the atmosphere to the cells of the palisade and spongy mesophyll
- large intercellular air spaces – for diffusion of carbon dioxide to all the mesophyll cells
- xylem to bring water and ions
- phloem to transport sucrose to the rest of the plant.

KEY POINTS

1 Leaves are the site of most photosynthesis that takes place in plants.

2 Leaves are green as they contain chlorophyll to absorb light energy; they have a large surface area to maximise light absorption and they are thin so that there are short distances for diffusion of carbon dioxide.

3 Internally, leaves are adapted for photosynthesis by having many cells closely packed in the palisade layer for maximum absorption of light and large intercellular air spaces to allow diffusion of carbon dioxide from the atmosphere to all the mesophyll cells.

SUMMARY QUESTIONS

1 Make a large drawing of the hibiscus leaf in Figure 4.3.1. Annotate your drawing to show how the external features are adaptations for photosynthesis.

2 Make a diagram of a cross-section of a leaf, showing each tissue with two or three cells. Annotate your diagram to show how the internal structure of a leaf is adapted for photosynthesis.

3 State the functions of the following in leaves: epidermis, vein, palisade mesophyll, guard cells and intercellular air spaces.

4 Use Figure 4.3.5 to draw a diagram to show a horizontal section through the palisade mesophyll.

4.4

Investigating photosynthesis

LEARNING OUTCOMES

At the end of this topic you should be able to:

- describe how to use iodine solution to test leaves for the presence of starch
- describe how to show that light and chlorophyll are necessary for photosynthesis
- explain what is meant by a *destarched* leaf
- outline how to investigate the effect of light intensity, temperature and carbon dioxide concentration on the rate of photosynthesis.

Testing leaves for starch

Testing leaves for starch is a good way to show that a plant has been photosynthesising. Some of the sugar produced in photosynthesis is converted into starch. Iodine solution is used to detect the presence of starch. The colour change with iodine solution cannot be seen if you simply put the solution on a leaf. The leaves must first be decolourised by removing the chlorophyll.

1 Put a leaf into boiling water for one minute. This destroys membranes, so you can extract the chlorophyll.

2 If you use a Bunsen burner to boil the water, turn it off afterwards.

3 Put the leaf into a test tube of ethanol. The chlorophyll dissolves in the ethanol.

4 Stand the test tube in a beaker of hot water for about 10 minutes.

5 Remove and wash the leaf in cold water. This removes the ethanol and rehydrates the leaf which softens it and makes it easy to spread out.

6 Spread the leaf out flat on a white surface and put iodine solution on it.

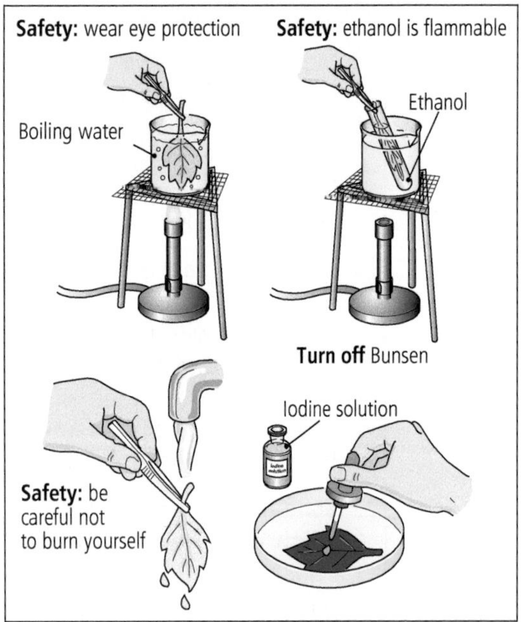

If the leaf goes blue-black, starch is present. If it stays a light yellow-brown colour there is no starch.

If you test a leaf from a plant that has been in a dark place for about a week you will find it has no starch in it. All of the starch has been converted to sugars and used in respiration. The plant is destarched. Plants that have been destarched are used to show that light is necessary for photosynthesis.

Is light needed for photosynthesis?

Follow these instructions to show that light is needed for the production of starch in photosynthesis.

1 Take a destarched plant and cover part of a leaf with some tin foil or black paper to prevent light getting through. Make sure you attach it firmly using tape or paper clips.

2 Leave the plant in the light for a few hours.

3 Test the leaf for starch as in Figure 4.4.1.

Safety: wear eye protection   **Safety:** ethanol is flammable

Boiling water   Ethanol

Turn off Bunsen

Iodine solution

Safety: be careful not to burn yourself

Figure 4.4.1 Testing a leaf for starch

STUDY FOCUS

The results from testing leaves for starch show whether starch is present or not; they do not tell us *how much* starch is present and therefore how much photosynthesis took place.

Results:

- Only the parts of the test leaf that were left uncovered and received light go blue-black.
- The parts of the leaf that were covered did not receive light and are a yellow-brown colour.

Is chlorophyll needed for photosynthesis?

Follow these instructions to show that chlorophyll is needed for the production of starch in photosynthesis.

1 Take a destarched, variegated plant such as a hibiscus (Figure 4.4.2). (*Variegated* means the leaves have different colours; in this case the leaves must be green and white. There is no chlorophyll in the white parts of the leaf.)

2 Place the plant in the light for about six hours.

3 Pick a leaf and draw it carefully to show the distribution of the white and green parts (or take a photograph).

4 Test this variegated leaf for starch as in Figure 4.4.1 and make a drawing of the results or take a photograph.

How much photosynthesis?

The effect of light intensity, carbon dioxide concentration and temperature on the rate of photosynthesis can be investigated with water weed as in Figure 2 on page 59. The three factors that affect the rate of photosynthesis can be investigated by changing:

- light intensity – by putting a lamp at different distances from the plant
- temperature – by putting the plant in beakers of water at different temperatures
- carbon dioxide concentration – by adding different quantities of sodium hydrogen carbonate ($NaHCO_3$) to the water.

Figure 4.4.2 | Variegated hibiscus leaves

LINK

Examples of these experiments and their results are shown in questions 9 and 10 on page 59. It is possible to test leaves for reducing sugar rather than iodine. This test using Benedict's solution is described in 5.1.

SUMMARY QUESTIONS

1 Explain why:
  a Leaves must first be decolourised when testing for starch.
  b Destarched leaves should be used when finding out whether light is needed for photosynthesis.

2 a Predict the result you would expect if variegated hibiscus leaves are tested for starch.
  b Explain your prediction.

3 In experiments to measure the effect of changing light intensity on the rate of photosynthesis it is important to keep the temperature constant. Suggest why this is so.

4 Suggest why counting bubbles is a good way to measure the rate of photosynthesis.

KEY POINTS

1 To test for starch, chlorophyll has to be removed from leaves first by boiling in ethanol and then testing with iodine solution.

2 A plant kept in the dark for a week uses up all the starch in its leaves and is destarched.

3 The need for light can be shown by using destarched leaves that are partially covered with light-proof material.

4 Variegated leaves with green and white parts are used to show that chlorophyll is needed for photosynthesis.

5 Counting the bubbles produced by a water weed can be used to determine the rate of photosynthesis.

Figure 4.5.1 Pride of Barbados is a legume. You can tell this by the characteristic shape of the seed pods.

Plants need mineral nutrients in order to make many different compounds. These nutrients are sometimes called mineral salts, salts, mineral ions or just minerals. These terms refer to the elements plants need other than carbon, hydrogen and oxygen. Most minerals are needed to make complex compounds, such as amino acids, proteins, chlorophyll and DNA. Plants absorb the mineral ions they require by active transport (see 3.4). Root hair cells provide a large surface area for the absorption of mineral ions.

Two of these elements are nitrogen and magnesium. Even though there is a huge quantity of nitrogen in the form of nitrogen gas (N_2) in the air, most plants are unable to use it. The exceptions are the flowering plants, known as **legumes**, such as Pride of Barbados (Figure 4.5.1). These plants have root nodules full of bacteria, which can take nitrogen gas from the air in the soil and convert it to amino acids (see 1.6). All other plants have to absorb nitrogen in the form of nitrate ions from water in the soil.

The roles of mineral nutrients in plants

Nitrate ions and magnesium ions are transported to leaves in the xylem. Both ions are needed to make chlorophyll. Magnesium is part of the chlorophyll molecule, which is responsible for trapping light energy. Plants constantly break down and rebuild chlorophyll in their leaves and so need a constant supply of magnesium.

Leaves make amino acids using the sugars they produce in photosynthesis and nitrate ions. Amino acids are exported from leaves in the phloem. The plant uses them to make proteins in areas of new growth, such as new leaves, flowers, root tips and seeds.

Investigating mineral deficiencies

We can investigate the effects that mineral nutrients have on plants by studying growth when they are not available.

Plants can be grown using **hydroponics**. This is where plants are grown in water or sand and supplied with the minerals they require in the water (solution). Solutions are prepared, containing all the mineral nutrients plants require normally (complete solution). When the minerals needed for plant growth are being investigated, the water may have different salts dissolved in it to give all the mineral nutrients that plants require (control). More solutions are prepared omitting one type of mineral nutrient in each case, e.g. without nitrogen and without magnesium.

Figure 4.5.2 shows how to use hydroponics to investigate the effect of mineral deficiencies.

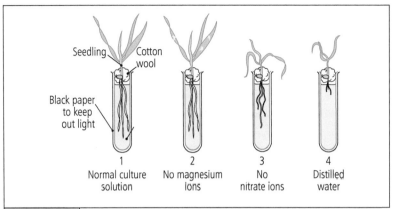

Figure 4.5.2 | How to use hydroponics to investigate the effect of mineral deficiencies

Figure 4.5.3 | Plants grown using hydroponics

Plants with nitrogen (nitrate) deficiency grow very slowly because they cannot make much protein. They have short roots and stems with few leaves. The lower leaves turn yellow as the plants cannot continually synthesise the chlorophyll they need. A plant with a deficiency of magnesium sends all the magnesium it has to the new leaves, so older leaves have a mottled yellow and green appearance.

Figure 4.5.6 | Bladderworts are green plants that have little bladders that trap small animals, such as this water flea.

Figure 4.5.4 | Crop plants grown in soils deficient in nitrogen do not grow well.

Figure 4.5.5 | A leaf showing symptoms of magnesium deficiency

SUMMARY QUESTIONS

1 a Explain why plants need mineral ions.

  b Describe how plants obtain their mineral ions.

2 Describe the appearance of plants grown without:

  a nitrate ions   b magnesium ions.

3 a Explain how carnivorous plants obtain the mineral nutrients that they need.

  b Suggest the trophic levels occupied by carnivorous plants, such as bladderworts in wetland ecosystems.

KEY POINTS

1 Plant roots absorb minerals including nitrate ions needed for healthy growth.

2 Nitrate ions are needed to make amino acids; magnesium ions are used by plants to make chlorophyll.

3 If mineral ions are lacking, a plant develops deficiency symptoms, such as yellowing of the leaves.

SECTION 1: Multiple-choice questions

1 Carnivorous plants trap and digest insects. They use proteins from the insects for growth. What do these plants produce in order to digest the insects?

  A   catalase

  B   proteases

  C   hormones

  D   hydrochloric acid

2 Green plants carry out gas exchange with the atmosphere. Which summarises the movement of gases at night and during the day?

	At night		During the day	
	oxygen	carbon dioxide	oxygen	carbon dioxide
A	in	out	out	in
B	out	in	in	out
C	in	out	in	out
D	out	in	out	in

3 Autotrophic nutrition involves

  A   converting chemical energy into light energy

  B   converting complex organic compounds into carbon dioxide and water

  C   converting simple inorganic compounds into complex organic compounds

  D   feeding on dead and decaying organisms

4 Which one of the following does *not* occur during photosynthesis?

  A   absorption of light by chlorophyll

  B   conversion of glucose to sucrose

  C   reduction of carbon dioxide to a carbohydrate

  D   splitting of water molecules using light energy

5 The mineral elements required in largest quantities by plants are:

  A   calcium, iron, magnesium

  B   nitrogen, magnesium, potassium

  C   nitrogen, phosphorus, potassium

  D   phosphorus, potassium, sulfur

6 The raw materials for photosynthesis are:

  A   carbon dioxide, light and water

  B   carbon dioxide and water

  C   chlorophyll and light

  D   chlorophyll, light and water

7 Most of the chloroplasts in a leaf are in the:

  A   palisade mesophyll

  B   lower epidermis

  C   spongy mesophyll

  D   upper epidermis

8 Which of the following would provide the conditions for the highest rate of photosynthesis of a tropical plant?

	Light intensity	Carbon dioxide concentration	Temperature/°C
A	high	low	30
B	low	high	20
C	low	low	30
D	high	high	35

9 A student used the apparatus shown in Figure 1 to investigate the effect of different light intensities on the rate of photosynthesis of a pond plant. The student monitored the room temperature throughout the investigation. The table shows the student's results.

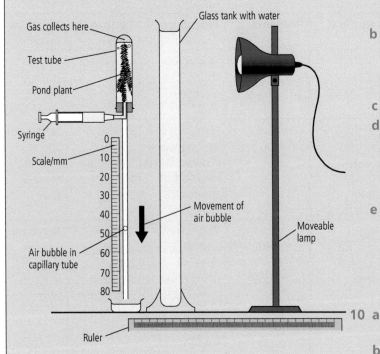

Figure 1

Distance of lamp from pond plant/mm	Distance travelled by air bubble in 5 minutes/mm	Rate of photosynthesis/ mm/min^{-1}
100	30	6.0
150	26	5.2
200	14	3.5
300	7	
500	3	0.6

a i Describe how the student would use the apparatus to obtain these results. (4)

ii State why gas is produced during the investigation. (1)

iii State why the air bubble moves down the tubing. (1)

b i Calculate the rate of photosynthesis missing from the table. (1)

ii Draw a graph of the results. (5)

c Explain the results. (4)

d Predict the results that would be obtained when the distance between the lamp and the pond plant is 50 mm and 600 mm. Explain your predictions. (4)

e i State two sources of error in this investigation. (2)

ii Suggest how this investigation could be improved. (3)

Total 25 marks

10 a Describe how photosynthesis occurs in a flowering plant. (5)

b Make a fully annotated diagram showing how the internal structure of a leaf is adapted for photosynthesis. (7)

c Describe the fate of the products of photosynthesis. (3)

Total 15 marks

Further practice questions and examples can be found on the accompanying CD.

5.1   Testing food substances

At the end of this topic you should be able to:

- describe how to carry out chemical tests to distinguish between starch, reducing sugars, non-reducing sugars, proteins and lipids
- explain that large molecules are formed by condensation and broken down by hydrolysis.

STUDY FOCUS

Reducing sugars are so called because they are reducing agents. Benedict's solution contains copper(II) ions. During the reaction reducing sugars donate electrons to the copper ions that become copper(I) ions. The red precipitate you see in the test for reducing sugars is copper(I) oxide.

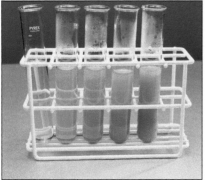

Figure 5.1.1 Testing for reducing sugars. The highest concentration of sugar is on the right.

The substances in our diet are carbohydrates, proteins, lipids (fats), vitamins, minerals, fibre and water. There are chemical tests to show that these substances are present in samples of the foodstuffs that we eat. Details of the tests are given in Table 5.1.1.

Table 5.1.1   Chemical tests for food substances

Nutrient	Reagents	Procedure	Positive result	Negative result
Starch	Iodine solution	Add a few drops to a sample of food	Blue-black	Yellow-orange
Reducing sugars (e.g. glucose and fructose)	Benedict's solution	Heat in boiling water bath with a solution of the food	Colour change from blue to green, orange or red	No colour change – solution remains blue
Non-reducing sugars (e.g. sucrose)	Hydrochloric acid (HCl), sodium hydroxide (NaOH), Benedict's solution	Boil sample with HCl; cool; neutralise with NaOH; test with Benedict's solution as above	Colour change from blue to green, orange or red	No colour change – solution remains blue
Protein	Biuret solution – a solution of sodium hydroxide (NaOH) and copper sulfate (CuSO$_4$)	Add few drops of biuret solution to a solution of the sample	Colour change from blue to lilac or purple	No colour change – solution is blue
Lipids (fats and oils)	Water and ethanol	Dissolve sample in ethanol, then pour solution into water	White emulsion	No white emulsion
	Filter paper	Rub the food sample into the paper and leave to dry	Greasy spot which is translucent	No greasy spot

Precautions: When you carry out the Benedict's test, put the test tubes into a water bath. The water must be at a temperature above 80 °C; it does not have to be boiling. Always wear eye protection when carrying out these tests. It is essential to neutralise the reaction mixture in the non-reducing sugar test because the Benedict's test does not work if acid is present.

Limitations of these chemical tests

These tests show whether the food substances are present, they do not tell us *how much* of each substance is present. It is possible to modify the tests so that iodine solution, Benedict's solution and biuret solution give ranges of colours. The colours become more intense as the concentration of the starch, reducing sugar or protein increases. However, results are obtained by comparing colours to a set of colour standards and people's judgment may differ.

Joining and breaking molecules

Boiling sucrose with hydrochloric acid breaks a bond between glucose and fructose. The breakage of this bond uses water; the hydrochloric acid acts as a catalyst (see 5.3). Breakage of bonds by using water is **hydrolysis**.

The synthesis of sucrose involves reacting glucose and fructose together. A chemical bond is formed between them when water is formed. This reaction is a **condensation** or a **dehydration** reaction. Making larger molecules, such as starch and protein, involves forming many bonds in this way – a process known as **dehydration synthesis**.

SUMMARY QUESTIONS

1 Define *hydrolysis* and *condensation*. Explain how these processes are involved in the formation and breakdown of a molecule of sucrose.

2 a Explain the term *reducing sugar*.

 b Name two reducing sugars and one non-reducing sugar.

 c Explain how starch differs from glucose.

3 A novel food has just been developed. How would you confirm that it contains non-reducing sugar, starch, protein and fat?

4 A food sample is thought to contain both glucose and sucrose. How would you prove this?

KEY POINTS

1 Benedict's solution is used to identify reducing sugars; iodine solution is used to test for starch; biuret solution tests for proteins; the emulsion and greasy spot tests identify lipids.

2 Sucrose and starch are formed by condensation reactions between smaller molecules. These bonds are broken by hydrolysis reactions.

EXAM TIP

You can call the reagent for the starch test 'iodine solution'. Do not call it 'iodine'.

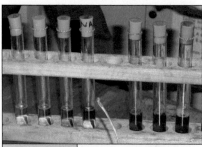

Figure 5.1.2 Different concentrations of a protein solution tested with biuret solution: on the left is 0%, with the highest concentration on the right

STUDY FOCUS

The non-reducing sugar test involves carrying out the testing with Benedict's solution twice. First test the sample with Benedict's to see if it has any reducing sugar. Then boil a separate sample with hydrochloric acid. The acid hydrolyses molecules of sucrose to form the reducing sugars glucose and fructose.

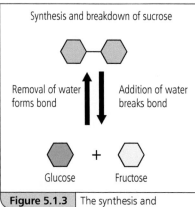

Synthesis and breakdown of sucrose

Removal of water forms bond

Addition of water breaks bond

Glucose + Fructose

Figure 5.1.3 The synthesis and breakdown of sucrose

5.2 Teeth and guts

LEARNING OUTCOMES

At the end of this topic you should be able to:

- identify the parts of the human alimentary canal on diagrams
- relate the structure of each part of the alimentary canal to its functions
- describe the structure of a tooth
- describe the role of teeth in mechanical digestion.

SUMMARY QUESTIONS

1 Distinguish between *mechanical* and *chemical* digestion.

2 Describe the role of teeth in feeding and digestion.

3 Describe what happens to food in the stomach and the small intestine.

4 Describe the roles of the liver and the pancreas in the digestive system.

The digestive system consists of all the organs, tissues and cells that **ingest** and **digest** food and then **egest** anything that is not digested. This system consists of the alimentary canal, the liver and the pancreas (Figure 5.2.1).

Mechanical digestion is the breakdown of food into smaller pieces by chewing in the mouth, churning of food in the stomach and emulsification of fat in the small intestine. These are physical processes that do not change the chemical nature of food.

Chemical digestion is the breakdown of large, insoluble molecules, such as starch, into small, soluble molecules. Large molecules are broken down by hydrolysis, catalysed by enzymes within the alimentary canal.

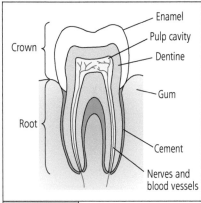

Figure 5.2.2 | A vertical section of a molar tooth

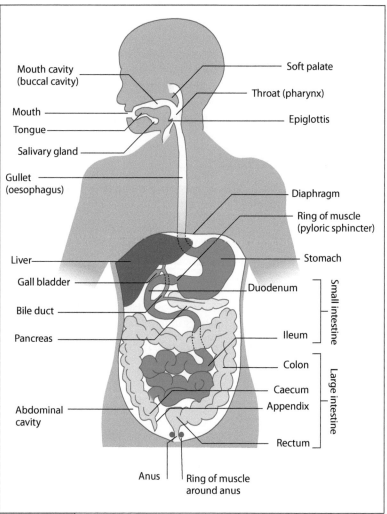

Figure 5.2.1 | The human alimentary canal

Table 5.2.1 Functions of the digestive system

Part of the digestive system	Functions
Mouth	• **mastication** – mechanical digestion of food using the teeth and tongue • secretion of saliva by salivary glands; salivary amylase begins the digestion of starch • food formed into boluses that can be swallowed
Oesophagus	• transfers food by peristalsis from mouth to stomach
Stomach	• wall of stomach secretes gastric juice containing hydrochloric acid and pepsin • muscular wall mixes food with gastric juice and breaks up large pieces of food into a creamy mixture • pepsin begins the digestion of protein • no digestion of starch as amylase does not function in acid environment
Liver	• secretes bile that contains bile salts to emulsify fats (see 5.3) • secretes sodium hydrogen carbonate to neutralise stomach acid
Gall bladder	• stores bile and releases it into the small intestine through the bile duct
Pancreas	• secretes pancreatic juice that contains amylase, trypsin and lipase • secretes sodium hydrogen carbonate to neutralise stomach acid
Small intestine	• secretes the enzymes sucrase, maltase, lactase and peptidase that complete the digestion of starch and protein • absorbs products of digestion into the bloodstream • absorbs water, ions and vitamins into the bloodstream
Large intestine	• absorbs the remaining water and ions • stores faeces in the rectum
Anal canal	• faeces pass out of the body

Teeth

Chewing food decreases its particle size so we are able to swallow it. It also increases the surface area that is exposed to saliva and gastric juice. Chemical digestion is much faster if the particles are smaller.

We have four types of teeth:

• **Incisors** are chisel-shaped for biting and cutting.
• **Canines** are pointed for piercing and tearing.
• **Premolars** have uneven 'cusps' for grinding and chewing.
• **Molars** are like premolars and are for chewing up the food.

Study the section through a molar tooth (see Figure 5.2.2).

• **Enamel** forms the hard, outer layer of the crown of the tooth, which is the part above the gum.
• Inside the enamel is the softer **dentine**, which is like bone in structure.
• A layer of **cement** fixes the root of the tooth into a bony socket in the jaw. The root is the part that is below the gum.
• The **pulp cavity** is a space in the tooth containing nerves and blood vessels.

KEY POINTS

1 Mechanical digestion is the breakdown of food into smaller pieces, e.g. mastication using the teeth.

2 Chemical digestion involves the breaking of chemical bonds by hydrolysis to change large molecules to small molecules.

3 In the stomach, food is churned up and mixed with gastric juice and hydrochloric acid. This starts the digestion of protein.

4 Bile emulsifies fats in the duodenum.

5 Enzymes produced by the pancreas and the small intestine complete the chemical digestion of starch, proteins and fat.

Enzymes

At the end of this topic you should be able to:

- define the term *catalyst*
- state that enzymes are biological catalysts
- describe the properties of enzymes
- describe the role of enzymes in chemical digestion.

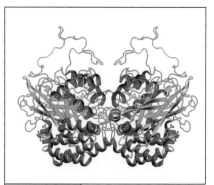

Figure 5.3.1 | A computer-generated image of the enzyme catalase

EXAM TIP

Never say 'the enzyme is killed'. Enzymes are not organisms. They are protein molecules. The correct word to use is denatured.

The food that we eat is composed of large, insoluble molecules such as starch, proteins and fats. They are too large to be absorbed through the wall of the intestine. This means that they need to be broken down into small, soluble molecules. The breakage of the bonds involves hydrolysis (see 5.1). The natural rate of hydrolysis at the temperature of our bodies is very slow. The rate needs to be speeded up by a **catalyst**.

A catalyst is a substance that increases the rate of a reaction without itself being changed. Biological catalysts are **enzymes** (Figure 5.3.1), which are proteins. All enzymes are made inside cells, where many of them work, for example in respiration. To digest our food the enzymes pass out from cells into the mouth, stomach and small intestine.

Properties of enzymes

Enzymes have the following properties:

- They are all proteins.
- Each enzyme catalyses one reaction.
- Only small numbers of enzyme molecules are needed to catalyse many reactions over a period of time.
- They can be used again and again.
- Their activity is affected by temperature.
- Their activity is affected by pH.

Enzymes are made of protein molecules. These can be folded into many different shapes. Each enzyme molecule has a shape that makes it specific for catalysing one reaction. This explains why there are many different enzymes – one enzyme for each reaction. Only the **substrate** molecule with a shape that fits into the enzyme will take part in the reaction catalysed by an enzyme. Other substrates have the wrong shape to fit in and are not involved in the reaction. This model of enzyme activity is known as the '**lock and key**'. The substrate (the 'key') must have a shape that fits exactly into the 'key hole' of the enzyme (the 'lock') as you can see in Figure 5.3.2.

Enzymes are influenced by the conditions of their surroundings. If the conditions become too hot, too acid or too alkaline their shape changes and they stop acting as catalysts. At high temperatures and at extreme pH, the bonds holding the enzyme molecule together start to break down. This changes the shape of the enzyme, so the substrate no longer fits. We say that **denaturation** has occurred and the enzyme can no longer catalyse the reaction.

Enzymes in digestion

The enzymes in our digestive system catalyse hydrolysis reactions to break down large molecules to smaller molecules, for example starch to glucose and proteins to amino acids. Information about these digestive enzymes is summarised in Table 5.3.1.

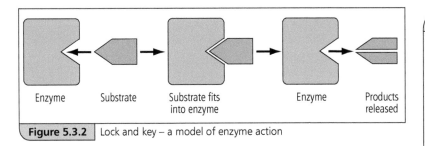

| Enzyme | Substrate | Substrate fits into enzyme | Enzyme | Products released |

Figure 5.3.2 Lock and key – a model of enzyme action

STUDY FOCUS

Your learning notes for this topic could include a large diagram of the digestive system (see 5.2). Label all the regions and annotate with the functions of each region. Include the sites of production of the enzymes in the table and their sites of action.

Table 5.3.1 Digestive enzymes made in the human digestive system

Type of enzyme	Name of enzyme	Site of production	Site of action	Reaction catalysed by enzyme
Carbohydrase	Amylase	Salivary glands	Mouth	starch $\longrightarrow$ maltose
		Pancreas	Small intestine	
	Sucrase	Wall of small intestine	Small intestine	sucrose $\longrightarrow$ glucose + fructose
	Lactase	Wall of small intestine	Small intestine	lactose $\longrightarrow$ glucose + galactose
	Maltase	Wall of small intestine	Small intestine	maltose $\longrightarrow$ glucose
Protease	Pepsin	Stomach wall	Stomach	protein $\longrightarrow$ peptides
	Trypsin	Pancreas	Small intestine	polypeptide $\longrightarrow$ shorter peptides
	Peptidases	Wall of small intestine	Small intestine	peptides $\longrightarrow$ amino acids
Lipase	Lipase	Pancreas	Small intestine	lipids (fats) $\longrightarrow$ fatty acids + glycerol

KEY POINTS

1 Catalysts speed-up a reaction and remain unchanged at the end; enzymes are biological catalysts that are made of protein.

2 Enzymes are specific to certain reactions.

3 In chemical digestion, enzymes catalyse the hydrolysis of large insoluble molecules to smaller, soluble molecules.

SUMMARY QUESTIONS

1 Define the following terms: *catalyst*, *enzyme*, *chemical digestion* and *denaturation*.

2 Make a table to summarise the digestion of these food nutrients: starch, protein, fat and sucrose. Your table should have the following headings: food nutrient, enzyme(s), site of production of enzyme(s), product(s) of digestion, site(s) of action in the human digestive system.

3 Some food contains starch, protein and fat. Use Table 5.3.1 to make a flow chart to show what happens to these three nutrients as they pass through the alimentary canal. Include the roles of the liver and pancreas in your flow chart.

STUDY FOCUS

Fat is insoluble in water. This makes it hard to digest as the fat forms into spherical globules exposing as little surface to the water in the alimentary canal as possible. When these globules of fat reach the duodenum, bile salts break up the globules of fat into smaller ones. This emulsification increases the surface area of the fat globules so molecules of lipase have easier access to the fat to break the bonds between fatty acids and glycerol.

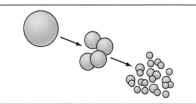

Figure 5.3.3 Large globules of fat are emulsified to smaller globules so that lipase can catalyse the formation of fatty acids and glycerol more easily.

Factors that affect enzymes

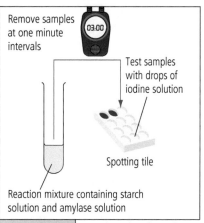

Remove samples at one minute intervals

Test samples with drops of iodine solution

Spotting tile

Reaction mixture containing starch solution and amylase solution

Figure 5.4.1 Samples taken from the reaction mixture in the test tube are added to drops of iodine solution every minute until there is no change in the colour.

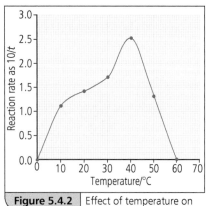

Figure 5.4.2 Effect of temperature on the activity of amylase

Effect of temperature on the activity of enzymes

Amylase is the catalyst for the breakdown of starch to maltose. You will remember from 5.1 that iodine solution is used to detect the presence of starch. As the starch is broken down by amylase, there is less and less starch present in the reaction mixture. You can follow this by taking samples from the reaction mixture and testing with iodine solution as shown in Figure 5.4.1.

Table 5.4.1 shows some results from an investigation in which seven reaction mixtures were kept at different temperatures.

Table 5.4.1 Effect of temperature on amylase

Temperature (°C)	Time taken for starch to be digested, t (minutes)	Rate of reaction as $10/t$
0	–	0
10	9	1.1
20	7	1.4
30	6	1.7
40	4	2.5
50	8	1.3
60	–	0

STUDY FOCUS

Divide 1, 10, 100 or 10 000 by the time taken for starch to be digested (reciprocal). This gives large numbers when the enzyme is working very fast. Then we have peaks on a graph when the enzyme is most active rather than when it is least active if we plotted time taken.

The graph in Figure 5.4.2 shows that the rate of reaction is slow at low temperatures, for example at 10 °C. It increases as the temperature increases to 40 °C and reaches a maximum at 40 °C (optimum temperature). The rate of reaction decreases at temperatures greater than 40 °C and is zero at 60 °C.

The **optimum temperature** is the best temperature for the enzyme. As the temperature increases towards the optimum, molecules of substrate and enzyme move faster and have more collisions so more reactions occur. At higher temperatures, the enzyme structure changes and at 60 °C all the enzyme molecules are denatured. We have to test temperatures between 30 °C and 50 °C to find the exact optimum temperature.

Effect of pH on the activity of catalase

Catalase is an enzyme found inside many cells. Its function is to catalyse the breakdown of hydrogen peroxide. This is a toxic substance that is produced by cells which can do damage if allowed to accumulate. It catalyses this reaction:

hydrogen peroxide $\longrightarrow$ oxygen + water

Catalase is found in many plant and animal tissues; it is also found in bacteria and fungi.

1 Use a cork borer to remove several cores from a potato. Cut the cores into smaller sections that are each about 2 mm in thickness.

2 Put three pieces into a solution with a pH of 7.0.

3 Put the same volume of hydrogen peroxide into some test tubes.

4 Put one potato disc into the test tube at pH 7.0. It will sink towards the bottom of the test tube.

5 As soon as the disc starts to rise to the surface, start timing and find out how long it takes the disc to reach the surface.

The reaction between catalase and hydrogen peroxide produces oxygen which forms inside the potato and underneath the disc, making the disc less dense so it floats.

6 Repeat with two more discs so that there are three readings for pH 7.0.

7 Repeat the whole procedure with discs at a range of other values of pH to find the optimum pH for catalase.

When investigating the effect of one factor on the activity of enzymes, all the other factors should be kept constant. This ensures the results are valid and due only to the factor that has been changed.

Table 5.4.2 Effect of pH on the activity of catalase

pH	Time taken for discs to reach the surface (seconds)			
	First disc	Second disc	Third disc	Mean (average)
4	36.03	37.13	38.59	37.25
5	15.77	12.93	14.35	14.35
6	12.06	10.05	11.03	11.05
7	9.13	10.13	9.63	9.63
8	9.67	10.29	9.98	9.98
9	10.81	12.69	11.87	11.79

Absorption and assimilation

At the end of this topic you should be able to:

- define the terms *absorption* and *assimilation*
- describe how the small intestine is adapted for absorption
- describe the role of the liver in assimilation.

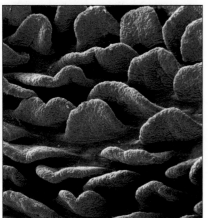

Figure 5.5.1 These are villi from the small intestine – they are leaf-like and are full of blood capillaries.

Absorption

Absorption is the movement of digested food molecules into the blood or the lymph. Simple sugars, amino acids, fatty acids and glycerol pass through the epithelial cells of the small intestine either by diffusion or by active transport.

The small intestine is very long (about 6 m in an adult) and is adapted for efficient absorption of food as it has:

- a very large surface area of about 9 m²
- a thin lining of epithelial cells (only one cell thick) so that food molecules can easily move into the blood and **lymph**
- epithelial cells with **microvilli** (see Figure 3.1.2 in 3.1)
- cell membranes with many carrier proteins for active transport (see 3.4).

The large surface area of the small intestine fits into the small space within the abdomen because it has a folded inner lining with millions of tiny, finger-like or leaf-like projections called **villi** (the singular of villi is **villus**) (Figure 5.5.1 and Figure 5.5.2).

The digested food enters the capillaries and **lacteals** (lymph capillaries) in the villi. Absorbed food molecules are transported quickly to the liver by the hepatic portal vein (Figure 5.5.3). Fatty acids and glycerol are transported more slowly in the lymph. The villi have muscle inside them. When this contracts the lacteals are squeezed causing the lymph to move into lymphatic vessels. These vessels are thin-walled, like veins, and they empty into blood vessels near the heart. As a result, fat does not enter the bloodstream too quickly.

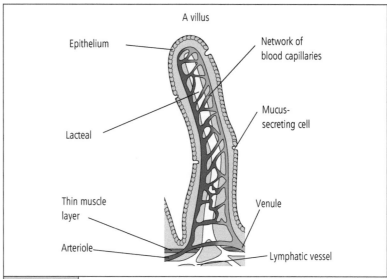

Figure 5.5.2 Longitudinal section through a villus

When the food gets to the colon there is not much left that is useful. What is left is now fibre, dead cells and bacteria. Most of the water has been absorbed in the small intestine; the rest is absorbed by the colon.

The solid waste or faeces is stored in the rectum. The undigested food, in the form of faeces, passes out of the body through the anus. Normally it takes between 24 and 48 hours for food to pass along the length of the digestive system.

Assimilation

The food molecules that have been absorbed are transported around the body and taken up by cells. **Assimilation** is the use of these molecules by the cells. The liver carries out a number of important functions as part of assimilation:

- It takes up glucose molecules from the blood and stores them as **glycogen**. This helps to regulate the concentration of glucose in the blood.
- It uses amino acids to make proteins, such as those involved in blood clotting.
- It breaks down surplus amino acids.
- It converts fatty acids and glycerol into fat which is stored around the body, e.g. under the skin.
- It produces cholesterol from fats.

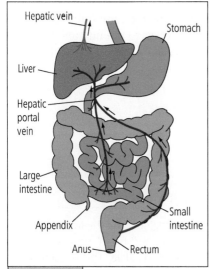

Figure 5.5.3 The hepatic portal vein carries blood from the stomach and intestines to the liver.

Hepatic vein · Stomach · Liver · Hepatic portal vein · Large intestine · Appendix · Anus · Rectum · Small intestine

KEY POINTS

1 Absorption is the movement of digested food molecules through the wall of the intestine into the blood and lymph.

2 Assimilation is the use of food molecules by the cells of the body.

3 The small intestine is adapted for absorption by being very long, having a folded inner lining with millions of tiny villi. Microvilli increase the surface area of each epithelial cell.

4 The liver stores glucose as glycogen, makes proteins, breaks down surplus amino acids and converts fatty acids and glycerol back into fat for storage.

SUMMARY QUESTIONS

1 Make a large labelled diagram of a villus. Annotate your diagram by writing notes about the functions of the parts that you have labelled.

2 Distinguish between absorption and assimilation.

3 Explain how the liver is involved in assimilating the products of digestion.

4 Suggest the danger in having too much fat in the blood.

Balanced diet

Figure 5.6.1 | Fresh fruit and vegetables should be a major part of everyone's diet.

A nutrient is a substance in food that provides benefit to the body. The energy that we need is provided by the major nutrients or **macronutrients**. These are the organic compounds we eat in large quantities: carbohydrates, fats and proteins. Not only do they provide energy but also the compounds like amino acids, sugars and fatty acids that we need to make our cells. Vitamins and minerals are the minor nutrients or micronutrients that do not provide energy and are needed in tiny quantities. Vitamins are organic compounds; the minerals that we need are inorganic and are often absorbed as ions.

A **balanced diet** provides all the energy and nutrients that a person requires for their immediate needs. A balanced diet provides:

- energy – carbohydrates, lipids and proteins provide this energy
- **essential amino acids** – eight to ten types of amino acid that the body cannot make from anything else
- **essential fatty acids** – two fatty acids that the body cannot make from anything else
- vitamins, e.g. vitamins A and C
- minerals, e.g. calcium and iron
- enough water to replace water that is lost each day
- fibre.

How much energy?

The energy that we need in our diet depends on age, gender, occupation and activity (how much exercise). People who play sport, do a lot of fitness training or have an occupation that involves taking much exercise require more energy than that shown in Table 5.6.1. American football players need to increase their energy intake by 8000 to 9000 kJ each day because of the intensity of their training and their large size. Basketball players only need to increase their energy intake by 1000 to 2000 kJ as their training is less intense and they have a lighter build. Female athletes should increase their energy intake by about 75–80% of that required by men.

Vegetarianism

Some people decide that they are not going to eat meat although they eat some animal products, such as eggs and milk. These people are vegetarians. Vegans are people who do not eat any foods of animal origin. We get many of our nutrients from eating animals, so people who are vegetarian or vegan have to make sure that their diet includes plant foods that provide these nutrients.

A properly balanced vegetarian diet is a healthy diet. However, people who do not eat meat and/or fish are at risk of vitamin B_{12} deficiency as this is only found in foods of animal origin. We need it to make red blood cells.

Table 5.6.1 Different energy needs for people who take little exercise

Age	Recommended energy intake per day (kJ)	
	Males	Females
0–3 months (fed on formula milk)	2280	2160
10–12 months	3850	3610
7–10 years	8240	7280
15–18 years	11510	8830
19–49 years	10600	8100
Last 3 months of pregnancy		8900
Breastfeeding		10900
50–59	10600	8000
60–64 years	9930	7990

Roles of vitamins and minerals

Vitamins and minerals are micronutrients, because you need very small quantities each day. Vitamins are complex molecules that we cannot make from anything simpler. Minerals are elements that we need for many different functions, as you can see in Table 5.6.2.

Table 5.6.2 Some micronutrients, their functions in the body and good dietary sources

Micronutrient		Function(s) in the body	Good sources
Vitamins	A	Helps rods in the eye to see light of low intensity (see 8.5)	Liver, chili powder, milk, sweet potatoes, carrots
	B₁	Helps aerobic respiration in mitochondria	Cereals
	C	Helps tissue repair and resistance to disease	Oranges, lemons and other citrus fruits
	D	Helps absorption of calcium in the gut and strengthening of bones and teeth (see 5.2 and 7.4)	Fish oil, milk, butter (also made in the skin exposed to sunlight)
Minerals	Iron	Forms part of haemoglobin in red blood cells that transports oxygen (see 6.4)	Liver, meat, cocoa, eggs
	Calcium	Gives strength to bones and teeth; needed for synapses in the nervous system; involved in blood clotting (see 5.2 and 7.4)	Milk, fish, green vegetables

KEY POINTS

1 A nutrient is a substance in food that provides benefit to the body.

2 Macronutrients are required in large quantities each day; micronutrients are needed in very small quantities.

3 Carbohydrates, proteins and lipids are the macronutrients providing energy and compounds for building cells; vitamins and minerals are the micronutrients and are required for other roles.

4 Vegetarians do not eat meat or fish, although some eat animal products, such as milk and eggs. Vegans do not eat any animal products.

SUMMARY QUESTIONS

1 Define the terms *nutrient*, *macronutrient*, *micronutrient*, *vitamin* and *mineral*.

2 Explain why the human diet must contain large quantities of the macronutrients.

3 Name four vitamins and two minerals that humans require in the diet.

4 Suggest some occupations that require a higher intake of energy than those given in the table.

Malnutrition

At the end of this topic you should be able to:

- explain the term *deficiency disease*
- describe the effects of protein energy deficiency
- state the causes, symptoms and treatment of night blindness, scurvy, rickets and anaemia
- describe the effects of eating more food than is necessary to maintain good health.

DID YOU KNOW?

Eating too much of vitamins and minerals rarely does harm, but eating too much vitamin A may be lethal. A group of fishermen once ate the liver of a large halibut and died of vitamin A poisoning.

Malnutrition

People who do not have a balanced diet may suffer from a form of **malnutrition**. There are forms of malnutrition caused by not enough of the macronutrients, or too much, which can lead to **obesity**.

Protein energy malnutrition (PEM) occurs in children, who do not receive enough energy and protein in their diet. Marasmus is mainly caused by not receiving enough energy-providing foods, so protein is used to provide energy. Growth is retarded and there is severe weight loss. Kwashiorkor is also the result of a protein deficiency and results in the swelling of body tissues and a swollen liver. Protein in the blood helps to absorb water from the tissues.

Deficiency diseases

Deficiency diseases are caused by the lack of micronutrients in the diet. Without vitamin A in the diet the rods in the eye do not work properly, causing **night blindness**. If the deficiency is serious then the front of the eye becomes cloudy and light cannot pass through easily.

Figure 5.7.1 | One of the major causes of blindness in children is vitamin A deficiency.

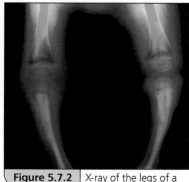

Figure 5.7.2 | X-ray of the legs of a child with rickets

Without Vitamin D bones become soft. Leg bones often bow outwards under the pressure of the body, indicating that a person has **rickets**. Children who do not go out in the sunshine, or who wear clothing that completely covers their body are most at risk of this deficiency disease. A deficiency of calcium can lead to weak bones and teeth, and slow blood clotting.

Vitamin C is required for the proper formation of collagen in the skin. A deficiency of vitamin C causes scurvy. Wounds are not repaired properly, gums bleed and teeth fall out (Figure 5.7.3).

Without iron, the red blood cells contain less haemoglobin so the quantity of oxygen transported in the blood decreases. This is iron-deficiency anaemia. People who are anaemic have less energy and feel tired and lethargic because they have less oxygen available for

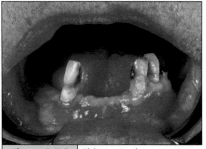

Figure 5.7.3 | This person has scurvy.

aerobic respiration. They are likely to grow and develop slowly. Girls and women are more at risk of iron-deficiency anaemia because they lose blood in their monthly periods.

Deficiency diseases are treated by making sure people have a balanced diet and by giving dietary supplements, such as pills with vitamins and minerals.

Obesity

Consuming more food energy than required increases the quantity of body fat. Two ways a person can be identified as obese are:

- being 20% above the recommended weight for his or her height
- having a **body mass index (BMI)** greater than 30.

BMI is calculated using the following formula:

$$\text{BMI} = \frac{\text{body mass (in kilograms)}}{\text{height}^2 \text{ (in metres)}}$$

There is an obesity epidemic in many regions of the World, including the Caribbean. The causes of this are:

- a change from traditional high fibre diets to 'Western' diets rich in fatty food and refined foods that contain much sugar (especially sucrose) and are low in fibre
- increase in incomes with more money to spend on food
- a change from physically active to more sedentary occupations
- the use of cars and public transport and a reduction in time spent walking to work, school, market or shops.

People who are overweight or obese are at high risk of developing serious health problems, such as **hypertension** (high blood pressure), coronary heart disease, diabetes, arthritis (damage to joints), many types of cancer, for example bowel and uterine cancers. People with diabetes and high blood pressure are given dietary advice:

- Avoid foods that increase the concentration of glucose in the blood immediately after eating.
- Eat plenty of starchy foods, fresh fruit and vegetables.
- Eat regular meals; avoid sugary foods and drinks especially between meals.
- Eat breakfast and do not skip meals.
- Eat low fat foods, e.g. low-fat dairy products and lean meat.
- Try to avoid eating fried and 'fast food'.
- Drink plenty of fluids to keep hydrated; drink alcohol moderately and do not binge drink.

People with hypertension should follow the advice given above, but in addition should:

- reduce their intake of sodium (should be between 1500 to 2300 mg a day)
- increase intake of foods rich in potassium, e.g. beans, bananas, leafy vegetables
- make sure their diet contains foods rich in calcium, e.g. low-fat dairy products, leafy vegetables, bread fortified with calcium.

KEY POINTS

1. Malnutrition is the result of an unbalanced diet where there is a shortage of nutrients or the person over-eats.

2. Deficiency diseases are caused by a lack of vitamin(s) or mineral(s) in the diet.

3. Obesity is a condition where a person is greatly overweight.

4. People with diabetes and hypertension should follow a strict diet, such as the DASH diet.

SUMMARY QUESTIONS

1. Define the terms *malnutrition*, *protein energy malnutrition*, *deficiency diseases* and *obesity*.

2. Describe the causes and effects of two vitamin deficiency diseases and two mineral deficiency diseases.

3. Surveys have discovered that many people in the Caribbean have anaemia. Suggest why.

4. Summarise the dietary advice that is given to people with diabetes and hypertension.

Respiration

At the end of this topic you should be able to:

• define the term *respiration*

• distinguish between aerobic and anaerobic respiration.

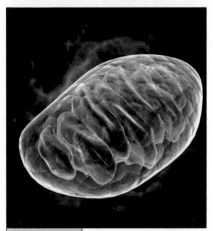

Figure 5.8.1 | A computer-generated image of a mitochondrion. Most of the ATP is made in these cell structures. Each is 0.002 mm long.

Figure 5.8.2 | Jamaican sprinter, Shelley-Anne Fraser Pryce, relying on anaerobic respiration in her muscles

Respiration takes place in *all* living cells *all of the time*. It provides a constant supply of energy for cells. They need this to stay alive and to carry out processes, such as active transport, protein synthesis and cell division. Glucose and fat are the fuels used to provide energy in the cells. During respiration, the energy is released very gradually in a series of small, enzyme-controlled reactions.

Aerobic respiration

In **aerobic respiration**, oxygen is used in the breakdown of glucose as shown by the word equation:

glucose + oxygen $\longrightarrow$ carbon dioxide + water + energy released

The balanced chemical equation is:

$$C_6H_{12}O_6 + 6O_2 \longrightarrow 6CO_2 + 6H_2O + \text{energy released}$$

This equation summarises many chemical reactions that occur in respiration. A specific enzyme catalyses each reaction. These reactions of respiration release energy from glucose which is used to convert **adenosine diphosphate (ADP)** to **adenosine triphosphate (ATP)**. Some energy is also released as heat.

ATP is good at transferring energy from respiration to the energy-consuming processes in cells. ATP diffuses easily through the cell and it breaks down readily to ADP with the transfer of energy.

The **mitochondrion** is where aerobic respiration occurs (Figure 5.8.1). Cells with a high demand for energy have many mitochondria.

Anaerobic respiration

In **anaerobic respiration** energy is released from glucose without using oxygen. The word equation for anaerobic respiration in animals shows that **lactic acid** is produced:

glucose $\longrightarrow$ lactic acid + energy released

Some bacteria produce lactic acid when they respire without oxygen. In humans, muscles respire anaerobically during fast bursts of exercise, such as sprinting and weightlifting.

Oxygen consumption does not return to resting levels immediately after the exercise finishes. Oxygen is required to repay an **oxygen debt**. During hard, strenuous exercise, such as sprinting, not enough oxygen may reach the muscles for aerobic respiration to supply all the energy needed. Muscle tissue therefore respires anaerobically so that there is enough energy released. Some glucose is broken down to lactic acid. The extra oxygen absorbed after exercise is used to respire the lactic acid.

When yeasts respire anaerobically they make alcohol and carbon dioxide as shown in this word equation:

glucose $\longrightarrow$ alcohol + carbon dioxide + energy released

Far less energy is released from each molecule of glucose in anaerobic respiration compared to aerobic respiration. This is because glucose is not completely broken down and a lot of energy remains in lactic acid and alcohol in the form of chemical bond energy.

When yeast is kept in a sugar solution with little access to air, it respires anaerobically to release energy for growth and produces alcohol and carbon dioxide as waste products. The carbon dioxide can be detected with limewater (see Figure 5.8.3).

To measure anaerobic respiration, you need to measure the amount of alcohol produced. As yeast produces more and more alcohol, the density of the liquid decreases. This decrease in density is measured with a hydrometer (Figure 5.8.4). As alcohol is produced, the density of the fermenting mixture decreases. Plants also respire anaerobically in the same way as yeast. This happens when soils get flooded and there is no air in the soil (see 1.3).

Figure 5.8.3 Limewater is used to detect the presence of carbon dioxide produced by anaerobic and aerobic respiration.

Biogas

Some bacteria respire anaerobically to make the gas methane (CH_4). This gas can be used as a source of energy. There are small-scale **biogas** generators like the one in Figure 5.8.5 that are filled with human, animal and plant waste and kept in anaerobic conditions. The gas is vented and used for cooking. There are also large-scale biogas generators that use solid waste from sewage treatment works. The energy made available is often used to power the treatment works.

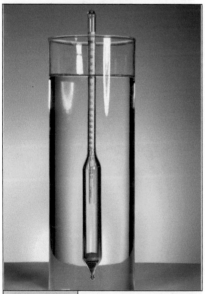

Figure 5.8.4 Hydrometers are used to follow the production of ethanol by yeast.

SUMMARY QUESTIONS

1 Define the terms *respiration*, *aerobic respiration*, *anaerobic respiration* and *oxygen debt*.

2 Make a table to compare aerobic and anaerobic respiration.

Figure 5.8.5 This small-scale biogas generator provides fuel for cooking.

Gas exchange surfaces

Figure 5.9.3 The gills of this giant catfish have many gill filaments.

Figure 5.9.4 Each gill filament is covered by tiny gill plates that are full of blood to provide a huge gaseous exchange surface (X 10).

You will remember *Amoeba* from its description and photograph in 3.2. Unicellular creatures like this use their body surface as their **gas exchange** surface. They are so small that their surface area to volume ratio is large enough to allow enough oxygen to enter and enough carbon dioxide to leave. Both gases move across the cell membrane of these protists by diffusion.

Earthworms are multicellular animals. They too use their body surface for gas exchange. An earthworm 10 cm in length is about 200 times longer and 1500 times thicker than *Amoeba*. This makes it much more difficult for oxygen to diffuse from the outer layer of the body to the centre of the animal and for carbon dioxide to diffuse in the reverse direction. Therefore earthworms have a blood system to transport gases and there are many tiny blood vessels (capillaries) for gas exchange (Figure 5.9.2).

Figure 5.9.1 Gas exchange occurs between the air in the soil and the earthworm's body surface.

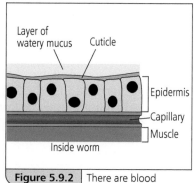

Layer of watery mucus · Cuticle · Epidermis · Capillary · Muscle · Inside worm

Figure 5.9.2 There are blood capillaries immediately below the earthworm's epidermis.

The gas exchange surface of a fish has tiny leaf-like plates along the gills. Water flows into the mouth and between gill filaments that are covered in tiny gill plates (Figures 5.9.3 and 5.9.4).

We breathe in and out to refresh the air in our lungs. Gaseous exchange occurs in the alveoli, in the lungs. Gas exchange is the diffusion of oxygen from alveolar air into the blood and the diffusion of carbon dioxide from the blood into the air. Our gas exchange surface shares features in common with other gas exchange surfaces, such as the gills of fish, the breathing tubes of insects and the internal surfaces of leaves. All gas exchange surfaces are in contact with the surroundings, even if they are enclosed deep inside the body.

Alveoli have features that adapt them for exchange of oxygen and carbon dioxide. These are:

- a very large surface area for the diffusion of gases
- a moist surface so that gases can dissolve before diffusion
- walls that are thin so that gases do not have to diffuse very far.

Steep concentration gradients for oxygen and for carbon dioxide are maintained because there is:

- a good blood supply, bringing carbon dioxide for efficient removal and absorbing lots of oxygen
- breathing that constantly supplies fresh oxygen-rich air and removes waste carbon dioxide.

When inspired (breathed in) air reaches the alveoli it contains a lot of oxygen. Oxygen dissolves in the watery lining of each alveolus and then diffuses through two layers of cells into the blood. There is a very short diffusion distance between the cells forming the walls of the alveoli and those of the capillary, which are all squamous cells (see Figure 5.9.5).

Gas exchange in plants

Gas exchange in leaves occurs on all the cell surfaces exposed to intercellular air spaces (see 4.3).

The stomata allow movement of gases in and out of the intercellular air spaces in the leaf. They do not form a gas exchange surface as there is air on both sides.

LINK

See 3.4 to remind yourself about diffusion and concentration gradients. A steep gradient is one where the concentrations on either side of the surface are very different.

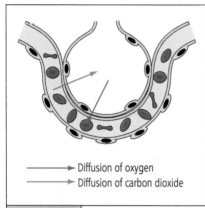

→ Diffusion of oxygen
→ Diffusion of carbon dioxide

Figure 5.9.5 Gaseous exchange in an alveolus

LINK

There is more about the structure and function of alveoli in 5.10. You should also look at 3.3 to remind yourself about squamous epithelial cells.

KEY POINTS

1. Gaseous exchange is the diffusion of oxygen and carbon dioxide between the surroundings and the body of an organism.
2. Gaseous exchange surfaces are thin, moist and large relative to the size of an organism.
3. Diffusion gradients in animals are maintained by blood flow and breathing movements.
4. Gas exchange in plants occurs on cell surfaces inside leaves.

SUMMARY QUESTIONS

1. Describe the features of a specialised gaseous exchange surface.
2. All vertebrates, such as mammals and fish, have specialised structures for gaseous exchange; protists such as *Amoeba* do not.
   a. Name these structures in mammals and fish.
   b. Explain why *Amoeba* does not have a specialised structure for gaseous exchange.
3. Explain why earthworms need a transport system.
4. Describe the gaseous exchange that occurs in plants:
   a. at night   b. during the day. Explain your answers.

EXAM TIP

Beware! We can say that alveoli and capillaries have walls made of cells, but not cell walls – remember plant cells have cell walls, but animal cells do not.

Breathing

LEARNING OUTCOMES

At the end of this topic you should be able to:

- define the term *breathing*
- describe the mechanism of breathing in humans
- describe the role of the diaphragm, ribcage and intercostal muscles in breathing.

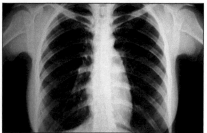

Figure 5.10.2 An X-ray of a pair of healthy lungs. Compare this with the X-ray of a smoker in 5.11.

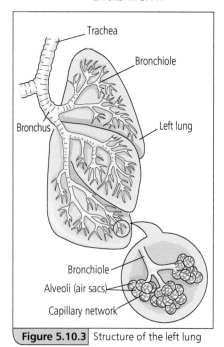

Figure 5.10.3 Structure of the left lung

The gaseous exchange system

The lungs are spongy organs situated within the **thorax** (chest). They are protected by the ribcage and the backbone. The diaphragm is a sheet of muscle and fibrous tissue separating the thorax from the abdomen. When the muscle contracts the **diaphragm** moves downwards and when it relaxes it is pushed upwards.

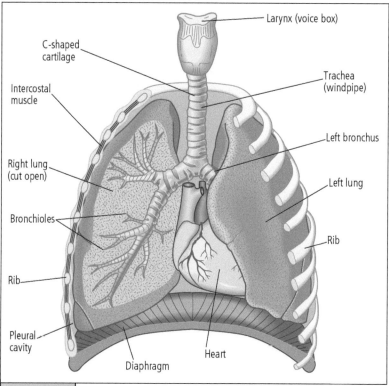

Figure 5.10.1 The gas exchange system

The pleural cavity is filled with fluid and lies between two pleural membranes (see Figure 5.10.1). This fluid is a lubricant preventing the lungs rubbing against the ribs. The **intercostal muscles** contract to move the ribs during breathing, especially when we take deep breaths.

Air enters the mouth or nose and passes through the throat to the **larynx**, which contains the vocal cords. Air then enters the **trachea**, which passes through the neck and into the thorax. The trachea branches into the two **bronchi** (singular bronchus), which enter each lung. Bronchi continue to branch to form many small **bronchioles**, which end in tiny air sacs each of which is called an **alveolus**. Around each alveolus are many blood capillaries for efficient gas exchange. The tubes through which air moves to reach the alveoli are often called the airways.

Breathing in (inspiration)

1 The muscles of the diaphragm contract and flatten the central part of the diaphragm, which is made of tough fibrous tissue. These muscles are strong and connect to the backbone, the lower ribs and the sternum (breastbone).

2 The external intercostal muscles *contract* and the internal intercostal muscles *relax*. This moves the ribs and sternum upwards and outwards.

3 These movements *increase* the volume inside the thorax, so *decreasing* the air pressure inside the lungs.

4 The air pressure inside the lungs is less than atmospheric pressure, so air moves in through your nose or mouth *into* the lungs and they inflate.

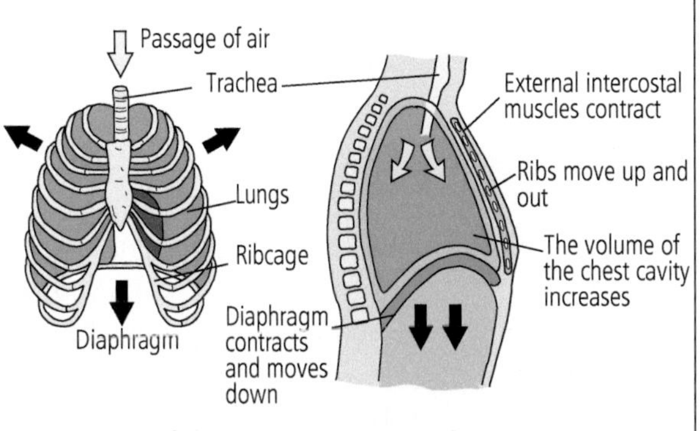

Figure 5.10.4 Breathing in

Breathing out (expiration)

1 The diaphragm muscles relax and the pressure exerted by the abdomen pushes the central fibrous tissue upwards.

2 The internal intercostal muscles contract and the external intercostal muscles relax to move the ribs downwards and inwards.

3 These movements decrease the volume inside the thorax so increasing the air pressure inside the lungs.

4 The elastic tissue around the alveoli recoils and this helps to force air out of the lungs.

During quiet or shallow breathing the diaphragm alone may be moving. Both the diaphragm and the ribcage move when taking deep breaths, for example during exercise.

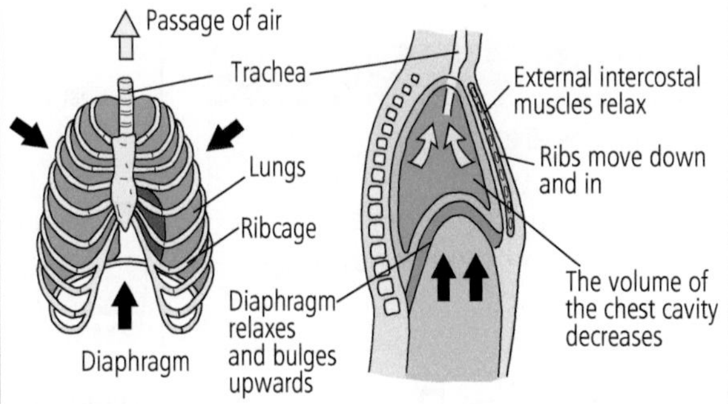

Figure 5.10.5 Breathing out

SUMMARY QUESTIONS

1 Distinguish between the terms *breathing* and *respiration*.

2 Describe the pathway taken by air as it moves from the atmosphere into the respiratory system. You could draw this as a flow chart diagram.

3 Make a table to show the functions of all the structures of the gas exchange system labelled in Figures 5.10.1 and 5.10.3.

4 Make a diagram of the gas exchange system. Add labels and annotate with the functions of the different structures.

KEY POINTS

1 Breathing is the movement of air in and out of the lungs.

2 Inspired air enters the nose or mouth, passes through the throat and then the larynx, which contains the vocal cords.

3 The air passes through the trachea, bronchi and bronchioles to the alveoli, where gas exchange occurs.

LINK

Synapses are tiny gaps between nerve cells (see 8.4). Many drugs including heroin and nicotine act on our synapses.

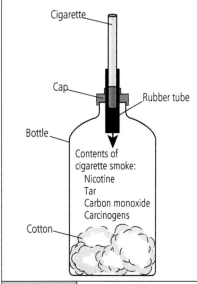

Figure 5.11.1 A simple smoking machine. Scientists have used more sophisticated machines to mimic our smoking behaviour to analyse the contents of tobacco smoke.

Cigarette

Cap

Rubber tube

Bottle

Contents of cigarette smoke:
Nicotine
Tar
Carbon monoxide
Carcinogens

Cotton

Addicted to smoking

If you smoke or know someone who smokes, you will know that it is very hard to give up the habit. Smokers have a craving that is only prevented by having another smoke. That craving is partly psychological but it is also physical. The body relies on the drug in tobacco smoke in order to function properly because its molecules interact with synapses in our nervous system. That drug is **nicotine** and it is one of the most addictive substances known.

Nicotine is a stimulant. It stimulates the release of adrenaline leading to an increase in heart rate and blood pressure. This gives an increase in mental alertness. **Marijuana** (ganga) contains a drug that has the opposite effect. It has a calming effect and may induce a trance-like state and also cause hallucinations.

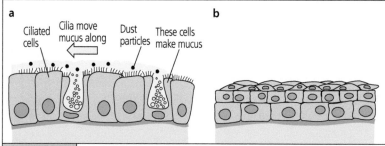

a Ciliated cells Cilia move mucus along Dust particles These cells make mucus

b

Figure 5.11.2 **a** Healthy lining of a bronchus of a non-smoker, **b** Lining of a bronchus of a long-term smoker: the ciliated cells are replaced by squamous cells.

Damage to the lungs

Tar is the black sticky material that collects in the lungs as smoke cools. It does not pass into the bloodstream. Tar irritates the lining of the airways stimulating the epithelial cells to produce more mucus. This tends to accumulate, narrowing the airways. Smokers cough to make this material move to the back of the throat (Figure 5.11.1).

Tar causes the cilia on the cells that line the air passages to stop beating. Mucus and the dust, dirt and bacteria that stick to it, are not removed from the lungs. The mucus accumulates and bacteria multiply. White blood cells congregate where this happens, particularly in the bronchi. The bronchi become blocked with **phlegm** (a mixture of mucus, bacteria and white blood cells), which people attempt to cough up. This condition is **chronic bronchitis**. People with this condition find it difficult to breathe as the bronchi are partly blocked (Figure 5.11.2).

Particles, bacteria and tar reach the alveoli. White blood cells digest a pathway through the lining of the alveoli to reach the bacteria. Eventually this weakens the walls of the alveoli so much that they break down and burst, reducing the surface area for gas exchange. This condition is **emphysema**, which leaves people gasping for breath. They cannot absorb enough oxygen or remove carbon dioxide efficiently. Many long-term smokers have both of these conditions.

Effects on transport of oxygen

Carbon monoxide combines permanently with haemoglobin in red blood cells so reducing the volume of oxygen that the blood can carry. There may be as much as a 10% decrease in the oxygen transported. This is particularly dangerous for pregnant women.

Lung cancer

90% of cases of lung cancer occur in people who smoke or who have smoked. The cause of lung cancer is the **carcinogens** in tar. These substances promote changes, known as mutation, to occur in the DNA of cells lining the airways. These mutations cause the cells to grow and divide out of control. This growth is very slow and it may take 20 years before there are any symptoms. The cells form a tumour. If this is not discovered it may grow to occupy a large area of the lung pushing against airways and blood vessels to block them. Worse, a part of the tumour may break off and spread into other organs. If a tumour is discovered before it has spread then it may be removed by surgery. If the tumour has spread, then the cancer is much more difficult to treat (Figures 5.11.3 and 5.11.4).

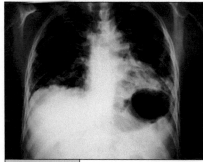

Figure 5.11.3 Lung cancer is often diagnosed by taking X-rays. Compare this with the X-ray of healthy lungs in 5.10.

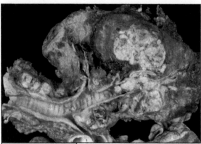

Figure 5.11.4 This cancer has spread through the lung, blocking blood vessels and airways.

SUMMARY QUESTIONS

1 State the components of tobacco smoke.

2 Smoking-related diseases are often classified as self-inflicted diseases. Discuss whether or not this is true.

3 Outline the effects of smoking on the gaseous exchange system.

4 Explain why smokers find it hard to give up their habit.

KEY POINTS

1 Nicotine is the addictive substance in tobacco smoke.

2 Tar damages the lining of the airways, stimulating excess production of mucus and destroying ciliated cells.

3 Carcinogens in smoke cause lung cancer.

4 Carbon monoxide combines with haemoglobin in red blood cells to reduce the blood's oxygen-carrying capacity.

SECTION 1: Multiple-choice questions

1 Which chemical reaction takes place inside the human stomach?

   A Cellulose in fibre is digested by cellulase enzymes.

   B Fats are digested into amino acids.

   C Proteins are digested by protease enzymes.

   D Starch is digested by lipase enzymes.

2 A person has anaemia. This could be caused by a lack of which nutrient?

   A calcium

   B iron

   C vitamin C

   D vitamin D

3 Which of the following is the word equation for anaerobic respiration in yeast?

   A glucose + oxygen $\longrightarrow$ carbon dioxide + water

   B glucose $\longrightarrow$ alcohol + carbon dioxide

   C glucose + oxygen $\longrightarrow$ alcohol + water

   D glucose $\longrightarrow$ lactic acid

4 Six test tubes were set up at temperatures between 15°C and 65°C. Each test tube contained identical solutions of starch and amylase. The time taken for each reaction to finish was recorded in this table.

Test tube	1	2	3	4	5	6
Temperature (°C)	15	25	35	45	55	65
Time taken (seconds)	135	75	30	15	95	185

The optimum temperature is:

   A 45°C

   B 65°C

   C between 35°C and 45°C

   D between 35°C and 55°C

5 A sample of food was tested with biuret solution. The solution changed colour from blue to purple. Which nutrient was present in the food sample?

   A fat

   B glucose

   C protein

   D starch

The rubber sheet in this model of the human thorax shows the effect of movements of the diaphragm. The diagram is needed to answer Questions 6 and 7.

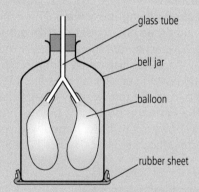

glass tube
bell jar
balloon
rubber sheet

6 When the rubber sheet is pulled downwards the balloons inflate. This is because:

   A air pressure in the balloons increases

   B air pressure in the bell jar increases

   C atmospheric pressure is greater than air pressure in the balloons

   D atmospheric pressure is less than air pressure in the balloons

7 When the rubber sheet is pushed upwards the balloons deflate. This is because:

   A air pressure in the balloons is greater than atmospheric pressure

   B air pressure in the bell jar is less than in the balloons

   C atmospheric pressure is greater than air pressure in the balloons

   D the balloons contract to force air out

8 Some students investigated the effect of temperature on the activity of the enzyme catalase. They used a 10% suspension of yeast cells as a source of catalase. The students determined the rate of reaction by collecting the oxygen produced. Table 1 shows their results.

Table 1

Temperature/ °C	Volume of oxygen collected/ cm³	Time taken to obtain oxygen/ seconds	Rate of reaction/cm³ of oxygen per second
0	0	–	0
10	5	100	0.05
20	10	65	0.15
30	10	12	0.83
40	10	5	2.00
50	10	9	
60	6	120	0.05
70	0	–	0

a i List the apparatus that the students would use in this investigation. *(3)*

ii Outline the method that the students would have to follow to obtain the results given in the table. *(4)*

b Calculate the rate of reaction at 50 °C. Show your working. *(2)*

c Plot a graph of the results. *(5)*

d Describe the results shown by your graph. *(4)*

e Explain the results. *(4)*

f i State *one* limitation of this investigation. *(1)*

ii Suggest *two* ways in which the investigation could be improved. *(2)*

Total 25 marks

9 Amylase catalyses the hydrolysis of starch.

a Write a word equation to show the reaction catalysed by amylase. *(2)*

A student investigated the effect of pH on the activity of amylase. The student made five reaction mixtures of amylase and starch using solutions of different pH.

The student took samples from each reaction mixture at intervals and tested them with iodine solution. The time taken for a yellow-brown colour to appear in samples taken from each reaction mixture is shown in Table 2.

Table 2

pH	Time taken for yellow-brown colour to appear/minutes
3	–
5	12
7	2
9	4
11	–

b i Use the student's results to make a table showing the rate of reaction at each pH. *(5)*

ii Describe the results shown in your table. *(4)*

c i Name the parts of the alimentary canal that secrete amylase. *(2)*

ii State what happens to the end products of starch digestion in the alimentary canal. *(2)*

Total 15 marks

10 a Make a fully annotated diagram to show how a villus in the small intestine is adapted for absorption of food. *(6)*

b i State the gas exchange surfaces of fish and humans. *(2)*

ii Compare the ways in which these surfaces are adapted for gas exchange. *(4)*

c Explain why animals require a continuous supply of oxygen. *(3)*

Total 15 marks

Further practice questions and examples can be found on the accompanying CD.

6.1 Transport

At the end of this topic you should be able to:

- explain why multicellular organisms need transport systems
- state the materials that are transported in animals and plants.

Tiny unicellular organisms, such as *Amoeba* (see 5.9), and some multicellular organisms, such as flatworms and tapeworms, have flat, thin bodies and rely on diffusion for transport of oxygen and carbon dioxide. However, most multicellular organisms are not flat and thin; they are more bulky and cannot rely on diffusion for transport of substances within their bodies.

Two problems come with increased bulk:

- the distances are too great to distribute oxygen throughout the body by relying on diffusion (think about the distance from your lungs to your big toe)
- the body surface becomes too small relative to body mass to function efficiently as a surface for gaseous exchange.

This practical demonstration will help you to understand the difficulty of relying on diffusion alone. Agar, a special jelly, is mixed with an alkali and a pH indicator. The jelly is cut into cubes of different sizes and placed into dilute hydrochloric acid. The colour of the pH indicator changes as the acid diffuses into the blocks. Eventually, the whole block changes colour. The time this takes is a measurement of how long the acid takes to diffuse to the centre of the block. The table shows some students' results for this investigation.

STUDY FOCUS

In question 2a, you should plot the time taken as the vertical axis. For the horizontal axis, you could plot the length of each side of the cubes (column 1) or the ratio given in column 4 (in which case plot 1, 1.2, 1.5, 2, 3 and 6). Remember to scale the axis correctly.

Table 6.1.1 Diffusion for different surface area:volume ratios

Cube of side/mm	Surface area/m^2	Volume/ mm^3	Ratio of surface area:volume	Time taken for block to change colour in acid/seconds
1	6	1	6:1	8
2	24	8	3:1	26
3	54	27	2:1	43
4	96	64	1.5:1	65
5	150	125	1.2:1	112
6	216	216	1:1	160

The time taken for acid to diffuse to the centre of the largest cube is 20 times slower than to the centre of the smallest cube.

Movement of substances by diffusion is not an efficient way of getting oxygen and glucose to cells far removed from the places where they are absorbed into the body.

STUDY FOCUS

The students calculated the surface area and the volume of the cubes and the ratios between surface area and volume. The ratios given in the table decrease as the cubes increase in size: the smallest cube has a ratio of surface area to volume of 6:1, whereas the largest cube has a ratio of 1:1.

The ratios of surface area to volume given in the table decrease as the cubes increase in size. This is because the volume of the cubes increases much more each time than the increase in the surface area. Your body is much bigger than these cubes, so your own surface area to volume ratio will be even smaller. With such a *small* surface area to volume ratio we cannot rely on diffusion to transport oxygen from the body surface to cells deep in the body. The distances are too great and there is not enough surface area to absorb enough oxygen.

Transport in flowering plants and mammals

Table 6.1.2 Transport in flowering plants and mammals

Feature of transport systems	Flowering plants	Mammals
Nutrients transported	Carbohydrates: sucrose Others: amino acids, mineral ions (6.8)	Carbohydrates: glucose Others: amino acids, fatty acids, vitamins, mineral ions (6.4)
Transport of water	In the xylem (6.6)	In the blood (6.4)
Transport of respiratory gases	No (supply of oxygen and carbon dioxide is by diffusion through air spaces and cells) (4.3)	Yes – oxygen and carbon dioxide (6.4)
Transport of hormones	In the xylem and phloem (8.2)	In the blood (9.3)
Fluid(s) transported	Xylem sap, phloem sap	Blood
Tubes used in transport	Xylem vessels, phloem sieve tubes (6.6, 6.8)	Arteries, capillaries and veins (6.2)
Mechanism for moving fluids	Xylem – transpiration pull (6.6) Phloem – pressure flow (6.8)	Heart pumps blood (6.3)
Rates of flow of fluids	Slower	Faster
Process of sealing wounds to prevent loss of fluids	Production of callose (a carbohydrate) to seal phloem sieve tubes	Blood clotting (6.4)

STUDY FOCUS

Another reason we do not absorb oxygen through our body surface is that we have skin. Look at 8.8 to find out why we do not use it for gas exchange.

SUMMARY QUESTIONS

1 The table shows information about three spherical organisms:

Feature	Spherical organisms		
	A	B	C
Radius/mm	1	2	3
Surface area/mm²	12.57	50.27	113.10
Volume/mm³	4.19	33.51	113.10

a State which organism has the highest surface area:volume ratio.

b Explain why **B** and **C** may need a transport system, whereas **A** may not.

2 a Plot a line graph of the results in Table 6.1.1.

b Use the graph you have drawn to explain why humans need a transport system.

3 Flowering plants have a transport system for water, mineral ions and organic substances, but not for oxygen and carbon dioxide. How do these gases reach cells in the leaves?

KEY POINTS

1 Transport systems move substances around multicellular organisms.

2 Mammals and flowering plants need transport systems because distances are too great for transport to occur throughout the body by diffusion.

3 Oxygen and carbon dioxide are transported in the blood in mammals, but move by diffusion through intercellular air spaces in flowering plants.

4 Carbohydrates, other organic nutrients, mineral ions and hormones are transported in both mammals and flowering plants.

DID YOU KNOW?

It would be better to say that the circulation system is an *enclosed* circulation as blood flows within blood vessels. Not all animals have blood vessels, animals such as crabs and insects have an open circulation with blood in large spaces in the body, not in blood vessels.

LINK

Squamous cells are very thin. They line the alveoli as well as capillaries. They are thin so that the diffusion distance from one side to the other is very short. Diffusion is more efficient if the distance is short (see 6.1).

STUDY FOCUS

Blood is red. Oxygenated blood is bright red; deoxygenated blood is dark red. It is a convention to use blue to represent deoxygenated blood. It doesn't mean that deoxygenated blood is *actually* blue. It isn't.

The transport system in humans consists of blood that is pumped by the heart through a system of blood vessels. Blood travels away from the heart in arteries and towards the heart in veins. We have a **double circulatory system** in which blood flows through the heart *twice* during one complete circulation of the body. To prove this, follow the blood around the diagram in Figure 6.2.1 from the lungs, around the system and back to where you started. The two circulations are:

- **pulmonary circulation** – deoxygenated blood flows from the heart, through the pulmonary arteries to the lungs and back to the heart in the pulmonary veins as oxygenated blood.
- **systemic circulation** – oxygenated blood flows from the heart, through the aorta and other arteries to all the other organs of the body and then back to heart through the vena cava as deoxygenated blood.

The circulation is also described as a **closed circulatory system** because the blood remains inside blood vessels during its journeys throughout the body.

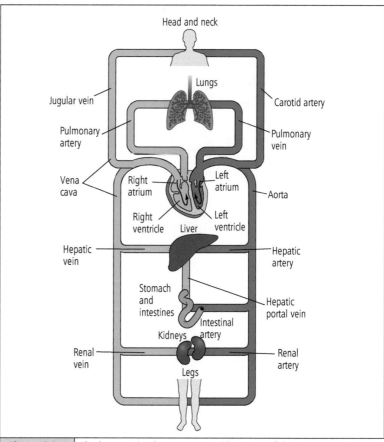

Figure 6.2.1 | The human circulatory system with names of the major blood vessels

Blood vessels

The walls of arteries and veins are made of three different tissues:

• squamous cells that form a smooth lining

• muscle tissue

• fibrous tissue that contains **elastic tissue** and **collagen** fibres.

The walls of capillaries do not have muscle or fibrous tissue; they are only composed of the squamous cells.

Table 6.2.1   The structure and function of blood vessels

Blood vessel	Relationship between structure and function
Artery (Figure 6.2.2)	• Blood flows away from the heart at high pressure • Elastic tissue in the walls withstands surges in blood pressure; it stretches and recoils to maintain the blood pressure • Blood is delivered to organs at a pressure slightly less than it left the heart • Walls have thick layers of muscle and fibrous tissue to withstand high blood pressures
Vein (Figure 6.2.3)	• Blood flows towards the heart at low pressure • Vessels expand to take increasing volumes of blood, e.g. during exercise • As blood pressure is low, backflow of blood is prevented by semi-lunar valves at intervals along veins • Walls have thin layers of muscle and fibrous tissue as they do not have to withstand high blood pressures
Capillary (Figure 6.2.4)	• Blood flows between arteries and veins at low pressure • Oxygen and carbon dioxide diffuse through the walls • Water and solutes, such as glucose and amino acids, pass across the walls into tissue fluid surrounding the cells • Walls are thin so there is a short diffusion distance between the blood and the tissue fluid

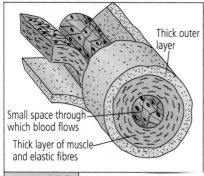

Figure 6.2.2 | An artery with the outer layers cut away

Thick outer layer

Small space through which blood flows

Thick layer of muscle and elastic fibres

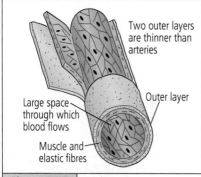

Figure 6.2.3 | A vein

Two outer layers are thinner than arteries

Outer layer

Large space through which blood flows

Muscle and elastic fibres

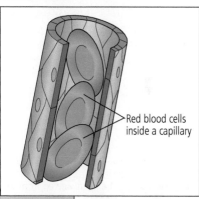

Figure 6.2.4 | A capillary magnified × 2000 to show the detail of the cells that make up the wall. Part is cut away to show the red blood cells inside.

Red blood cells inside a capillary

KEY POINTS

1 In a double circulation system, blood travels through the heart twice in one complete circulation of the body.

2 Blood flows from the heart to the lungs and back in the pulmonary circulation and from the heart to the rest of the body and back in the systemic circulation.

3 Blood flows away from the heart in arteries, towards the heart in veins and through tissues in capillaries.

4 Arteries have thick walls to withstand high pressure; veins have thin walls as blood pressure is low; capillaries are exchange vessels and have very thin walls.

SUMMARY QUESTIONS

1 Explain how blood flows in one direction in the circulatory system.

2 Relate the structure of the artery, vein and capillary to the function(s) of each of these blood vessels.

6.3

The heart

LEARNING OUTCOMES

At the end of this topic you should be able to:

- describe the structure of the heart including the four chambers, valves and the major blood vessels
- explain how the heart functions to move blood to the lungs and to the rest of the body
- describe what happens during one heart beat.

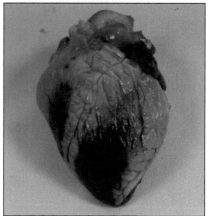

| Figure 6.3.1 | The heart viewed from the front of the body |

| Figure 6.3.3 | A heart dissected to show the inside of the left ventricle and the base of the aorta |

The human heart consists almost entirely of **cardiac muscle** tissue. This is specialised muscle that can contract about 70 times a minute for up to a hundred years or more without tiring.

We need a heart to pump blood around the body. The heart contracts and 'squeezes' the blood, applying pressure to it. The blood can then flow through the vessels and overcome the pressure exerted on our bodies by the atmosphere. The heart is a 'double pump': the right side of the heart pumps blood to the lungs and the left side pumps blood to the rest of the body.

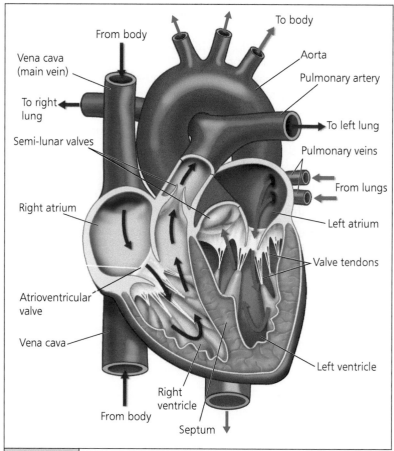

| Figure 6.3.2 | The heart |

The septum separates the two halves of the heart. This prevents the mixing of deoxygenated and oxygenated blood. On each side of the heart there are two chambers. The upper chamber is the atrium. Blood empties into the atria from veins. When each atrium contracts it pumps blood into a ventricle. The ventricles have much more muscular walls than the atria as they have to pump the blood at higher pressure over a great distance.

Between each atrium and ventricle is an **atrioventricular valve**. These valves prevent the blood flowing back into the right and left atrium when the right and left ventricles contract. At the base of the **pulmonary artery** and the **aorta** there are **semi-lunar valves**. These prevent blood flowing back into the ventricles when they relax.

The left ventricle has a more muscular wall than the right ventricle. This is because it has to pump blood around the body. It has to overcome much more resistance to flow around the body than the blood that flows through the lungs, which have a spongy texture.

Heart action

The heart is not 'told' to contract by the brain. In the wall of the right atrium are some specialised cardiac muscle cells that act as the heart's pacemaker. These cells send out pulses of electricity that instruct the atria and then the ventricles to contract.

The heart pumps blood when its muscles contract. When the muscle contracts the chamber gets smaller and squeezes the blood out. After each chamber contracts it relaxes so it fills up with blood again.

Systole is when the heart muscles contract.

Diastole is when the heart muscles relax.

During systole, the atria contract to force blood into the ventricles (see Figure 6.3.4a). The valves between the atria and ventricles open due to the higher pressure of blood in the atria pushing against them. The atria relax and then the ventricles contract to force blood out into the arteries (see Figure 6.3.4b). The higher pressure in the ventricles closes the atrioventricular valves to prevent blood flowing back into the atria. The increase in pressure also causes the semi-lunar valves at the base of the arteries to open. This allows blood to flow from the right ventricle to the lungs in the pulmonary arteries and from the left ventricle to the rest of the body in the aorta (main artery).

The chambers fill with blood during diastole. Deoxygenated blood returns to the right atrium in the **vena cava** (main vein). Oxygenated blood returns to the left atrium in the **pulmonary veins** (see Figure 6.3.4c).

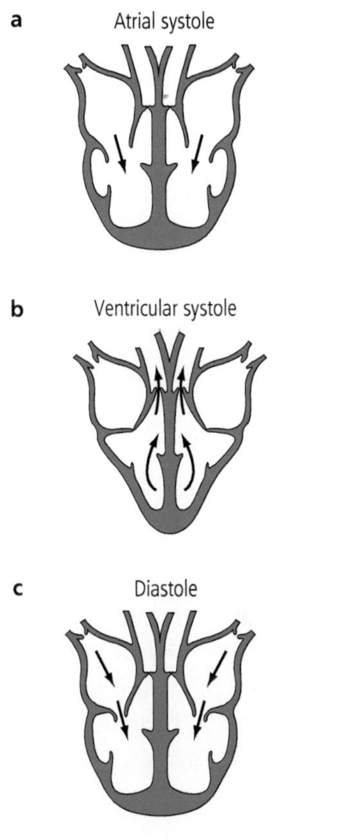

a   Atrial systole

b   Ventricular systole

c   Diastole

Figure 6.3.4 | The changes that occur in the heart during one heart beat

KEY POINTS

1   The heart consists of two muscular pumps divided by a septum.

2   Each side has two chambers: an atrium and a ventricle.

3   Ventricles contract to force blood into arteries; two atrioventricular valves and two semi-lunar valves ensure that blood flows in one direction through the heart.

4   The right ventricle pumps blood into the pulmonary circulation; the left ventricle pumps blood into the systemic circulation.

SUMMARY QUESTIONS

1   Explain why we need a heart.

2   Describe the pathway taken by blood as it flows through the heart.

2   Explain the difference between diastole and systole.

3   The heart is sometimes described as a 'double pump'. Explain what this means.

4   Explain how one-way flow of blood through the heart is achieved.

5   Make a large labelled diagram of the human circulatory system showing all the organs included in 6.2 and 6.3.

6.4 Blood

LEARNING OUTCOMES

At the end of this topic you should be able to:

- list the components of the blood
- state the function of each component
- explain how the structure of red blood cells (erythrocytes), phagocytes and lymphocytes are related to their functions
- explain how blood is involved in defence against disease
- define the terms *immune system* and *natural immunity*.

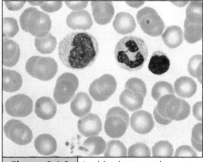

Figure 6.4.2 In this photograph you can see red blood cells, a phagocyte and a lymphocyte. Compare with Figure 6.4.3 to identify them (× 800).

Blood is the fluid that is pumped around the circulatory system by the heart. As blood flows through capillaries in the organs, substances are exchanged with the surrounding tissues. We have seen that in the lungs there is gaseous exchange with the air in the alveoli. In respiring tissues there is exchange with the cells that require oxygen and need to have their carbon dioxide removed.

Blood is a tissue that consists of cells and fragments of cells suspended in plasma (Figure 6.4.1).

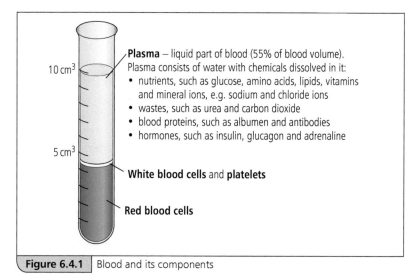

Plasma – liquid part of blood (55% of blood volume). Plasma consists of water with chemicals dissolved in it:
- nutrients, such as glucose, amino acids, lipids, vitamins and mineral ions, e.g. sodium and chloride ions
- wastes, such as urea and carbon dioxide
- blood proteins, such as albumen and antibodies
- hormones, such as insulin, glucagon and adrenaline

White blood cells and **platelets**

Red blood cells

Figure 6.4.1 Blood and its components

Table 6.4.1 shows the features of the blood cells you can see in Figures 6.4.2 and 6.4.3.

Table 6.4.1

Type of blood cell	Features	Relationship between structure and function
Red blood cell	• Small cell • Shape: biconcave disc • No nucleus, no mitochondria • Cytoplasm is full of haemoglobin	Can change shape and fit easily through capillaries More space to fill with haemoglobin to transport oxygen and carbon dioxide
Phagocyte	• Large cell • Lobed nucleus • Cytoplasm with mitochondria and many small vacuoles containing enzymes	Lobed nucleus helps cells leave blood through small gaps in the capillary walls Vacuoles contain enzymes to digest bacteria
Lymphocyte	• Small cell • Small quantity of cytoplasm with few mitochondria	When activated during an infection the cytoplasm enlarges to produce antibodies that are made of protein (see 6.5)

Defence against disease

Blood is involved in preventing pathogens from entering the body by the formation of blood clots at the site of a damaged blood vessel. If pathogens enter the body, specialised white blood cells destroy them.

This is how blood clots are formed:

1 **Platelets** are small cell fragments which release substances that interact with calcium ions in the plasma to activate **prothrombin**.

2 Inactive prothrombin changes into the active enzyme **thrombin**.

3 Thrombin then catalyses the conversion of the soluble protein **fibrinogen** into fibrin, an insoluble protein.

4 **Fibrin** forms a meshwork of fibres to trap platelets and blood cells, which dry to form a scab (see Figure 6.4.4).

Blood clotting seals wounds to restrict the loss of blood and prevents the entry of pathogens through open wounds. When there is a wound in the skin, the stem cells at the base of the epidermis divide by mitosis to form new skin cells to repair the damage.

Phagocytes engulf and destroy pathogens. If bacteria invade the body, cells in the area release chemicals that attract phagocytes from the blood. Phagocytes engulf bacteria into food vacuoles where they are digested by enzymes. The enzymes are stored in small vacuoles in the cytoplasm.

Blood clotting, the action of phagocytes and other **non-specific defences** may defeat the invasion. These are part of our defence or **immune system** that we all inherit and they form our **natural immunity**. The defences that specifically target the pathogens that invade us are not inherited. They are discussed in 6.5.

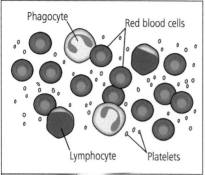

Figure 6.4.3 | A drawing made from a photograph similar to the one in Figure 6.4.2 ($\times$ 800)

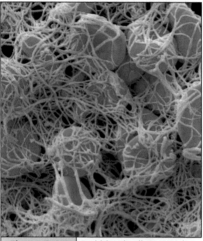

Figure 6.4.4 | Red blood cells trapped in a meshwork of fibrin ($\times$ 2000)

SUMMARY QUESTIONS

1 a List the components of blood.
   b What percentage of the total volume does each component occupy?

2 Blood consists of cells and fragments of cells suspended in plasma.
   a Make a labelled drawing of each type of cell found in blood.
   b State the function of each cell.
   c What are the fragments of cells called and what is their function?

3 Explain how each of the cell types you have drawn in question **2a** is adapted to its function.

4 Outline how blood defends the body against disease.

5 Make a flow chart diagram to show what happens during blood clotting.

KEY POINTS

1 Blood is composed of red blood cells, white blood cells (phagocytes and lymphocytes) and platelets suspended in liquid plasma.

2 Red blood cells are filled with haemoglobin to transport oxygen; phagocytes contain enzymes to digest bacteria; lymphocytes produce antibody molecules.

3 Natural immunity refers to the forms of defence that we all inherit; blood clotting and phagocytosis are examples.

LINK

The reason HIV is such a serious infection is that it destroys the body's lymphocytes that are responsible for much of our defence against infectious diseases. See 10.3.

EXAM TIP

Take care with all the words that begin with 'anti-' in this unit. An antigen is a chemical that stimulates lymphocytes to produce antibodies. Antibodies are proteins that help to destroy pathogens. Antitoxins neutralise the toxins (poisonous chemicals) that some bacteria produce.

If you have an infection, such as the common cold, you will be ill for a while and have a variety of symptoms. You will then begin to feel better and within a week or two you will be back to your normal, healthy self. If the same strain of the common cold virus invades again, you will not get the same symptoms. You will not be ill. This is another role of the immune system: to provide highly effective defences against specific pathogens. Lymphocytes are responsible for this specific immunity.

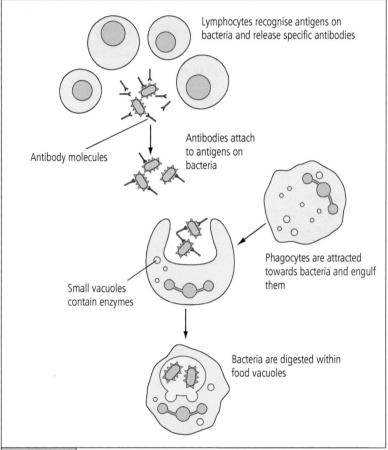

Lymphocytes recognise antigens on bacteria and release specific antibodies

Antibody molecules

Antibodies attach to antigens on bacteria

Phagocytes are attracted towards bacteria and engulf them

Small vacuoles contain enzymes

Bacteria are digested within food vacuoles

Figure 6.5.1 Lymphocytes secrete antibodies that make it easier for phagocytes to engulf bacteria and destroy them.

You are born with a very large number of different types of lymphocyte. These cells are specific to different surface chemicals, known as **antigens**. These are found on the surface of bacteria, viruses and other pathogens. When a pathogen enters the body, phagocytes 'cut it up' and display antigens to lymphocytes. Those lymphocytes that recognise the antigens divide by mitosis and multiply.

- Some of these lymphocytes become bigger and fill with cytoplasm so that they can secrete protein molecules into lymph and into the blood. These proteins are **antibodies**.

- Some antibodies stick to the surface of pathogens and cause them to clump together as in Figure 6.5.1.
- **Antitoxins** are antibodies that combine with the toxic waste products of bacteria, such as those that cause tetanus and diphtheria, neutralising them so that they have no effect.

The production of antibodies takes a week or so and during this time people are ill.

Many pathogens invade our cells. During an infection, other lymphocytes are activated to patrol the body looking for infected cells. When they find infected cells they destroy them so the pathogens cannot reproduce and spread to other cells.

The first time you have a certain infection, the response is very slow. This is why you have fallen ill. The response to another infection by the same pathogen is much faster; so fast that you are unlikely to have any symptoms. This is because during the first infection many lymphocytes are produced that recognise the specific pathogen. Some of these do not produce antibodies, but remain in the body as **memory cells**. A second invasion of the same pathogen stimulates the large number of memory cells to respond immediately. Memory cells remain in the body for many years, perhaps a lifetime, giving us long-term **immunity**.

Vaccination

It is possible to promote the same type of immunity artificially without having to be ill. **Artificial immunity** may be achieved by injecting a **vaccine** that contains live pathogens, dead pathogens or antigens taken from the surface of pathogens (Figure 6.5.2). Some vaccines stimulate immunity to just one specific disease. Others contain antigens for several diseases. For example, MMR protects against measles, mumps and rubella. It is important that children begin a vaccination programme early in life to reduce the risk of catching infectious diseases that can be life-threatening. Many vaccines require booster injections to ensure that there are enough memory cells in the body to mount a rapid and effective defence against an invasion of a pathogen.

Countries have **vaccination** programmes to protect their populations. The **vaccines** included protect everyone against common diseases. Some vaccines are only given to travellers and to special categories of people, such as vets and medical staff. Vaccination is used to protect the whole population, including people who cannot be vaccinated. This happens because pathogens have no place to reproduce if everyone (or nearly everyone) is vaccinated. Smallpox has been eradicated from the world in this way and other infectious diseases, such as polio, are likely to be eradicated in the near future.

STUDY FOCUS

Artificial immunisation is provided in two ways. **Long-term immunity** is given by vaccination; **short-term immunity** is given by injecting antibodies that are prepared from the plasma of blood isolated from blood donations.

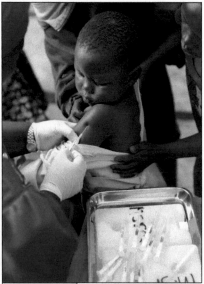

Figure 6.5.2 Vaccination is a key part of protecting populations against infectious diseases.

KEY POINTS

1 Immunity is the ability to resist the spread of an infection.

2 During an infection, lymphocytes are activated to produce antibodies that act against specific pathogens.

3 Vaccines are an artificial way to promote immunity against diseases.

SUMMARY QUESTIONS

1 Define the terms *immunity*, *vaccine* and *vaccination*.

2 Distinguish between
  a specific and non-specific immunity (see 6.4)
  b natural and artificial immunity (see 6.4).

3 Explain how immunity may be gained.

4 Discuss the importance of vaccinating young children.

Xylem and transpiration

At the end of this topic you should be able to:

- define the terms *transpiration*, *transpiration stream* and *transpiration pull*
- outline the pathway taken by water as it travels through a plant
- state that xylem is a tissue composed of xylem vessels
- explain how the structure of xylem vessels is suited to their function
- discuss the roles of transpiration in plants.

EXAM TIP

Be prepared to explain that transpiration is a consequence of having a large surface area for gas exchange in leaves.

Plants require large volumes of water. Most of the body of a plant is water and plants lose large quantities as water vapour from their leaves. You will remember from 4.3 and 5.9 that leaves have a very large internal surface for gaseous exchange for photosynthesis. Each cell has a surface in contact with air. The cell walls of all these cells are damp. Evaporation occurs at any damp surface in contact with air. Leaves have stomata to allow carbon dioxide to diffuse into the intercellular air spaces. The air inside the leaf is fully saturated with water vapour, so there is a concentration gradient between the air inside the leaf and the air outside. **Transpiration** is the evaporation of water at the surfaces of mesophyll cells, followed by the diffusion of water vapour through stomata.

Water molecules tend to 'stick together', a force called cohesion. The loss of water by evaporation creates a pull on the water between the cells in the leaf. This pull causes water to move from the xylem in the leaf veins to replace the water in the cell walls. The pulling effect of evaporation is transmitted to water in the xylem in the stem and then all the way down to the roots in the **transpiration stream**. This **transpiration pull** moves columns of water under tension. On hot, dry, sunny days the loss of water occurs faster than water can be absorbed from the soil. As a result the tension can be so great that the trunks of large trees are pulled inwards.

Root hair cells absorb water. Water moves by osmosis from the soil, through the fully permeable cell wall and the differentially permeable cell membrane into root hair cells. From here water moves across the root tissue and into the xylem.

The photographs in Figure 6.6.1 show the pathway taken by water inside celery stalks, which are the petioles of leaves.

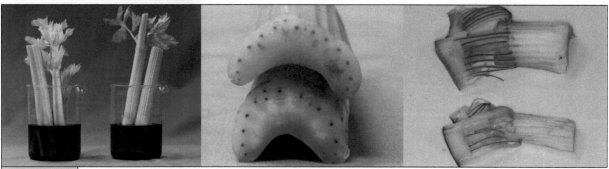

Figure 6.6.1 | Xylem tissue is stained by the dyes and dissected out from celery petioles.

The coloured strands in the photographs of the celery are **xylem vessels**.

They are columns of cells that have the following features to help transport water:

- wide tubes, so that plenty of water can flow
- no cell contents, therefore hollow tubes that provide little resistance to the flow of water (xylem vessels are dead)
- cellulose cell walls that water molecules tend to 'stick' to
- no end walls separating the cells from one another
- thick cell walls that are strengthened with lignin, which prevents the vessels collapsing from the tension of the water.

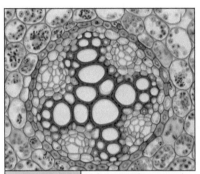

Figure 6.6.2 Xylem vessels are made from cells that are much wider than other plant cells (×100).

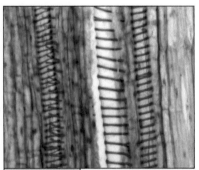

Figure 6.6.3 Lignin is laid down in the walls of xylem vessels in spirals and in rings (×450).

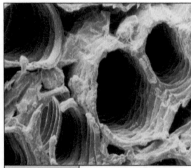

Figure 6.6.4 Xylem vessels viewed in an electron microscope (×300)

Advantages of transpiration

The movement of water through the xylem does not require the plant to use any energy. It is a passive process driven by energy from the Sun. Transpiration provides all the parts of the plant with a supply of water. This water is needed:

- as a raw material for photosynthesis
- to fill the vacuoles of cells so they support the plant
- for evaporation to cool plants in hot weather
- to dissolve mineral ions such as nitrate ions and magnesium ions that are transported in the transpiration stream.

One disadvantage of transpiration is that plants require large volumes of water. They do not need to use energy to move the water, but they do need continually to grow roots to reach fresh sources of water, which may not always be available.

SUMMARY QUESTIONS

1 Define the following terms: *transpiration*, *transpiration pull* and *transpiration stream*.

2 Explain why transpiration is a consequence of photosynthesis.

3 Describe the pathway taken by water as it passes through a plant.

4 Explain how xylem vessels are adapted to their function.

5 Outline the advantages and disadvantages of transpiration to plants.

KEY POINTS

1 Transpiration is the evaporation of water at the surfaces of mesophyll cells followed by the diffusion of water vapour through stomata.

2 Evaporation drives the transpiration pull to move water.

3 The transpiration stream is the pathway taken by water in xylem vessels from the roots to the leaves.

4 Xylem vessels are columns of wide empty cells without end walls that provide little resistance to the flow of water. Their cell walls are strengthened with lignin to prevent collapse when under tension.

Investigating transpiration

At the end of this topic you should be able to:

- outline how to use a potometer to investigate rates of transpiration
- explain the effects of external factors on rates of transpiration
- describe and explain the adaptations of plants to conserve water.

Figure 6.7.1 A potometer for measuring the rate of water uptake by leafy shoots. Figure 1 on page 101 is a diagram of a potometer like this one.

DID YOU KNOW?

Potometers can measure both water uptake and transpiration if they are put on a balance to measure loss in mass. The balance has to measure to 0.01 g if results are to be taken over a short period of time.

A **potometer** is used to measure transpiration *indirectly* by finding out how much water plants take up. The volume of water lost is slightly less than the volume of water taken in by the roots. This is because some of the water is used for photosynthesis and to keep cells turgid.

To measure rate of water uptake

1 Leafy shoots are cut under water and kept there to prevent air entering xylem vessels and blocking them.

2 The potometer is put into a large basin of water and submerged.

3 The tap on the reservoir is opened so that there is water inside the glass tubing. It is then closed.

4 The stem should be cut at an angle to give a large surface for absorbing water and placed inside the rubber tubing, making a tight fit. There should be no leaks.

5 The potometer is removed from the water. After a while air will be taken into the glass tubing. Put the glass tubing into a bowl of water so that there is an air bubble inside the tubing.

6 The apparatus is left for a while, so that the leafy shoot adjusts to the conditions and water uptake reaches a constant rate.

7 Measure the distance travelled by the air bubble over a suitable period of time. This may be a different period of time for each set of conditions that you investigate.

8 The air bubble can be re-set to the end of the capillary tube by opening the reservoir tap.

The effect of environmental conditions on the rate of water uptake may be investigated by:

- placing a black bag over the leafy shoot to find out the effect of darkness
- placing a clear bag over the leafy shoot to investigate the effect of still air
- using a fan or hair dryer to increase the wind speed
- use shading and lamps to provide different light intensities.

Environmental factors affecting transpiration

- Light – Stomata close in darkness and open in light. As most water vapour diffuses out of leaves through stomata their width is a major factor in determining how much transpiration occurs.
- Humidity – The air inside leaves is fully saturated with water vapour. The humidity of the surrounding air determines the concentration gradient for water vapour. In humid conditions there is less transpiration because the concentration gradient for water is less steep than in dry air.

- Temperature – Warm conditions increase the rate of evaporation inside the leaves. This is because warmer air holds more water vapour than cooler air.
- Wind speed – In still air, water vapour remains near the leaves reducing the concentration gradient. In windy conditions, water molecules are blown away from the leaf surface, so increasing the steepness of the concentration gradient (Figure 6.7.2).

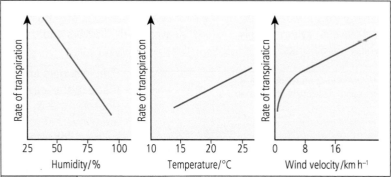

Figure 6.7.2 | The effect of increasing humidity, temperature and wind speed on rates of transpiration

Adaptations of plants to obtain and conserve water

There are many plants that live in places where there are high rates of transpiration and/or water is in short supply. They have special features, which allow them to obtain sufficient water and retain it rather than losing it in transpiration:

- deep roots, that extend to great depths
- extensive, shallow roots that cover a wide area
- thick, waxy cuticles over the stems and leaves to reduce the water loss through the upper and lower epidermis
- thick leaves and/or stems to store water; plants like this are called succulents.

Figure 6.7.3 | Some plants have leaves that roll to keep water vapour near the lower epidermis, so reducing the rate of transpiration.

Figure 6.7.4 | Sea grape has an extensive root system and leaves with thick cuticles. The leaves are arranged to shade each other.

SUMMARY QUESTIONS

1 State what happens to water taken up by plants that is *not* transpired.

2 List the precautions that should be taken when using a potometer to measure the rate of water uptake by a leafy shoot.

3 List the factors that influence rates of transpiration.

4 a Describe and explain the adaptations of plants that grow where water is in short supply.

   b Outline the abiotic factors that make these adaptations necessary.

KEY POINTS

1 Rates of water uptake and transpiration are measured with a potometer.

2 Light intensity, humidity, temperature and wind speed are factors that influence rates of transpiration.

3 Plants have adaptations for water absorption, water storage and reducing the rate of transpiration.

Phloem and storage

At the end of this topic you should be able to:

- define the term *translocation*
- state that substances are transported in the phloem from source to sink
- explain how the structure of phloem is suited to its function
- identify storage compounds in plants and animals and the places where they are stored
- discuss the importance of storage in organisms.

Sources to sinks

In plant transport, the organ where substances start their movement is described as a **source** and any destination is a **sink**. Water and mineral ions are absorbed by the root system, which is the source, and travel in xylem vessels to stems, leaves, buds, flowers and fruits, which are all sinks.

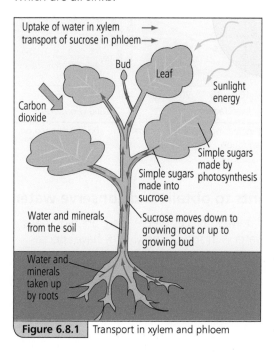

Figure 6.8.1 | Transport in xylem and phloem

Simple sugars are made in the leaves by photosynthesis. These are converted to sucrose, for transport in phloem tissue to the rest of the plant. In the transport of sucrose and other products, such as amino acids, the leaves are the source and other organs are sinks. This transport is called **translocation,** which means 'from place to place' (Figure 6.8.1).

Substances are transported in the phloem in different directions: downwards from leaves to roots, upwards from leaves to flowers, fruits and buds and also from storage organs to new stems and leaves.

Running parallel to xylem vessels throughout plants are phloem **sieve tubes**. These are columns of living cells that contain some cytoplasm and have end walls between them. The end walls are perforated by many small pores to form **sieve plates**. It is thought that they prevent the cells bursting under pressure of their contents and are perforated to reduce the resistance to flow (Figures 6.8.2 and 6.8.3).

Sucrose is moved into the sieve tubes at the source in the leaves. This is an active process, requiring energy. Cells surrounding sieve tubes have many mitochondria to provide the energy for this loading of sucrose. The high concentration of sucrose in the sieve tubes in the veins of the leaf causes water to diffuse in by osmosis. This builds up a 'head of pressure' that forces the phloem sap out of the leaf veins into the stem and on to the sinks. This mechanism is called pressure flow. The highest rates of translocation occur on warm, sunny days, when plants are producing lots of sugar.

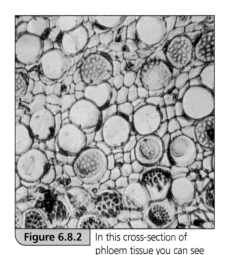

Figure 6.8.2 | In this cross-section of phloem tissue you can see some sieve plates, each with many sieve pores (× 130).

Storage in plants and animals

When growing conditions are good, plants transport sucrose to leaves, stems or roots that are modified for storage. These **storage organs** swell with the stored food, which may be starch, lipids or protein or a combination of all three. Storage organs provide a supply of energy and nutrients when conditions are too harsh for photosynthesis. Conditions may be too dry, too hot, too wet or too cold.

In plants, food storage is associated with reproduction. Structures that are produced for asexual or vegetative reproduction store food, often because they have to survive harsh periods before growing again. Tubers, corms, bulbs and rhizomes are all storage organs that are also used for vegetative reproduction. Plants store food in seeds to provide enough energy for the embryo during germination and, once germinated, for the seedling to become established.

Fat provides animals with a long-term energy store. Mammals store fat in a layer under the skin and around the large organs, such as the heart and the kidneys. Humans are good at storing fat; this was probably a useful adaptation for times when food was scarce. This is rarely the case now, yet we still store fat easily and have an epidemic of obesity to show for it (see 5.7). The liver also stores some fat as well as vitamins and minerals, such as vitamin B_{12} and iron – both needed for the production of red blood cells.

Fat stores are put to good use; for example, marine mammals use it for buoyancy and as a thermal insulator. It also stores fat-soluble vitamins, such as vitamin A.

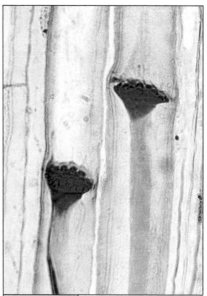

Figure 6.8.3 Sieve plates are also clearly visible in this longitudinal section of phloem sieve tubes.

Figure 6.8.4 A seed in an early stage of germination. The embryo is respiring starch and lipid to provide energy for growth.

SUMMARY QUESTIONS

1 Define the terms *translocation*, *source* and *sink*.

2 Describe briefly how sucrose is transported in the phloem.

3 Make a table to compare xylem and phloem.

4 Explain **a** why plants have storage organs and **b** the roles of fat stored by mammals.

KEY POINTS

1 Translocation is the movement of sucrose and other organic compounds in the phloem.

2 A source is the organ where a substance begins its movement through a plant; a sink is its destination.

3 Movement in the phloem is by pressure flow as the result of active processes in leaves.

4 Plants and animals store carbohydrate, lipids and proteins to provide energy and materials, often during times when food is scarce.

5 Animals store fat as a long-term energy store and to provide thermal insulation and buoyancy.

Figure 6.8.5 Hunter gatherers from the Kalahari where food may often be scarce. The ability to store fat in times of plenty provides them with energy in times of scarcity.

SECTION 1: Multiple-choice questions

1 Plants absorb water from the soil and lose it to the atmosphere. Through which structures does water pass from soil to atmosphere?

A palisade mesophyll cells ⟶ xylem vessels ⟶ root hair cells

B root hair cells ⟶ mesophyll cells ⟶ xylem vessels

C root hair cells ⟶ xylem vessels ⟶ mesophyll cells

D spongy mesophyll cells ⟶ root hair cells ⟶ xylem vessels

2 Water is lost from leaves to the atmosphere by which process?

A photosynthesis

B respiration

C translocation

D transpiration

3 Which substances are dissolved in human blood plasma?

A carbon dioxide, haemoglobin and glycogen

B carbon dioxide, protein and starch

C glucose, hormones and urea

D oxygen, urea and sucrose

4 Which is the correct description of the human circulation? In each complete circuit of the whole body, blood passes

A from the alimentary canal to the liver before returning to the heart

B through the pulmonary circuit and the systemic circuit

C through the four chambers of the heart before going to the lungs

D through arteries, arterioles and capillaries before returning to the heart in veins

5 Which is an effect of smoking on the gas exchange system?

A bladder cancer

B chronic bronchitis

C heart disease

D high blood pressure

6 When blood clots the following occur:

1 fibrinogen is converted to fibrin

2 prothrombin is converted to thrombin

3 platelets release substances that interact with calcium ions

4 blood cells are trapped in a mesh of fibres

Which is the correct sequence of these stages in blood clotting?

A 1 ⟶ 2 ⟶ 3 ⟶ 4

B 2 ⟶ 1 ⟶ 4 ⟶ 3

C 3 ⟶ 2 ⟶ 1 ⟶ 4

D 4 ⟶ 1 ⟶ 2 ⟶ 3

The following list of features of blood cells is needed for Questions 7 and 8.

1 Cytoplasm is full of haemoglobin.

2 Nucleus is lobed.

3 Cytoplasm has many small, enzyme-filled vacuoles.

4 Shape is a biconcave disc.

5 Cell has no nucleus.

6 Nucleus occupies most of the cell.

7 Which of these features describes red blood cells?

A 1, 2 and 3

B 1, 4 and 5

C 2, 3 and 6

D 3, 4 and 5

8 Which of these features describes phagocytic white blood cells?

A 1 and 5

B 2 and 6

C 2 and 3

D 3 and 5

9 Which carbohydrate is transported in phloem tissue?

A Fructose

B Glucose

C Maltose

D Sucrose

10 A student used the potometer shown in Figure 1 to investigate the effect of different conditions on the rate of water uptake.

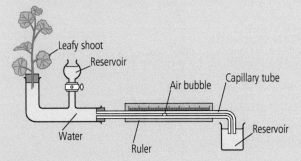

Figure 1

The student set up the potometer in a brightly lit laboratory at room temperature and provided three sets of conditions, A, B and C, as follows:

A still, humid air

B moving, humid air

C moving, dry air.

In each case, the student waited for 10 minutes before taking any readings. The student's results are shown in Table 1.

Table 1

Time/ minutes	Distance travelled by the air bubble in different conditions/mm		
	A	B	C
2	3	6	8
4	4	12	16
6	7	17	30
10	9	21	57
12	11	25	86

a Describe *three* precautions that the student should take when setting up the potometer. (3)

b Explain why the student waited for 10 minutes before taking readings for each set of conditions. (2)

c Draw a graph of the results in the table. (6)

d Use the results to:

i Describe the effect of humidity and air movement on the rate of water uptake by the leafy shoot.

ii Explain the effect of increasing air speed and decreasing humidity in the investigation. (6)

e The lower surfaces of all the leaves of the shoot in Figure 1 were coated in petroleum jelly, which is impermeable to water. The shoot was then exposed to dry, moving air.

i Predict the result that would be obtained. (2)

ii Give an explanation for your prediction. (3)

f The student repeated the investigation, but this time placed the potometer on a balance to record any changes in mass.

Explain the advantage of measuring changes in mass as well as the uptake of water. (3)

Total 25 marks

11 Figure 2 shows a ginger rhizome at the beginning of the growing season.

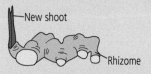

Figure 2

a Describe how you could find out what types of carbohydrate are stored in the rhizome. (7)

b Explain the advantages of storing carbohydrate in structures such as rhizomes. (3)

c Explain why the cells at the tips of the new shoots are a sink for the transport of materials, rather than a source. (5)

Total 15 marks

Further practice questions and examples can be found on the accompanying CD.

7.1   Excretion

Metabolism is all the chemical and physical changes that occur in bodies. Some of the chemical processes produce substances that are of no use and may even be toxic if allowed to accumulate.

Excretion in humans

Waste substances produced by humans are:

• carbon dioxide from aerobic respiration

• **urea** from the breakdown of excess amino acids

• **bile pigments**, bilirubin and biliverdin, from the breakdown of haemoglobin in dead red blood cells

• water from aerobic respiration.

Carbon dioxide is the waste product of aerobic respiration. Produced in mitochondria, it is carried in the blood to the lungs where it is excreted. If carbon dioxide accumulated in the body it would be toxic as it causes acidosis – a condition that leads to cell damage.

Amino acids that are absorbed from the gut can be used to make proteins, but they cannot be stored as amino acids. Any amino acids that are excess to our requirements are broken down in the liver (Figure 7.1.1). This process forms ammonia and compounds that can be used in respiration or converted into carbohydrates or fat for storage. Ammonia is toxic in low concentrations because it increases the pH of cytoplasm making enzymes less active. It is immediately converted by the liver into urea, which is less harmful and requires less water for its excretion.

Figure 7.1.1 | This shows what happens to the amino acids that are absorbed from the small intestine.

The liver also breaks down old red blood cells to release haemoglobin. Molecules of haemoglobin are broken down and the iron is recycled to make new haemoglobin. The rest of the *haem* part of haemoglobin molecules is converted into bile pigments, which are excreted in urine and faeces. If not excreted, bile pigments accumulate in the skin and eyes giving them a yellow colour.

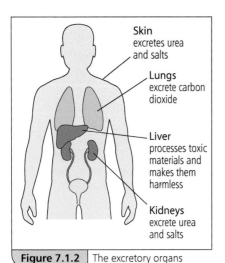

Figure 7.1.2 | The excretory organs

Skin
excretes urea
and salts

Lungs
excrete carbon
dioxide

Liver
processes toxic
materials and
makes them
harmless

Kidneys
excrete urea
and salts

Additionally, the liver breaks down hormones into inactive substances that are removed from the body.

The body also has more than enough of some substances. Water for example, is absorbed into the blood from food and drink. It is also produced as a waste product of aerobic respiration. If water builds up in the body, cells could swell and even burst! The body can also have too many ions (from mineral salts), especially potassium, sodium and chloride. If these accumulate, the blood and tissue fluids become too concentrated so that water leaves cells by osmosis and the cells function less efficiently.

The organs involved in excretion (Figure 7.1.2) in humans are:

• Lungs – excrete carbon dioxide, which is lost from the blood by diffusion across the walls of the alveoli (see 5.9).

• Kidneys – filter the blood to produce **urine**, which is water in excess of requirements with dissolved waste substances such as urea and salts (see 7.2).

• Liver – produces bile pigments and spent hormones.

• Skin – urea, sodium and chloride ions are excreted when we sweat.

Egestion

Egestion is the removal in the faeces of anything that has been ingested, but not digested and absorbed. Fibre or roughage from plant material, such as fruit and vegetables, is the main component of our diet that is egested. Bile pigments, some of which are excreted in the faeces, are *not* egested since they have been produced in the liver by our metabolism.

Excretion in plants

Oxygen is the waste product of photosynthesis; carbon dioxide is the waste product of respiration. Some of the oxygen is used by plants during the day for their respiration; the rest diffuses out of their leaves. Other excretory compounds cannot be lost so easily. Plants use waste compounds to make substances, such as tannins and calcium oxalate, that are used before being excreted in leaves and bark that fall from plants. Calcium oxalate crystals are very sharp (Figure 7.1.3) and damage the mouths of herbivores; tannins also deter herbivores, although how they do this is not known for certain.

LINK

See 3.4 to remind yourself why cells swell and possibly even burst if there is too much water in the body.

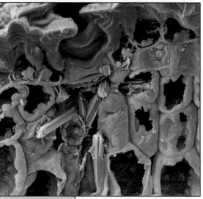

Figure 7.1.3 The sharp needle-like objects in this *Agave* leaf are calcium oxalate crystals that are good at deterring herbivores. Notice the thick waxy cuticle and the stoma at the top of the leaf.

KEY POINTS

1 Metabolism is all the chemical and physical changes that occur in the body; excretion is the removal from the body of waste products of metabolism, toxic substances and substances in excess, such as water and ions.

2 Egestion is the removal of undigested material through the anus.

3 The main metabolic wastes in humans are urea and carbon dioxide.

4 The kidneys, lungs, liver and skin are excretory organs.

5 Plants excrete oxygen and carbon dioxide by gas exchange; organic compounds such as calcium oxalate are stored (e.g. in leaves and bark) and used for protection.

SUMMARY QUESTIONS

1 Define the terms *metabolism* and *excretion.*

2 Distinguish between excretion and egestion.

3 a Make a table to show the waste products of plants and animals and the ways in which each is excreted from the body.

   b Explain why wastes must be excreted.

4 Distinguish between excretion in animals and in plants.

5 Explain why plants excrete oxygen during the day and carbon dioxide at night.

The human urinary system

One of the main excretory organs in humans is the kidney. It is part of the urinary system (Figure 7.2.1).

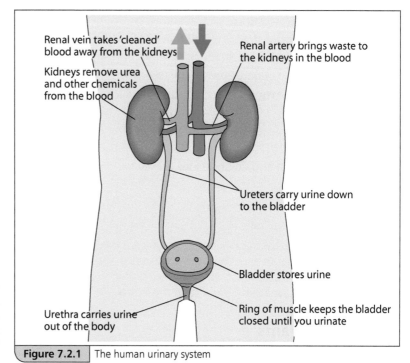

Renal vein takes 'cleaned' blood away from the kidneys

Renal artery brings waste to the kidneys in the blood

Kidneys remove urea and other chemicals from the blood

Ureters carry urine down to the bladder

Bladder stores urine

Urethra carries urine out of the body

Ring of muscle keeps the bladder closed until you urinate

Figure 7.2.1 | The human urinary system

The functions of the kidney are:

• excretion

• **osmoregulation** – maintenance of constant water content of the body

• maintenance of constant concentration of ions, e.g. sodium and potassium, in the blood

• control of the pH of the blood.

The internal structure of the kidneys

The photographs in Figures 7.2.2 and 7.2.3 and Figure 7.2.4 show the external and internal structure of the kidney.

Inside each kidney are thousands of tiny tubes called **nephrons**, or kidney tubules, which you can only see under a microscope. The function of nephrons is to filter the blood, remove waste chemicals, reabsorb useful substances and allow water to be excreted or reabsorbed. The waste chemicals and excess water are removed from the body in urine.

Figure 7.2.2 | A kidney with part of the ureter attached

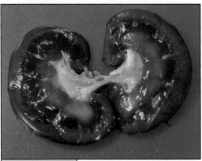

Figure 7.2.3 | A kidney cut open vertically to show the cortex, medulla, pelvis and ureter

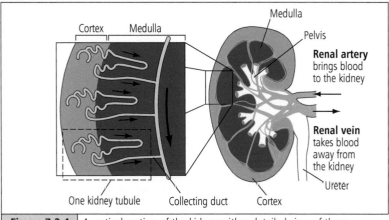

Figure 7.2.4 A vertical section of the kidney with a detailed view of three nephrons on the left

Structure of a nephron

Blood flows in a renal artery into a kidney. Inside the kidney, the renal artery branches many times to form arterioles. Each of these arterioles supplies blood to a closely packed group of capillaries called a **glomerulus** (Figure 7.2.5) that fits inside **Bowman's capsule**, which is a cup-like structure. Blood is filtered as it flows through the glomerulus to form **glomerular filtrate**. Blood flows from the glomerulus in another, thinner arteriole and then into capillaries around the rest of the nephron. Blood from these capillaries flows into the renal vein to leave the kidney.

Each nephron is a coiled microscopic tube. Cells lining the nephron reabsorb many of the substances in the filtrate back into the blood. At the end of the nephron, filtrate drains into a **collecting duct**, which goes through the **medulla** and empties into the **pelvis** of the kidney. Water may be reabsorbed as urine flows through the collecting ducts. Urine collects in the pelvis and then flows into the ureter to be stored in the bladder. Urine is a solution of excretory wastes dissolved in water. Water always has to be present as the solvent for these wastes, such as urea and excess mineral salts. The yellow pigment in urine is made in the body from the bile pigments.

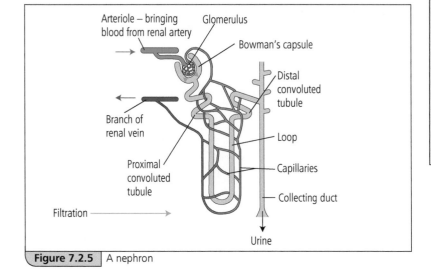

Figure 7.2.5 A nephron

SUMMARY QUESTIONS

1 Make a diagram of the urinary system and annotate it with the functions of each part.

2 Make a diagram to show the internal structure of a kidney that you would see with the naked eye. Label the main regions of the kidney.

3 Make a large, labelled diagram of a nephron and its associated blood vessels. You will need this to answer question 1 in 7.3.

4 a Suggest how blood in the renal vein differs from blood in the renal artery.

   b Suggest why blood must flow continuously through the kidneys.

STUDY FOCUS

Annotate a drawing of the nephron (see question 3 in 7.2) as you read this section.

STUDY FOCUS

It is important that the concentration of blood and tissue fluid is kept constant. When there is plenty of water in the body, the hypothalamus does not secrete ADH, the collecting ducts are impermeable, no water is reabsorbed and dilute urine is produced. The control of water in the body by the hypothalamus, ADH and the kidney is an example of **homeostasis** – maintaining near constant conditions in the body (see 8.8).

Pressure filtration

The kidneys are close to the heart, so the blood pressure in the renal artery is high. You can see from Figure 7.2.5 that the blood vessel entering the glomerulus is wider than the one leaving it. This causes pressure inside the glomerulus to increase so that blood is filtered. Ions, water and small molecules are forced out of the blood plasma through the walls of the capillaries. The lining of the capillaries is like a net with tiny holes in it. Blood cells and large molecules, like blood proteins, are too big to pass through the capillary lining and so stay in the blood. Small molecules, like urea, glucose, amino acids, ions and water, are filtered into Bowman's capsule to form filtrate (Figure 7.3.1).

The blood that flows from the glomerulus has less plasma than the blood entering it.

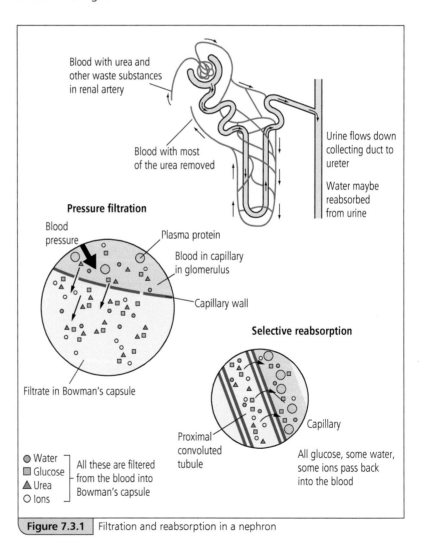

Figure 7.3.1 | Filtration and reabsorption in a nephron

Selective reabsorption

The body needs glucose, amino acids, some ions and much of the water. The cells lining the first part of the nephron (proximal convoluted tubule) reabsorb these from the filtrate. Glucose, ions and amino acids are reabsorbed by active transport; water is reabsorbed by osmosis. The filtrate is now mostly water with urea and excess ions. As the filtrate flows on through the nephron, more water may be reabsorbed if the body is low in water. The fluid that enters the collecting ducts is urine. The blood, with a lower concentration of waste chemicals, leaves the kidney in the renal vein.

Anti-diuretic hormone and conserving water

The kidney controls how much water passes out in the urine. If the body is well supplied with fluids, the collecting ducts are impermeable to water. The urine is a dilute solution of urea, salts and other compounds. If you are dehydrating because it is hot, you have been sweating a lot and not drinking anything, the hypothalamus in the brain (see 8.4) responds to the concentration of the blood. It stimulates the pituitary gland to release **anti-diuretic hormone** (ADH). ADH makes the epithelial cells lining the collecting ducts become permeable to water. The surrounding blood vessels in the medulla have a high concentration of salt, so water diffuses from the urine into the blood by osmosis. This forms concentrated urine conserving water that would otherwise have been passed out.

Kidney dialysis

Some people have kidney failure, perhaps because they have been in accident or have an infection. If nothing is done about it they will die in a very short time. These people can be treated using **kidney dialysis**. Their blood flows through a dialysis machine that removes most of the excretory waste without unbalancing the salt, glucose and water content of the plasma (Figure 7.3.3).

LINK

Try question 11 on page 113 to find out more about kidney dialysis.

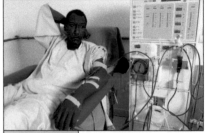

Figure 7.3.2 Kidney dialysis involves visits to a clinic three times a week.

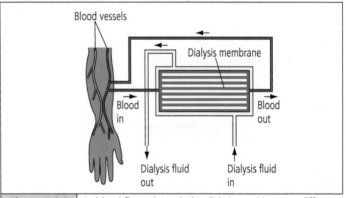

Figure 7.3.3 As blood flows through the dialysis machine urea diffuses out and concentrations of glucose and ions are stabilised.

KEY POINTS

1 Pressure filtration occurs as blood flows through the glomerulus; urea, ions, glucose and water leave the blood plasma to form filtrate in the Bowman's capsule.

2 Useful materials such as glucose, some salts and most of the water are reabsorbed from the filtrate into the blood capillaries along the nephron.

3 ADH is secreted by the hypothalamus when the blood is too concentrated. It stimulates the uptake of water from urine in collecting ducts.

SUMMARY QUESTIONS

1 Annotate your diagram of a nephron (from 7.2) with the functions of the different parts.

2 Make a flow chart diagram to show how the hypothalamus, pituitary gland, blood, kidneys and ADH are involved in the control of the concentration of urine.

3 Distinguish between pressure filtration and selective reabsorption.

4 Explain the role of ADH in the body.

5 Explain how kidney dialysis saves the lives of people with kidney failure.

Figure 7.4.1 | The cotyledons (seed leaves) of this peanut have moved apart so the shoot can grow into the light to absorb light for photosynthesis.

Figure 7.4.2 | Eat or be eaten. Both gazelle and cheetah are running for their lives.

Movement in plants and animals

Movement is an action by an organism or part of an organism that changes its position or place.

Plants are fixed in one position and have spreading bodies that absorb light, carbon dioxide, water and mineral ions. Some plant movement occurs quite fast: the leaves of mimosa and the Venus flytrap are examples (see 8.1). When plants reproduce they make pollen grains that move from one plant to another. Their seeds are dispersed from the parent plant to colonise new areas and reduce competition (see 9.6).

Most plant movements are due to *growth* and are slow (see 8.2 for examples). They relate to their nutrition. Shoots grow towards light to expose their leaves to as much light as possible so that they can photosynthesise efficiently. Roots grow downwards towards sources of water.

Most animals are not fixed in one place. They move their whole body, which is known as **locomotion**. Movement in animals is brought about by muscle contraction.

Locomotion is necessary to:

- find food
- hide and escape from predators
- migrate to avoid harsh conditions or in search of food
- find mates
- find nesting sites and make nests

Some animals are fixed and only move part of their bodies, for example coral polys, sea anemones and barnacles. Parts of their body move to gain food and defend themselves.

The human skeleton

Locomotion is crucially important to humans. We are bipedal (we walk on two legs). Compared with four-legged animals, we have our front limbs free to manipulate objects. We have opposable thumbs, which allow us to grasp objects and make and use tools.

The functions of the skeleton are shown in Table 7.4.1.

STUDY FOCUS

Try answering question 15 which you will find on the CD. This will help you to locate the important parts of the skeleton, learn the names of the bones and identify the positions of the joints (see 7.5).

Table 7.4.1   Functions of the skeleton

Function	Comments
Locomotion	• Bones are a firm structure for muscle attachment by tendons. • The skeleton has systems of levers to move the whole body from place to place, or move parts of the body relative to one another.
Protection	• The cranium protects the brain, the eyes and ears. • The ribcage protects the lungs and heart. • The vertebral column protects the spinal cord. • The pelvis protects the internal urinary and genital organs, e.g. uterus, ovaries and bladder.
Support	• The bones provide a framework for all the other systems of the body, such as the digestive, excretory, nervous, endocrine and muscular systems. • The backbone provides support for the limbs and the head. • The jawbones support the teeth.
Breathing	• The ribcage is moved up and down by the intercostal muscles to increase and decrease the volume of the thorax (see 5.10).
Production of red blood cells	• Red bone marrow in the interior of the short bones and at the ends of long bones have **stem cells**, that divide by mitosis to produce red blood cells to replace those that are removed from the circulation.

The human fore limb

The **humerus** is the long bone of the upper arm (Figure 7.4.3).

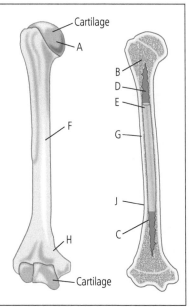

A Rounded head fits into the shoulder blade to form a ball and socket joint, allowing movement in three planes.
B The ends of the humerus are made of spongy bone, which is light and strong and withstands stresses in all directions.
C Growth of the bone occurs here.
D Red bone marrow in the ends of the bone produces red blood cells.
E Yellow bone marrow is a store of fat.
F The long shaft is hollow, which reduces the chances of a break occurring across the bone.
G The outer part of the shaft is made of strong, compact bone.
H Rounded ends form a hinge joint with the radius and ulna.
J The triceps and other muscles attach to the surface of the shaft, but not the biceps as this is attached to the scapula.

Cartilage
A
B
D
E
F
G
J
H
C
Cartilage

Figure 7.4.3	The humerus bone showing how it is adapted for its functions

KEY POINTS

1 Movement is an action by an organism, or part of an organism, causing a change of position or place. Locomotion is movement of the whole organism.

2 The types of movement in plants and animals are related to their forms of nutrition and reproduction.

3 The functions of the skeleton are: locomotion, protection, support, breathing and the production of red blood cells.

4 Long bones, e.g. the humerus, are adapted for support and movement.

SUMMARY QUESTIONS

1 Define the terms *movement* and *locomotion*.

2 Write a food chain for the three organisms visible in Figure 7.4.2.

3 a Make a table to compare movement in plants and animals.

  b Explain the differences in your table from part **a**, by referring to the forms of nutrition and reproduction in plants and animals.

4 a List the functions of the human skeleton.

  b State the bones of the body that are involved in each of the functions listed.

5 Explain how the human skeleton is involved in blood formation, breathing, locomotion, protection and support.

6 Explain how the humerus is adapted for its functions.

Joints, muscles and movement

Figure 7.5.1 You can see the cartilage at the end of the bones of these pig's trotters.

Joints

Locomotion involves the skeleton, joints between the bones and the skeletal muscles.

The place where two bones meet is a **joint**. There are two types of joint:

• a fixed joint where there is no movement, e.g. between the bones of the cranium

• a moveable (or synovial) joint where there is movement.

Two types of moveable joint are (Figure 7.5.2):

• a hinge joint in which movement occurs in one plane, e.g. at the elbow and the knee

• a ball and socket joint where movement occurs in all three planes, e.g. at the shoulder and the hip.

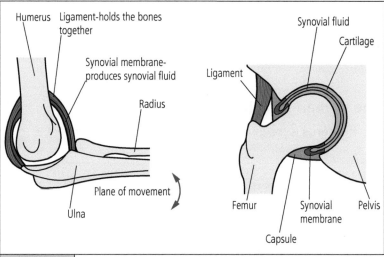

Figure 7.5.2 A hinge joint (elbow) and a ball and socket joint (hip)

Muscles are attached to bones by **tendons**. These are full of tough, inelastic collagen fibres that run deep into bones to form the origin and insertion of each muscle. When muscles contract and shorten they pull on the tendons which move the bone. The end where the muscle inserts moves; the origin is the fixed end.

Ligaments attach bones together and support the joints. Most of these are also made of collagen and are tough, but they have some elastic tissue which means that they can stretch a little.

Cartilage covers the end of bones at moveable joints. It is softer than bone and smooth so it glides over the ends protecting the bone from wear and tear.

Synovial fluid is secreted by the synovial membrane surrounding the joint. This fluid is an oily liquid that lubricates the joint.

Muscles only *contract*, they do not expand. To move about or to move part of your body, muscles contract and *shorten* and pull on a bone. Muscles cannot push the bone to move it back to where it started. In order to get a bone to move back another muscle is needed. For example, there are two muscles that move the forearm and they form an **antagonistic pair** (Figure 7.5.3). They are the **biceps** and **triceps** muscles.

Contraction and shortening of the *biceps muscle* raises the forearm. This type of movement is called flexion and the biceps is the **flexor muscle**. When this happens the antagonist muscle, the triceps, relaxes and is pulled to become longer.

Contraction and shortening of the *triceps muscle* lowers the forearm. This type of movement is called extension and the arm is now extended. The triceps is the **extensor muscle**. When this happens the antagonist muscle, the biceps, relaxes and is pulled to become longer.

Lever action

Levers are the most efficient way of moving or supporting a load. There is a lever action in every moveable joint in the body. Joints act as fulcrums. These are the points about which a lever pivots. Muscles provide the effort to move levers.

Levers in the body support the weight of the body. The arm acts as a lever (Figure 7.5.4): the muscle provides the *effort*, the joint is the *fulcrum* and what is held in the hand is the *load*. The arrangement of the muscle minimises the effort needed to move the load. In the arm, for example, a movement of 25 mm of the biceps results in a movement of 457 mm of the hand at the end of the lever.

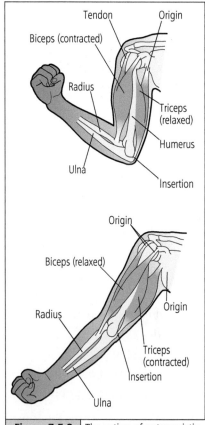

Figure 7.5.3 The action of antagonistic muscles in flexing (left) and extending (right) the forearm

KEY POINTS

1 Joints are where bones meet.

2 Ligaments and tendons are both tough tissues. Ligaments attach bones together; tendons attach muscles to bones.

3 Fixed joints occur where there is no movement; hinge joints where there is movement in one plane; ball and socket joints where there is movement in three planes (rotational).

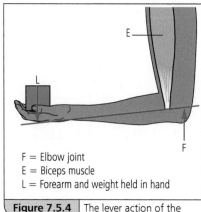

F = Elbow joint
E = Biceps muscle
L = Forearm and weight held in hand

Figure 7.5.4 The lever action of the arm: F is the fulcrum, E is effort and L is load.

SUMMARY QUESTIONS

1 Explain what is meant by the terms *fixed joint* and *synovial joint*.

2 State the locations in the body of hinge joints and ball and socket joints.

3 Describe the functions of the following in movement about a joint: cartilage, ligament, tendon, muscle tissue and synovial fluid.

4 Explain how the human forearm is **a** extended, and **b** flexed.

SECTION 1: Multiple-choice questions

1 Where in the human body is urea made?
   A   bladder
   B   kidney
   C   liver
   D   stomach

2 Which substance is not in the urine of a healthy person?
   A   glucose
   B   sodium ions
   C   urea
   D   water

3 Excretion is the removal from the body of
   A   dead skin
   B   excess heat
   C   undigested materials
   D   waste products of metabolism

4 What happens when the forearm is raised?

	Biceps muscle	Triceps muscle
A	contracts	contracts
B	contracts	relaxes
C	relaxes	contracts
D	relaxes	relaxes

5 Collecting ducts can reabsorb water from urine before it leaves the kidney. Which of the following occurs when there is excess water that is removed from the body?
   A   ADH is secreted to increase the permeability of the collecting ducts to water.
   B   ADH is not secreted and the collecting ducts remain permeable to water.
   C   ADH is secreted to decrease the permeability of the collecting ducts to water.
   D   ADH is not secreted and the collecting ducts remain impermeable to water.

6 Bones are attached firmly together by:
   A   cartilage
   B   ligaments
   C   synovial membranes
   D   tendons

7 Pairs of muscles that bring about movement across a hinge joint are known as:
   A   antagonistic muscles
   B   extensor muscles
   C   flexor muscles
   D   skeletal muscles

8 Blood is filtered in the glomeruli in the kidney. Which part of the nephron does the filtrate collect in after leaving a glomerulus?
   A   Bowman's capsule
   B   Collecting duct
   C   Distal convoluted tubule
   D   Proximal convoluted tubule

9 Urine flows from nephrons in the kidney into the pelvis. Which is the correct sequence of structures through which urine passes to be voided from the body?
   A   collecting duct ⟶ bladder ⟶ urethra
   B   collecting duct ⟶ urethra ⟶ bladder
   C   ureter ⟶ bladder ⟶ urethra
   D   urethra ⟶ bladder ⟶ ureter

10 Which of the following correctly pairs an excretory organ with the metabolic waste substance that it excretes?
   A   kidney and urine
   B   liver and bile pigments
   C   lungs and oxygen
   D   skin and carbon dioxide

11 a Ammonia is produced by all animals as a waste product of their metabolism.

Ammonia produced by humans is converted to *urea*.

Explain why this is necessary. *(3)*

b The table shows the composition of blood plasma in the renal artery, filtrate in Bowman's capsule and urine.

Substance	Concentration/g dm⁻³		
	Blood plasma in renal artery	Filtrate in Bowman's capsule	Urine
Urea	0.2	0.2	20.0
Glucose	0.9	0.9	0.0
Amino acids	0.05	0.05	0.0
Mineral ions	9.0	9.0	16.5
Protein	82.0	0.0	0.0

Explain why

i Four of the substances shown in the table are present in the filtrate, but protein is not. *(2)*

ii Glucose and amino acids are not present in the urine. *(2)*

iii The concentration of urea and mineral ions is higher in the urine than in the filtrate. *(3)*

iv The blood in the renal artery has a higher concentration of urea than blood in the renal vein. *(1)*

c Explain how filtrate is formed in the kidney. *(4)*

d A man with kidney failure received regular dialysis treatment for 20 days. Figure 1 shows how the concentration of urea in his blood changed over the 30 days from the start of his treatment.

Further practice questions and examples can be found on the accompanying CD.

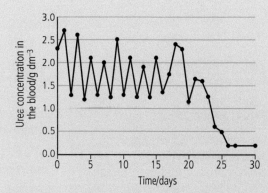

Figure 1

i State how many times the man received dialysis treatment; give the evidence from Figure 1 to support your answer. *(2)*

ii Calculate the decrease in the concentration of the man's urea in the blood from the start of dialysis until the end of his treatment on day 20. Show your working. *(2)*

iii Describe the changes that occur in the urea concentration in the blood over the 20 days. *(3)*

iv Explain the changes you have described in **iii**. *(3)*

Total 25 marks

12 a Distinguish between movements of plants and those of animals. *(2)*

b i Make a large diagram to show the major bones of the shoulder, the upper arm and the forearm. *(3)*

ii Label the following on your diagram: ball and socket joint, hinge joint, humerus, radius, scapula and ulna. *(3)*

iii Draw on your diagram the biceps and triceps muscles. Label the two muscles and their sites of origin and insertion. *(3)*

c Explain why the movement of the forearm requires a pair of antagonistic muscles and not just one muscle. *(4)*

Total 15 marks

8 Irritability

8.1 Coordination and survival

In order to survive in their habitat each organism needs to sense changes in its environment and make suitable responses. A **stimulus** is a change in the environment. A **response** is a change in position or behaviour of an organism as a direct result of a stimulus. **Irritability**, also known as **sensitivity**, is the ability to detect stimuli and respond to them.

Figures 8.1.1 to 8.1.6 show some examples of responses of plants and animals.

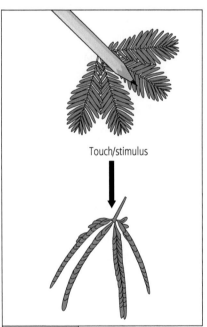

Touch/stimulus

Figure 8.1.1 Lightly touch the leaves of mimosa ('sensitive' or 'shy' plant) and the leaflets fold up. Keep touching the leaf and the petiole bends downward so the leaf is parallel to the stem.

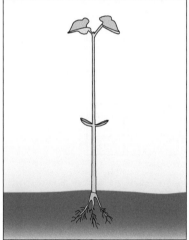

Figure 8.1.2 This kidney bean seedling germinated in the dark. The roots are growing downwards and the stem is growing upwards as the plant responds to gravity.

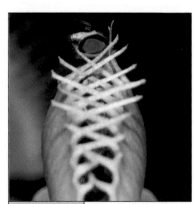

Figure 8.1.3 Venus fly trap. The fly touched the sensitive hairs on the surface of the leaf and has been well and truly trapped. There is a drawing of a whole plant in the questions at the end of Unit 8.

Figure 8.1.4 Earthworms are sensitive to vibrations in the ground. This earthworm has detected a bird pecking at the soil showing an escape response.

Figure 8.1.5 This Caribbean reef octopus changes its appearance to match its surroundings.

Receptors and effectors

In each of these cases a stimulus is detected by **receptors**. These detect certain stimuli and send information about them to **effectors** which carry out the response. Communication between receptors and effectors is the function of a coordinator.

Receptors in animals are generally specialised cells that convert the energy of stimuli such as light or movement into electrical impulses that travel along nerve cells. The outer ear funnels sound waves towards the ear drum which vibrates, causing the three bones of the middle ear to move and convert sound waves into movement of a fluid that causes the 'hairs' that you can see in Figure 8.1.6 to bend. Some animal receptors are simply the endings of nerves, such as some of those in the skin that detect touch and temperature.

Venus fly traps have hairs over their surface that detect movement. Other plant receptors are less obvious. There are no specialised receptor cells; instead stimuli are detected in other ways: light by pigments and gravity by starch grains.

Effectors in animals are muscles and glands. When stimulated by nerves, muscles contract to move parts of the body and carry out a response. Some glands release hormones into the blood; others release substances into ducts that lead elsewhere in the body or, in the case of sweat glands onto the body surface to cool down when it is hot.

Most plant responses are growth responses and the effectors are the regions where growth occurs known as **apical meristems**. Here cells elongate by absorbing water. If cells on one side of a stem or root elongate more than the other, the plant organ bends away from the side where most growth occurs. Leaves also move upwards in the morning to intercept the light and move downwards in the evening. To achieve this cells on the upper side of the petiole grow faster than those on the lower side so the leaf bends downwards. The opposite movement is caused by faster growth of cells on the lower side of the petiole.

LINK

The roles of receptors and effectors in plants are discussed in 8.2.

STUDY FOCUS

Identify the survival value of each response to each organism in Figures 8.1.1–8.1.5, and then answer question 2.

Figure 8.1.6 Sensory hair cells from the cochlea in the inner ear (× 600)

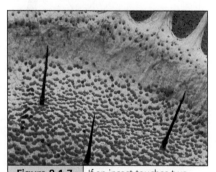

Figure 8.1.7 If an insect touches two of these hairs on a leaf of the Venus fly trap, the trap shuts within 20 seconds. Enzymes to digest the insect are secreted by the red glands all over the surface (× 15).

KEY POINTS

1 Irritability is the ability to make responses to stimuli that are changes in the environment.

2 A response is a change in position or behaviour of an organism; responses have survival value.

3 Receptors detect stimuli, effectors carry out responses; communication between receptors and effectors is the role of coordination systems, such as the nervous system.

SUMMARY QUESTIONS

1 a List all the different stimuli that are mentioned in this topic.

  b List the effectors in plants and animals.

2 Explain how each of the responses in Figures 8.1.1–8.1.5 helps to ensure survival.

Plant responses

At the end of this topic you should be able to:

- describe the responses of stems and roots of seedlings to light, touch and gravity
- relate these responses to the behaviour of plants in their habitats
- outline how to make controlled investigations of plant responses
- record results of investigations in tables.

Figure 8.2.1 Seedlings growing in light from one side only

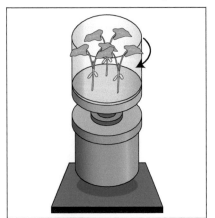

Figure 8.2.2 Seedlings growing in a clinostat

Responses to light and gravity

Plant responses depend on the direction of the stimulus.

Plant responses can be investigated with seedlings of plants, such as peas, beans, cress, corn or peanuts.

Seeds are soaked in water so that they start to germinate. They are then arranged as in investigations 1 to 3.

Investigation 1 The responses of seedlings to light

Seedlings that have been grown in the dark are put in conditions A to D:

A Kept in the dark.

B Put into an environment with uniform light (light from all around).

C Put into an environment with light from one side only.

D Put onto a revolving disc with light from one side.

The plants in groups A to D must all experience the same conditions of temperature and other factors.

The piece of apparatus in Figure 8.2.2 is a *clinostat* – it revolves once every 15 minutes to give light to all sides of the seedlings.

The results

A The seedlings continue to grow upwards, leaves are yellow, seedlings are taller than those in B.

B The seedlings continue to grow upwards, leaves are green, seedlings are not as tall as those in A.

C The seedlings grew as in Figure 8.2.1.

D The seedlings grew as in Figure 8.2.2.

Plants have pigments, which detect light. Chemicals diffuse through the plant. They coordinate the response by stimulating more elongation growth to occur on one side of roots and shoots.

Investigation 2 The response of seedling roots to gravity in the dark

The results are shown in Figure 8.2.3.

Investigation 3 The response of seedling shoots to gravity in the dark

The results are shown in Figure 8.2.4.

Roots use starch grains inside cells to detect the direction of gravity. Downward growth has survival value as roots grow towards a source of water. Growth into the soil also anchors the young plant. Shoots

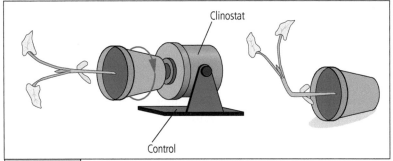

Figure 8.2.4 Seedling shoots grown in the dark

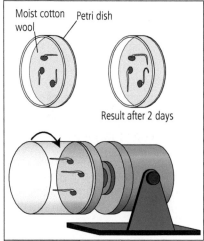

Figure 8.2.3 Seedling roots grown in the dark

may not be pointing upwards. They have a similar system to detect the direction of gravity and respond by growing upwards towards the source of light for photosynthesis.

Response to touch

Plants show two types of response to touch. Mimosa ('sensitive' plant) and the Venus fly trap, for example, show sudden responses that are not dependent on the direction of the stimulus. The response of tendrils, such as those of morning glory, is slower and is dependent on the position of the stimulus (Figure 8.2.5). They are best observed by taking observations or photographs at intervals of time (time-lapse photography).

When roots touch an object in the soil they grow in a different direction to avoid the obstruction. In this way roots use less energy for growth as they push their way through the air spaces in the soil.

Plant responses are particularly noticeable in young plants. When a seed germinates it can be orientated in any direction, it needs to change position so the root grows downwards and the shoot upwards.

A plant kept in the dark will continue to grow upwards at a fast rate. The leaves remain yellow and do not unfurl or expand until they reach the light source. This is to ensure that the seedling's energy is used most effectively – growing through the soil to reach the light; then leaves unfurl and expand.

Figure 8.2.5 Use a pencil to stimulate a tendril and observe how it grows over several hours.

SUMMARY QUESTIONS

1 a Make a table to record the results of Investigation 1.

 b State three ways in which the seedlings in Investigation 1 have responded to light.

2 Describe the responses of the roots to gravity as shown in Figure 8.2.3.

3 Explain the advantages of using the clinostat in Investigations 1 to 3.

4 Explain why Investigations 2 and 3 are set up in the dark.

5 Explain the advantages to plants of these responses to light, gravity and touch.

KEY POINTS

1 Some plant responses are fast, such as the closing of the Venus fly trap; most plant responses are slow because they are growth responses.

2 Plants respond to the direction of light, gravity and touch.

3 Plant responses are investigated under controlled conditions so the effect of each stimulus can be determined.

4 Plant growth responses ensure that plants gain sufficient light, carbon dioxide, water and ions for their survival.

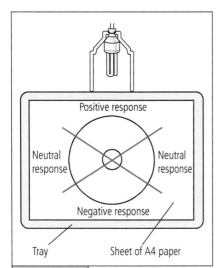

Figure 8.3.1 Apparatus for investigating responses of invertebrates to light

The responses of small terrestrial invertebrates, such as woodlice, maggots, millipedes and earthworms, can be investigated in the school lab with some simple apparatus. The responses that they show involve

- moving directly towards or away from a source of a stimulus
- changing their speed in response to the intensity of the stimulus
- changing direction with the intensity of the stimulus.

The way in which results are recorded is determined by the type of response shown by the invertebrates.

Investigation 1 The response of invertebrates to light

The apparatus in Figure 8.3.1 is arranged so that the desk-lamp is about 100 mm from one end of the tray, shining at a shallow angle along the tray. Put the marked A4 paper in the tray.

Place one active maggot exactly at the centre of the small circle and place a transparent cover over the tray. Mark the position of the centre on the cover.

Start timing as soon as the head of the maggot crosses the inner circle. Mark this position on the beaker with a small 'a'. Every 10 seconds, mark the maggot's position again, using the same symbol. If the maggots are very lively, five seconds may be a better interval.

Record, in a suitable table, across which sector (+ve, −ve, or neutral) the maggot left the outer circle. Continue marking its position at regular intervals until it reaches the edge of the marked paper.

Repeat these steps until you have recordings from 10 maggots: use a new symbol ('b', 'c', 'd', etc. for each one). Take care to place the cover in the same position for each trial.

Place the transparent cover on a large sheet of paper, and mark the relative position of the lamp. Make a table for your results as in Table 8.3.1.

Table 8.3.1

Sector	Number of maggots	Mean speed at 2 second intervals/mm s^{-1}				
		2	4	6	8	10
Positive	1	1.75	0.75	1.00	0.00	0.00
Negative	15	12.40	9.00	8.30	5.50	3.50
Neutral	4	1.56	0.59	0.35	0.25	0.00

This method and Figure 8.3.1 were provided by the late John Cheverton.

Investigation 2 The response of invertebrates to temperature

Draw a line across the middle of the base of a beaker. Place the beaker in a bowl of cold water from the tap. Record the air temperature in the small beaker, not the temperature of the water bath. Put an active invertebrate inside the beaker and record how often the animal crosses the line in a given period of time. Use hot and cold water and ice in the bowl to give different air temperatures in the beaker.

Table 8.3.2 shows some results after following this procedure. Each temperature was repeated with three different millipedes.

Choice chambers

Figure 8.3.2 shows a **choice chamber**. This can be used to give two halves that have different conditions, such as light versus dark, damp versus dry, and combinations of conditions such as light and dry versus dark and damp. A drying agent, such as anhydrous calcium chloride or silica gel, placed in the lower compartment gives air with a low humidity; cotton wool soaked in water gives a higher humidity in the air immediately above. Bench lamps and black paper can be used to give light and dark compartments.

Woodlice (Figure 8.3.3) are released into the choice chamber. Results can be collected in a number of ways, for example the total number of woodlice in each compartment or the number that are moving can be counted at timed intervals.

Table 8.3.3 shows some data from a student's choice chamber investigations.

Table 8.3.2

Temp. /°C	Number of times millipedes crossed the line in 3 minutes			
	1	2	3	mean
10	4	3	6	4
20	9	8	7	8
25	12	15	12	13
30	16	17	15	16
40	3	5	4	4

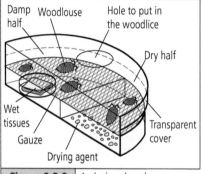

Damp half · Woodlouse · Hole to put in the woodlouse · Dry half · Wet tissues · Gauze · Drying agent · Transparent cover

Figure 8.3.2 | A choice chamber

Table 8.3.3

Time/ min	Investigation 1		Investigation 2	
	Number of woodlice in each area		Number of woodlice moving in each area	
	Light	Dark	Dry	Humid
0	10	0	5	5
2	6	4	7	1
4	3	7	3	2
6	3	7	1	0
8	1	9	0	0
10	1	9	0	0

Figure 8.3.3 | The common woodlouse

SUMMARY QUESTIONS

1 Draw graphs of the results shown in Tables 8.3.1–8.3.3. What conclusions can you make from the results?

2 Explain how to use choice chambers to investigate the responses of small invertebrates to light.

3 Explain the survival value of the responses shown by small terrestrial invertebrates to light, temperature and moisture.

Nerves and the brain

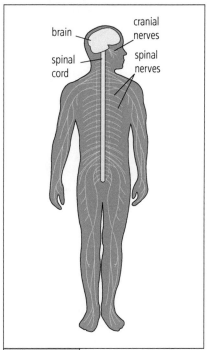

Figure 8.4.1 The human nervous system

EXAM TIP

Do not confuse the spinal cord with the spine. See 7.4 to be sure of the difference.

Coordination

Animals have two coordination systems:

- a nervous system consisting of nerve cells
- an endocrine system consisting of organs that secrete hormones, such as adrenaline and insulin, into the blood.

Figure 8.4.1 shows the structure of the human nervous system. The brain and spinal cord form the **central nervous system (CNS)**; all the nerves that spread throughout the body from the CNS form the **peripheral nervous system (PNS)**.

The cranial and spinal nerves are bundles of many nerve cells surrounded by tough fibrous tissue. **Neurones** are specialised nerve cells that send electrical impulses to and from the CNS over long distances. There are three types of neurone:

- **Sensory neurones** conduct electrical impulses from sensory cells, such as rods and cones in the eye, to other neurones in the CNS.
- **Motor neurones** conduct electrical impulses from the central nervous system to effectors. These effectors are muscles and glands, such as sweat glands and the adrenal glands.
- **Relay neurones** are only found in the CNS and they transmit information between sensory and motor neurones. In addition, there are other types of neurone in the CNS for integrating and storing information and for decision making.

The brain

The brain is the body's main coordination centre which receives information from receptors, makes decisions, stores memories and sends instructions to effectors. Parts of the brain are specialised for certain functions (Figure 8.4.2).

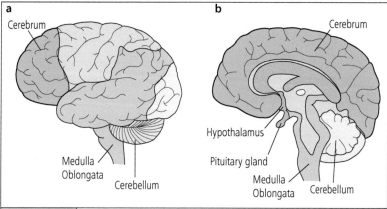

Figure 8.4.2 The brain showing the location of the four regions listed in Table 8.4.1. **a** left side of the brain, **b** vertical section through the brain.

Table 8.4.1   Functions of the parts of the brain

Region of the brain	Functions
Cerebrum consisting of the left and right cerebral hemispheres	Conscious thought Coordination of voluntary actions Memory, learning and reasoning Understanding language and control of speech Interpretation of sensory information from sense organs
Cerebellum	Receives information from balance receptors in the ear and from stretch receptors in muscles and tendons Coordination of balance, posture and movement
Hypothalamus	Monitors and controls body temperature and water content of the blood Controls release of hormones from the **pituitary gland**: ADH to control the kidney (see 7.3) and FSH and LH to control the menstrual cycle (see 9.3)
Medulla oblongata	Controls many involuntary actions, such as: • rate and depth of breathing • heart rate and blood pressure • peristalsis – movement of food in the alimentary canal

Coordination of simple reflexes

When a person touches a hot object without realising that it is so hot, there is a very quick, automatic response that the person does not think about.

This is an example of a **simple reflex**, which is an **involuntary action**.

The sequence of events is:

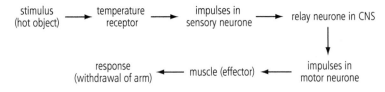

Many simple reflexes like this are protective.

Knee jerk reflex

This reflex is used to check that the nervous system is functioning correctly. A tap on the knee stretches a tendon; this stimulates stretch receptors in the tendon that send impulses along a sensory neurone to the spinal cord. In this reflex there is no relay neurone, so the sensory neurone stimulates a motor neurone that conducts impulses to a muscle in the upper leg. The effector muscle contracts to move the lower leg. Try it and see!

SUMMARY QUESTIONS

1   Define the terms *neurone*, *effector*, *receptor*, *simple reflex* and *involuntary action*.

2   Make a simple drawing of the nervous system and use colour coding to distinguish between the CNS and the PNS.

3   Make a large drawing of the brain, label the parts from Table 8.4.1 and annotate with their functions.

4   Describe the response to each of the following stimuli:

 a   touching a very hot object

 b   a bright light shining into the eye

 c   a piece of grit in the eye

 d   an insect bite.

At the end of this topic you should be able to:

- describe the structure of the eye and state the functions of each part
- explain how images are formed in the eye
- define the term *accommodation*
- describe how focusing is achieved.

The eye is one of our sense organs. It contains receptor cells in the retina with a number of extra structures that are involved in moving, focusing and protecting the eye (Figure 8.5.1). Receptor cells respond to light by stimulating sensory neurones to conduct impulses to the brain via the optic nerve. The brain interprets all the impulses that it receives to form an image of what we are looking at.

Rods and **cones** are highly specialised sensory cells located in the retina at the back of the eyeball. Rods detect light of low intensity and are used for night vision. They need vitamin A to function properly (see 5.7). Cones are only stimulated by light of high intensity so only function in daylight. There are three types that respond best to different wavelengths of light. The brain interprets information from these three types of cone to give us our colour vision. All the receptors in the fovea are cones. Each has its own neurone to the brain so they also give us acute, detailed vision.

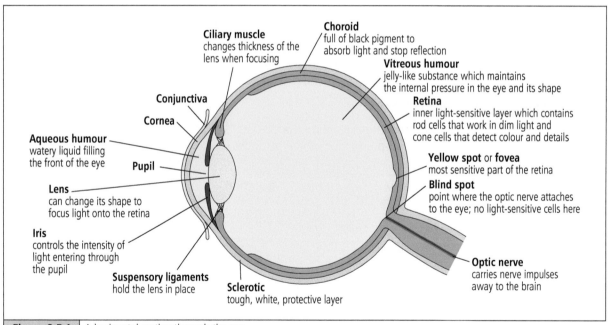

| **Figure 8.5.1** | A horizontal section through the eye |

A horizontal section of the eye includes both the fovea and the blind spot. A vertical section includes either the fovea or the blind spot or neither of them.

Image formation

When light enters the eye it is focused onto the retina. Most light is focused as it passes through the cornea. This is because it was travelling through the air and now enters a denser medium. If we relied on the cornea to focus light we would see a very blurred image of the world around us. The lens provides the fine focusing so that we see sharp images. Figure 8.5.2 shows how the cornea and the lens focus the light. Each medium has a refractive index and when light passes from one medium to another it is refracted or 'bent'.

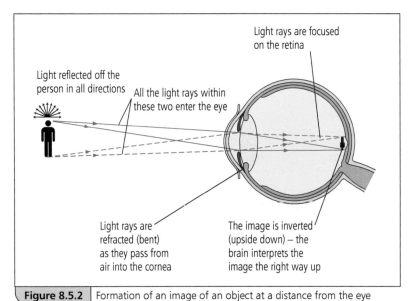

Light rays are focused on the retina

Light reflected off the person in all directions

All the light rays within these two enter the eye

Light rays are refracted (bent) as they pass from air into the cornea

The image is inverted (upside down) – the brain interprets the image the right way up

Figure 8.5.2 | Formation of an image of an object at a distance from the eye

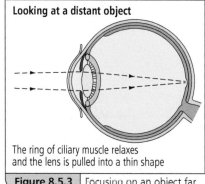

Looking at a distant object

The ring of ciliary muscle relaxes and the lens is pulled into a thin shape

Figure 8.5.3 | Focusing on an object far away from the eye

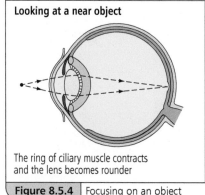

Looking at a near object

The ring of ciliary muscle contracts and the lens becomes rounder

Figure 8.5.4 | Focusing on an object close to the eye

Accommodation

Accommodation is the term used to describe the changes that occur in the eye when focusing on far and near objects. As light enters the eye it must be refracted (bent) so that we can see the image clearly. We call this focusing. About 60% of the refraction of the light rays is done by the cornea and the rest is done by the lens. The lens is surrounded by elastic tissue which can be stretched and can recoil. The shape of the lens is controlled by the ciliary muscles and suspensory ligaments (see Figure 8.5.1).

Looking at a distant object

The ciliary muscles *relax*. The pressure of the fluids inside the eye pulls the suspensory ligaments tightly (or taut) so the lens is pulled into an elliptical (thin) shape. Light rays are refracted as they pass through the lens and focused on the retina (Figure 8.5.3). The distant object is in focus. The lens does not need to do too much focusing as the light rays from each point are nearly parallel when they enter the eye.

Looking at a near object

The ciliary muscles *contract* to counteract the pressure inside the eye. The suspensory ligaments are not pulled and become slack. This lets the elastic tissue around the lens recoil so the lens becomes more spherical (fatter). Light rays are refracted more than they were when looking at the distant object. The near object is in focus. This time the lens needs to do more focusing as the light rays are diverging as they enter the eye (Figure 8.5.4).

The control of the shape of the lens by the ciliary muscles in accommodation is another reflex. This too is protective – if you cannot clearly see where you are going, you will damage yourself.

KEY POINTS

1 The eye is a complex sense organ that focuses light on the retina which is full of rods and cones.

2 Light is refracted (bent) as it passes through the cornea and the lens.

3 Accommodation is the focusing of the lens to form a sharp image on the retina. For distant objects the suspensory ligaments are taut and the lens is thin. For near objects the suspensory ligaments are slack and the lens much fatter.

SUMMARY QUESTIONS

1 Use the information in Figure 8.5.1 to make a table showing the functions of the parts of the eye.

8.6

Eye defects and the pupil reflex

Eye defects

Having an eyeball that is too short or a lens that is not convex enough causes **long sight**. If you are long-sighted then objects close to the eye are blurred and out of focus because the light rays are not focused to a point as they reach the retina. Opticians correct long sight by using **converging** or convex lenses in spectacles or contact lenses (Figure 8.6.1).

Short sight is caused by having a long eyeball or a lens that is too convex. If you are short-sighted then distant objects are blurred and out of focus because the light rays are focused in front of the retina. Opticians correct short sight with **diverging** or concave lenses (Figure 8.6.2).

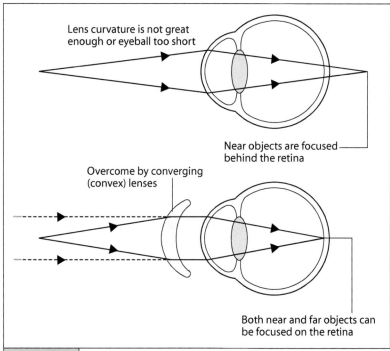

Figure 8.6.1 Long sight is corrected by using converging lenses.

Glaucoma is the result of increased pressure in the eyeball which obstructs the blood vessels supplying the optic nerve, reducing supplies of oxygen and nutrients. Neurones in this nerve start dying; first those that supply the periphery of the retina and later those from the yellow spot or fovea. The pressure increases because of poor drainage of the fluids in the eye. Glaucoma usually develops slowly and people are often unaware of the changes as there is a slow deterioration in their peripheral vision. Some children are born with it and their eyes often have a cloudy appearance and are very watery.

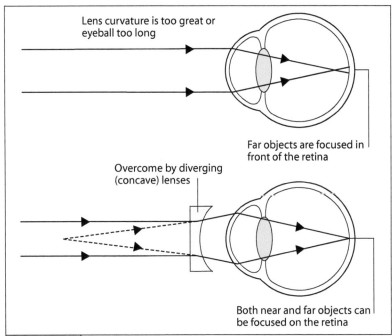

Lens curvature is too great or eyeball too long

Far objects are focused in front of the retina

Overcome by diverging (concave) lenses

Both near and far objects can be focused on the retina

Figure 8.6.2 Short sight is corrected by using diverging lenses.

Pupil reflex

Move from a very bright well-lit place and walk into somewhere dark. For a while you cannot see much. Now think about the reverse – going from a dark place and entering somewhere very bright. For a moment you are almost blinded by the light until your eyes adjust. These adjustments are made by muscles in the iris. Circular muscles in the iris contract to *decrease* the diameter of the pupil; radial muscles contract to *increase* its diameter. A simple reflex controls them. Sensory neurones transmit impulses from the retina to the brain along the optic nerve; motor neurones transmit impulses to the iris muscles along another one of the cranial nerves.

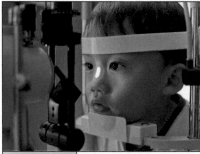

Figure 8.6.3 Children should have their eyes tested from a young age to make sure that any defects are detected and treated.

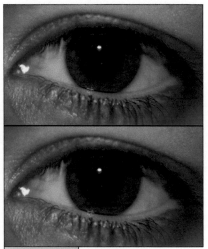

Figure 8.6.4 Constriction of the pupil protects the retina from damage by bright light in this simple reflex.

SUMMARY QUESTIONS

1 Define the terms *accommodation*, *glaucoma*, *long sight* and *short sight*.

2 Explain how opticians correct long and short sight.

3 Make a flow chart diagram to show how the pupil reflex is controlled when you walk from a dark room into bright light.

4 Explain the purpose of constricting and dilating the pupils in the eyes.

8.7 Drugs

The term drug refers to any substance that is taken into the body or applied to the skin which alters a chemical reaction in the body or interferes with any pathogen.

Drugs can be divided into those that are for medical use and those that are not. Most medical drugs are available only on prescription from a doctor; others are freely available 'over the counter' from pharmacies, shops and supermarkets. **Non-medicinal drugs** which are used for the pleasure that they are supposed to give are often known as recreational drugs. Some, such as **caffeine** and **alcohol**, are part of everyday life for many people. Others, such as cocaine, **heroin** and marijuana, are illegal as they are considered a risk to health. People found in possession of illegal drugs or involved in their production, trafficking and supply are prosecuted by law enforcement agencies.

Medicinal drugs

Some drugs are prescribed for short periods of time and some for much longer, in some cases for a lifetime. Almost all drugs can be abused and this includes drugs bought over the counter and obtained on prescription (Table 8.7.1). See 10.1 to find out why the drug insulin is prescribed for a person's lifetime.

Table 8.7.1 Effects of certain drugs

Type of drug	Examples	Effects on the body	Effects of abuse
Sedative or **tranquilliser**	Valium, Librium	Slows down body functions to relieve anxiety; induces sleep	Overdose of some sedatives may be fatal, especially if taken with alcohol
Antidepressant	Prozac, Citalopram	Relieves depression; also taken for many other conditions including for pain relief	Even without taking more than the prescribed dose, these can have severe side effects, such as untypical violent behaviour
Pain killer (analgesics)	Paracetamol, Aspirin, Ibuprofen	Relieves pain by interfering with production of chemicals that cause inflammation	Aspirin causes bleeding of the stomach; an overdose of paracetamol can lead to liver failure and may be fatal
Steroid	Testosterone and other anabolic steroids	Increases muscle mass and athletic performance	High blood pressure, heart attack, male infertility, male baldness and growth of hair in females
Diet pill	Ephedrine	Promotes weight loss by suppressing the appetite and increasing metabolic rate so increasing use of fat in respiration	Used to help concentration (e.g. while studying); a stimulant, it can become addictive and have serious side effects, such as heart attack and stroke

The distinction between legal and illegal drugs varies from country to country. Alcohol, for example, is legal in many countries but is banned for general consumption in some countries, such as Saudi Arabia.

Non-medicinal drugs

Caffeine is a **stimulant** present in beverages, such as coffee, tea, some soft drinks and energy drinks. It stimulates the CNS, increasing alertness and improving concentration. The dose needed to cause harm is very high, so it is regarded as a safe drug. The effects of too much caffeine are anxiety, insomnia, hallucinations and other severe effects.

Alcohol is a **depressant** drug that slows down the transmission of impulses along neurones. At low concentrations it reduces concentration and our inhibitions. It impairs our sensory awareness and increases the time we take to respond to stimuli. Long term, alcohol causes damage to nerves and to the liver causing cirrhosis, which is an irreversible condition.

Heroin is a powerful depressant that slows down impulses along neurones transferring information from pain receptors to the brain. The molecular structure of heroin is similar to one of the body's own painkillers. When people take heroin for the first time they usually feel a warm rush of contentment and intense happiness. This state is known as **euphoria**.

People who start taking heroin want to repeat the feelings they first experienced, but they quickly become dependent on the drug and in two to three weeks are addicted. The body develops a tolerance to heroin. More painkillers are needed to prevent nerve cells sending impulses to the brain. But the body does not produce more of its own natural painkillers. Addicts have to take heroin in ever greater quantities to just deaden the pain.

Social and economic effects of drug abuse

People dependent on illegal drugs may not maintain normal social behaviour. The withdrawal effects of drugs often involve mood swings and violent behaviour. They may lose their friends, become distant from their family and join a drug sub-culture. They may resort to crime in order to buy drugs because they are not able to obtain an income. Many crimes are associated with drug abuse; women turn to prostitution to gain enough money to buy drugs.

The cost to society of drugs is very high. Communities have to provide the facilities to treat drug addiction, cope with drug-related criminal offences, and rehabilitate drug users. Resources are devoted to apprehending drug traffickers and suppliers. But the social cost of alcohol is much higher than the costs of dealing with illegal drugs, as a greater proportion of the population abuse alcohol.

Figure 8.7.1 Heroin addiction is a serious form of addition, but far more people put their lives at risk from nicotine and alcohol addiction.

SUMMARY QUESTIONS

1 Make a table similar to Table 8.7.1 for caffeine, alcohol and heroin.

2 Explain the meanings of the following terms: *drug*, *legal* and *illegal drugs*, *medicinal drugs*, *prescription drugs* and *non-medicinal drugs*.

3 Discuss the social and economic effects of drug abuse.

8.8 The human skin

LEARNING OUTCOMES

At the end of this topic you should be able to:

- describe the structure of the human skin
- describe the role of melanin
- describe the role of the skin in temperature control
- define the term *homeostasis*
- discuss the use of skin creams, sun protection factors and skin bleaching.

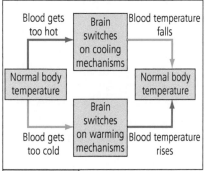

Figure 8.8.2 The control of body temperature is an example of homeostasis.

LINK

Homeostasis is the maintenance of near constant conditions in the body. The hypothalamus is the body's thermostat. It regulates other aspects of homeostasis. See 8.4 to see its location in the brain and see 10.1 for another example of homeostasis.

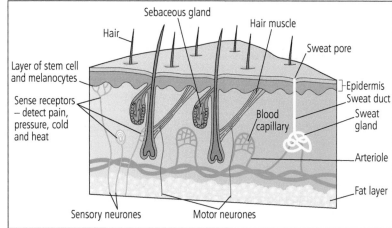

Figure 8.8.1 The skin – the part between the epidermis and the layer of fat is the dermis.

The skin and its functions

The skin is the largest organ in the body and one with important roles in the interactions between our bodies and our surroundings. The functions of the structures labelled in Figure 8.8.1 are:

- **Epidermis** – this is made of layers of squamous cells filled with the tough fibrous protein keratin; these cells provide mechanical protection against injury and are gradually rubbed away.
- Layer of **stem cells** – these cells divide by mitosis to replace cells lost from surface of the epidermis.
- **Melanocytes** – these cells are between the stem cells and make **melanin**, which absorbs ultraviolet light protecting the body from its harmful effect.
- Hair – provides some insulation on the head
- Sweat glands – secrete sweat which travels up sweat ducts to sweat pores; sweat evaporates to lose heat
- Arterioles – control flow of blood to capillaries which lose heat to the surroundings
- Sensory nerve endings and sensory cells – detect changes in temperature, pressure and pain
- Sensory neurones – conduct nerve impulses to the CNS
- Motor neurones – conduct nerve impulses to instruct the hair muscles to contract and raise the hairs
- Fat – store of energy and a thermal insulator

Temperature control

No matter what the weather is like, your body temperature stays at 37 °C, unless you have a fever. Sensors in the skin detect changes in air temperature. Receptors in the spinal cord and hypothalamus detect changes in the temperature of the blood.

If the temperature of the blood flowing through the hypothalamus in the brain increases, it sends nerve impulses to the skin to promote heat loss:

- Arterioles *widen* so more blood flows through the capillaries and loses heat to the surroundings by convection and radiation.
- Sweat glands produce sweat by filtration from the blood plasma. The heat of the body causes the sweat to evaporate having a cooling effect.

When we feel cold and our blood temperature decreases, the hypothalamus sends nerve impulses to the skin to reduce heat loss by stimulating:

- Arterioles to *contract* so reducing blood flow through the capillaries.
- Sweat glands to stop producing sweat.

If the blood temperature continues to fall, the hypothalamus stimulates heat production in the liver and sends impulses to skeletal muscles to contract to release heat by shivering. Blood flowing through the liver and muscles is warmed and distributes heat to the rest of the body.

Temperature receptors in the skin are useful in the cold, as they give an early warning about possible loss of heat to the surroundings before the blood temperature falls.

The effects of the adjustments made by the body in response to changes in temperature are continually monitored by the hypothalamus to detect whether they have had the desired result (Figure 8.8.2).

Skin care

All people, whatever their skin colour, are at risk of developing skin cancer. Melanin in the skin provides protection against ultraviolet light, which causes cancer. Creams and lotions are available to provide protection against UV light. These products absorb and/or deflect the UV light. The higher the sun protection factor (SPF) the more protection is afforded. Although the actual length of time able to be spent in the sun differs between people, it depends on their skin colour and the time of day (the UV light is more intense in the middle of the day).

People may wish to lighten their skin because they have vitiligo in which areas of skin lighten, they have areas of skin that are particularly dark, e.g. under the arms, or they believe that it is preferable or fashionable to have a light skin.

The ingredients of some skin bleaching products have severe effects. Some products contain hydroquinone which is banned in the European Union as it is thought to be carcinogenic (cancer-causing) (Figure 8.8.3).

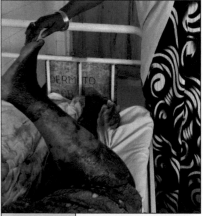

Figure 8.8.3 The danger of using some skin bleaching products

SUMMARY QUESTIONS

1 Make revision notes by drawing a large, labelled, diagram showing the structure of the skin. Annotate your diagram with information on the functions of the skin in protection, temperature control and sensitivity.

2 Make a large flow chart diagram to show how the hypothalamus controls body temperature.

KEY POINTS

1 Body temperature is monitored and controlled by the hypothalamus in the brain.

2 The skin protects the body against injury and is an effector in temperature control; it has receptors for touch, pain and temperature.

3 Skin care includes using products to protect against UV light which can cause cancer; skin lightening products should be used with caution as some contain potentially harmful substances.

SECTION 1: Multiple-choice questions

1 The type of cells that all sense organs contain are called:

  A ciliated

  B effector

  C receptor

  D squamous

2 Which of the following happen when the eyes adjust to light from a near object?

    The ciliary muscles

  A contract increasing the tension in suspensory ligaments and increasing the curvature of the lens

  B contract reducing the tension in suspensory ligaments and increasing the curvature of the lens

  C relax increasing the tension in suspensory ligaments and decreasing the curvature of the lens

  D relax reducing the tension in suspensory ligaments and decreasing the curvature of the lens

3 When a bright light is shone into the eye, the diameter of the pupil decreases.

    This is an example of

  A accommodation

  B a simple reflex

  C homeostasis

  D a voluntary response

4 Which of the following are responsible for loss of heat at the end of a sprint?

	Arterioles in the skin	Blood flow through capillaries in the dermis	Secretion of sweat by sweat glands
A	constrict	decreases	decreases
B	constrict	increases	decreases
C	widen	decreases	increases
D	widen	increases	increases

5 A man injures his arm in an accident. Afterwards, he can feel objects touching his hand, but he cannot move his hand away from them. The cause of this could be that:

  A all the receptors in his hand are damaged

  B all nerves between the receptors in his hand and his CNS are cut

  C all nerves between his CNS and the effectors in his arm are cut

  D all nerves between his hand and the CNS are damaged

6 Which part of the brain controls the breathing rate and the heart rate?

  A cerebrum

  B cerebellum

  C hypothalamus

  D medulla oblongata

7 The movement of a tendril around a stick is an example of

  A an effector

  B a growth response

  C a stimulus

  D a reflex

8 Which is a medicinal drug?

  A caffeine

  B heroin

  C nicotine

  D paracetamol

9 Woodlice are terrestrial animals that do not have a very waterproof body surface. They feed on decaying wood and shelter underneath stones and logs. Some students investigated the behaviour of woodlice in three different investigations.

Investigation 1

The students made a choice chamber with moist cotton wool on one side and a drying agent on the other. Both sides received the same light intensity. 10 woodlice were released into the choice chamber. After 20 minutes, 9 woodlice were in the damp side.

a State why the light intensity was the same on both sides of the choice chamber. *(1)*

b State the stimulus and the response for the behaviour shown by the woodlice. *(2)*

c Suggest how the behaviour of the woodlice is coordinated. *(3)*

Investigation 2

The students made 5 chambers with different humidities. The different humidities were made by using different concentrations of glycerol. 20 woodlice were placed into each chamber and left for 5 minutes. At the end of this time, the number of woodlice moving in each chamber was recorded. This was repeated three times with different groups of woodlice.

Investigation 3

Single woodlice were placed into chambers with the same humidities as in investigation 2. The speed of each woodlouse was recorded over a two-minute period. This was repeated with 10 woodlice.

d Explain why the speed of the woodlice was recorded from the time when they were placed into the choice chamber and not after 5 minutes. *(2)*

The table shows the results of Investigations 2 and 3.

Relative humidity/%	Mean percentage of woodlice moving/%	Mean speed of woodlice/ mm min^{-1}
10	95	300
25	90	280
50	77	270
75	35	250
100	15	100

e Draw a graph to show these results. *(6)*

f Describe the results. *(3)*

g Explain how the behaviour of woodlice in the three investigations that the students carried out increases the chances of survival of the animals in their habitat. *(4)*

h Explain how you would use choice chambers to find out if humidity or light is more important in determining the behaviour of woodlice. *(4)*

Total 25 marks

10 a Make a diagram of a horizontal section of the eye. Label the following structures on your diagram:

ciliary muscle, cornea, iris, lens, optic nerve, retina and fovea (yellow spot). *(7)*

b Explain how an image is formed in the eye. You may use a diagram to help with your answer. *(3)*

c Describe and explain what is wrong with the eyesight of people who have:

i short sight

ii long sight

iii glaucoma *(5)*

Total 15 marks

Further practice questions and examples can be found on the accompanying CD.

9 Growth and reproduction

9.1 Growth

LEARNING OUTCOMES

At the end of this topic you should be able to:

- define the term *growth*
- describe the structure of a seed
- describe the events that occur during germination
- state where growth occurs in the bodies of plants and mammals
- discuss ways to measure growth.

Growth of a multicellular organism is a permanent increase in its size as a result of an increase in the number of cells and the mass of the organism. There is more about the type of cell division that occurs during growth in 11.2.

Flowering plants begin their growth from seeds (Figure 9.1.1), each of which contains a multicellular embryo with stores of energy-rich compounds (such as starch and lipids).

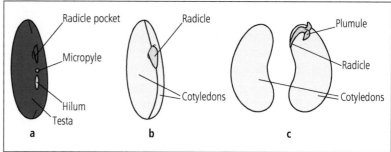

Figure 9.1.1 | Seeds of the kidney bean **a** external view, **b** embryo after removal of the seed coat, **c** with cotyledons separated to show radicle and plumule

STUDY FOCUS

Germination is the process of growth from absorption of water by the seed until a seedling is self-sufficient so it does not need to use its stores of energy. Look at 5.1 to help you answer question 1 and 5.3 to remind yourself about the properties of enzymes.

Seeds absorb water through the **micropyle** by osmosis. This hydrates the tissues inside the seed and they swell. The **testa** or seed coat splits and the embryo starts to grow: **germination** begins.

The following events occur during germination of seeds, such as kidney beans (Figure 9.1.2).

- Water activates the enzymes inside the seed that catalyse the hydrolysis of starch to maltose, maltose to glucose, lipids to glycerol and fatty acids, and proteins to amino acids.
- Glucose and amino acids are translocated in the phloem from the cotyledons to the growth points at the tips of the radicle and the plumule.

DID YOU KNOW?

There are two groups of flowering plants: dicotyledonous plants (dicots) have seeds with two cotyledons; monocotyledonous plants have seeds with one cotyledon. There are examples of both groups in this Unit. You only need to know about the seeds of dicot plants such as beans.

- Water activates mitochondria so that the rate of respiration increases to provide the cells with ATP for growth (see 5.8). Seeds have high rates of respiration and absorb much oxygen.
- Cells divide by mitosis. The new cells fill with water and form vacuoles that exert pressure on the cell walls to stretch them causing the cells to enlarge.
- The radicle breaks through the testa and begins growing downwards into the soil (see 8.2).
- The plumule breaks through the testa and grows upwards. Once the leaves have unfurled and expanded, the plant can begin to photosynthesise and gradually becomes independent of the energy reserves stored in the cotyledons.

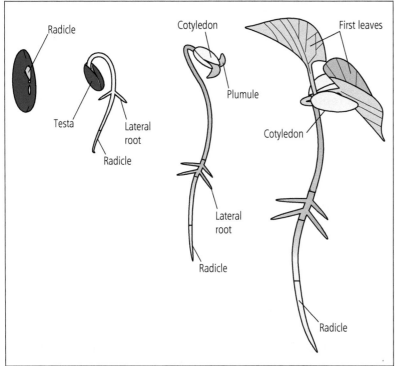

| **Figure 9.1.2** | Stages of germination of kidney bean plants |

LINK

See 6.8 to remind yourself about translocation and movement from sources to sinks.

KEY POINTS

1 Growth is a permanent increase in size and dry mass by an increase in cell number, or cell size, or both.

2 Germination involves the activation of tissues inside the seed; water is absorbed, the seed swells, the seed coat breaks, a radicle and then a plumule emerge.

3 Growth in plants occurs by cell division in meristems: apical meristems are at the tips of roots and shoots; lateral meristems are cylinders of tissue that produce new xylem and phloem.

Growth in plants is localised to tissues of unspecialised cells, known as meristems. **Apical meristems** are at the tips of all shoots and roots. They are where growth in length occurs. **Lateral meristems** are cylinders of tissue that extend the length of the shoots and roots. These meristems produce new cells that become the transport tissues xylem and phloem. Lateral meristems are especially important in perennial plants, such as trees and shrubs, which keep growing year after year and producing new woody tissue for support. In mammals, growth occurs all over the body, but there are specialised growth regions at the end of the long bones (see 7.4). Growth in mammals stops at a certain age.

Ways to measure growth

Growth of plants can be measured in many different ways:

• linear increase, e.g. in length of root and shoot

• area increase, e.g. in surface area of a leaf

• numerical increase, e.g. in number of leaves

• mass increase, e.g. using wet (fresh) mass and dry mass.

One of the best indicators of growth is dry mass, since this measures the new organic compounds that have been produced as a result of photosynthesis and absorption of mineral ions. Unfortunately, this involves killing the organism concerned in order to remove all the water. This can be done by dividing some seeds or seedlings into batches and harvesting each batch at intervals over the time period (see question 6 at the end of Unit 9).

SUMMARY QUESTIONS

1 Maize grains are rich in starch. Describe how you would show that starch is changed to reducing sugars during their germination.

2 Describe, in detail, how you would investigate the differences in growth of plants kept in full sunlight and in deep shade.

3 Explain the roles of meristems in plants.

4 Make fully annotated diagrams to show the germination and early growth of kidney beans.

5 Suggest the advantages and disadvantages of counting leaves as a way to measure growth.

Sexual and asexual reproduction

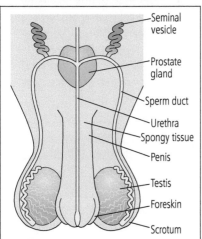

Figure 9.2.1 The male reproductive system viewed from the front

(Labels: Seminal vesicle, Prostate gland, Sperm duct, Urethra, Spongy tissue, Penis, Testis, Foreskin, Scrotum)

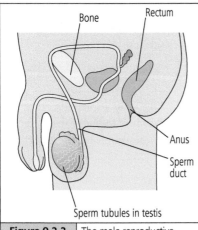

Figure 9.2.2 The male reproductive system viewed from the side

(Labels: Bone, Rectum, Anus, Sperm duct, Sperm tubules in testis)

Sexual reproduction involves the fusion of male and female sex cells, known as **gametes**, to form a **zygote**. The offspring produced are *genetically different* from each other and from their parents. This gives rise to much variation among the offspring.

In **asexual reproduction** there is only *one* parent. All the offspring are *genetically identical* to the parent as they inherit exactly the same genetic information. This means there is very little variation amongst the offspring. Any variation is due to the effect of the environment, for example the availability of nutrients and water determine how well organisms grow. A group of individuals that are all genetically identical is called a **clone**.

The male reproductive system

The **testes** are the male gonads. They produce the male gametes or **spermatozoa**, or sperm for short, and secrete the male hormone **testosterone**.

Functions of the organs labelled in Figures 9.2.1–2 are summarised in Table 9.2.1.

Table 9.2.1 The male reproductive organs

Organ	Function
Testis	• Produces sperm (male gametes) in huge numbers from puberty throughout the rest of life • Secretes testosterone that stimulates sperm production and development of secondary sexual characteristics
Scrotum	• Holds the testes at a temperature slightly lower than body temperature
Sperm duct	• Transfers sperm from the testes to the urethra in the penis
Prostate gland	• Secretes seminal fluid containing sugars as food for the sperm
Penis	• Inserted into vagina, releases semen that contains sperm • Has many sensory cells that are stimulated during sexual intercourse

The female reproductive system

The structure of the female reproductive system is shown in Figures 9.2.3–4 and the functions of the main organs are summarised in Table 9.2.2. The **ovaries** are the female **gonads,** which are the organs that make and release gametes or eggs, and secrete the hormones oestrogen and progesterone.

Table 9.2.2   The female reproductive organs

Organ	Functions
Ovary	• Produces and releases eggs (female gametes) • Secretes oestrogen that stimulates development of secondary sexual characteristics • Secretes progesterone that maintains the soft lining of uterus during the second half of the menstrual cycle and during pregnancy
Oviduct	• Moves eggs from ovary to uterus using cilia and peristalsis • Site of fertilisation.
Uterus	• Lining provides site for implantation and early development of the embryo • Foetus develops within the uterus • Muscle in the outer layer contracts during birth
Cervix	• Ring of muscular and glandular tissue at the base of the uterus • Secretes different forms of mucus during the menstrual cycle • Retains contents of uterus during pregnancy
Vagina	• Lining secretes mucus • Sperm are deposited in the vagina • Widens to form the birth canal
Clitoris	• Sensitive region at entry to vagina with many receptors that are stimulated during sexual intercourse

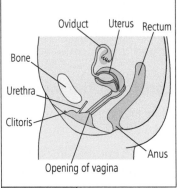

Figure 9.2.3	The female reproductive system viewed from the front

Figure 9.2.4	The female reproductive system viewed from the side

LINK

11.4 and 11.5 explain why the offspring of sexually reproducing organisms are genetically different from one another.

KEY POINTS

1 Eggs and sperm are specialised cells known as gametes. Fusion of gametes occurs in sexual reproduction, but not in asexual reproduction.

2 Sexual reproduction produces genetic variation in the offspring; asexual reproduction does not.

3 Human ovaries produce eggs that are released at ovulation into the oviduct where fertilisation occurs. The uterus is the site of internal development.

4 Human testes continually produce sperm that are released during intercourse to travel through the sperm ducts to the urethra.

5 The prostate gland produces seminal fluid.

SUMMARY QUESTIONS

1 Make a table to compare asexual and sexual reproduction.

2 Make large labelled diagrams of the female and male reproductive systems. Annotate the diagrams with the functions of the organs that you have labelled.

3 State **a** where the male and female gametes develop, and **b** where fertilisation occurs.

The menstrual cycle

At the end of this topic you should be able to:

- define the terms *menstrual cycle* and *ovulation*
- describe the changes that occur in the ovary and the uterus during the menstrual cycle
- outline the role of the pituitary gland in controlling the menstrual cycle by releasing hormones
- outline the roles of oestrogen and progesterone
- describe the effect of pregnancy on the menstrual cycle.

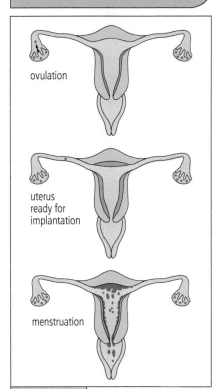

ovulation

uterus ready for implantation

menstruation

Figure 9.3.1 | During the menstrual cycle the activities of the ovaries and the uterus are synchronised.

The monthly changes in the ovary and the uterus are synchronised so that the lining of the uterus is ready to receive an embryo if fertilisation occurs. This monthly cycle of changes is the **menstrual cycle**. During puberty, girls start to have periods. This is when the lining of the uterus breaks down, and blood and cells are passed out through the vagina. When **menstruation** happens for the first time it shows that a girl has had her first menstrual cycle (Figure 9.3.1).

Girls are born with a very large number of potential egg cells in their ovaries, and they do not produce any more during their lifetime. Each potential egg is surrounded by a small group of cells and together they form a **follicle**.

Each month one or two follicles develop. Each egg cell divides by meiosis and increases in size as the cytoplasm fills with stores of fat and protein.

As the follicle grows it enlarges and fills with fluid and moves towards the edge of the ovary. About two weeks after menstruation, the pressure inside the follicle is so great that it bursts releasing the egg, some follicle cells and the fluid into the oviduct. This is **ovulation**. Some follicle cells remain in the ovary to form the **yellow body**. If fertilisation occurs, it will grow and remain in the ovary throughout pregnancy.

At the same time as the follicle is developing, the lining of the uterus starts to thicken. In the week after ovulation it is thick and full of glands and blood vessels with the potential to nourish and protect the embryo. If fertilisation occurs the embryo arrives in the uterus and sinks into this lining. This stage of reproduction is **implantation**.

If fertilisation does not occur the egg dies and passes out of the vagina and the yellow body in the ovary breaks down. The thick lining of the uterus breaks down and is passed out during menstruation. The cycle then begins again.

If pregnancy occurs the embryo releases a hormone that stimulates the yellow body to remain active which in turn stimulates the lining of the uterus to continue to thicken, supplying the embryo with nutrients and oxygen as it continues its development. This also ensures that menstruation will not occur.

Control of the menstrual cycle

There are four hormones that control the menstrual cycle (Figure 9.3.2). The pituitary gland secretes:

- **follicle stimulating hormone** (FSH), and
- **luteinising hormone** (LH).

The ovary secretes:

- **oestrogen**, and
- **progesterone**.

FSH starts the cycle by stimulating a follicle to develop and the follicle cells to secrete oestrogen into the bloodstream.

Oestrogen causes the lining of the uterus to thicken in preparation to receive a fertilised egg and prevents any more eggs developing. Oestrogen in the blood passes to the pituitary gland and prevents it making any more FSH. Instead it stimulates the production of LH, which stimulates ovulation and the remaining follicle cells to form a yellow body.

The yellow body secretes progesterone, which makes the uterus lining thicken even more and prevents it breaking down. Both oestrogen and progesterone are needed to prepare the lining of the uterus for implantation of the fertilised egg.

If pregnancy occurs these two hormones continue to be produced. They make sure that the lining of the uterus stays thick and they stop the woman's menstrual cycle starting again.

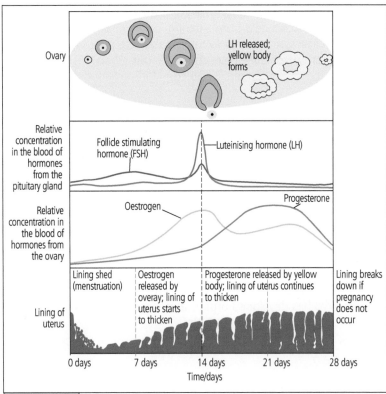

Figure 9.3.2 Changes in the ovary and uterus are coordinated by FSH and LH secreted by the pituitary gland.

STUDY FOCUS

The menstrual cycle involves a complex series of events controlled by hormones from the pituitary gland. Compare different ways to show these changes and make your own annotated diagrams and charts to summarise all the information you find.

SUMMARY QUESTIONS

1 Define the following terms: *menstruation*, *ovulation* and *implantation*.

2 Draw a time line to show the changes that occur in the ovary and in the uterus during a menstrual cycle.

3 a Name four hormones involved in coordinating the menstrual cycle and state where they are secreted.

  b Describe the roles of these hormones in controlling the menstrual cycle.

4 Make a timeline for the human gametes from production until fertilisation.

Reproduction and birth control

LEARNING OUTCOMES

At the end of this topic you should be able to:

- describe the events leading up to and including fertilisation
- describe the process of *implantation*
- describe the functions of the amnion, placenta and umbilical cord
- discuss the advantages and disadvantages of methods of birth control.

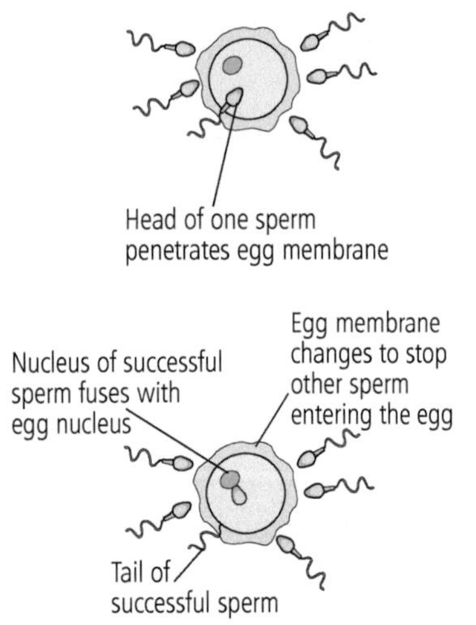

Human fertilisation

After sperm are deposited in the vagina, some sperm swim through the mucus in the cervix into the uterus and then to the oviduct. Many sperm cells do not survive this difficult journey. A man produces huge numbers of sperm to increase the chances of success.

If there is an egg in the oviduct, a sperm cell may succeed in fertilising it. First enzymes are released by the tip of the sperm to digest a pathway through the jelly coat around the egg.

The cell membrane of the sperm fuses with the membrane around the egg and the sperm nucleus enters the egg cytoplasm (Figure 9.4.1). A membrane immediately forms around the fertilised egg or zygote to stop other sperm cells from entering. Only *one* sperm is successful. The two nuclei fuse together to form the zygote nucleus. Sperm can stay alive for two or three days, so if intercourse happens just before ovulation the sperm can fertilise an egg, if it is released during this time.

Implantation

After fertilisation the zygote divides by mitosis to form a two-celled embryo. Then it continues dividing. After a few hours, the embryo is a hollow ball of cells, which moves down the oviduct. The embryo is moved by cilia on the epithelial cells along the oviduct and also by muscular contractions, similar to peristalsis in the gut.

It may take several days for the embryo to reach the uterus. The embryo embeds into the soft lining of the uterus. This is called **implantation**. The uterus lining is thick with many glands and blood vessels, which provide food and oxygen to the embryo by diffusion. Carbon dioxide and chemical wastes diffuse out of the embryo. Once the embryo has developed organs and is recognisably human, it is known as a **foetus** (Figure 9.4.2).

Table 9.4.1 shows the functions of the structures labelled in Figure 9.4.2.

Figure 9.4.1 | Fertilisation

Head of one sperm penetrates egg membrane

Nucleus of successful sperm fuses with egg nucleus

Egg membrane changes to stop other sperm entering the egg

Tail of successful sperm

Table 9.4.1   How the foetus develops

Organ	Structure	Function
Amnion	• Thin layer of cells and fibrous tissue	• Encloses foetus in a watery fluid – the **amniotic fluid**, which provides protection against mechanical damage
Placenta	• Disc of tissue that has many villi giving a large surface area	• Exchange of substances between foetal blood and maternal blood
Umbilical cord	• Rubbery cord, containing an artery and two veins	• Deoxygenated blood flows to the placenta • Oxygenated blood returns to the foetus

Birth control

Birth control is any method that prevents the birth of a baby. This involves methods to prevent fertilisation or implantation occurring, removing the embryo or foetus at some stage during pregnancy. Methods that prevent fertilisation are methods of **contraception**. If conception and implantation have occurred and the embryo or foetus has started to develop, then the destruction of this is an abortion. Abortion is birth control but *not* a method of contraception.

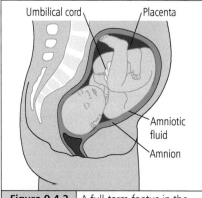

Figure 9.4.2 | A full-term foetus in the uterus

Table 9.4.2 Methods of birth control

Type of birth control method	Details	Advantages	Disadvantages
Barrier:	prevents sperm reaching the egg in the oviduct		
condom	fits over the penis to prevent release of semen into vagina	protects against transmission of STIs	can split during intercourse
diaphragm and cervical cap	fits over cervix to prevent entry of sperm into uterus	the woman is in control	does not protect against STIs
Hormonal (the pill)	contains oestrogen and/ or progesterone – prevents development of follicles in the ovary	very low failure rate	not all women can use this method; some women are at risk of developing blood clots
Surgical: vasectomy	sperm duct is cut and tied; prevents sperm being ejaculated	no other form of contraception is necessary	do not protect against STIs; these are permanent methods of birth control
sterilisation	oviduct is cut and tied; prevents eggs reaching site of fertilisation		
Natural	monitoring body temperature or changes in cervical mucus to determine fertile time during menstrual cycle	no costs involved; no need to obtain condoms, pills, etc.	higher failure rate than other methods

People have used birth control methods for centuries. The development of the contraceptive pill in the 1960s gave women far more control over their fertility and gave greater opportunities for people to plan how many children to have and when. Widespread provision of contraception has allowed governments to take steps to limit population growth. In some countries birth control methods have been so successful that birth rates have fallen below the level needed to maintain the population.

KEY POINTS

1 Male and female gametes fuse together at fertilisation to form a zygote.

2 After fertilisation the zygote divides by mitosis to form a ball of cells known as an embryo. After further development, the embryo develops organs and is called a foetus.

3 The amnion holds fluid to protect the foetus, which is connected to the placenta by the umbilical cord.

4 The placenta is the site of exchange of substances between maternal blood and foetal blood.

SUMMARY QUESTIONS

1 State what happens at fertilisation and at implantation.

2 Distinguish between the following: ovum and sperm; zygote and embryo; embryo and foetus.

3 Describe the roles of the amniotic sac, placenta and umbilical cord.

4 Explain the biological principles involved in each of the methods of birth control in Table 9.4.2.

Flowers

At the end of this topic you should be able to:

- outline the stages in flowering plant reproduction including pollination and fertilisation
- describe the structure of an insect-pollinated flower and state the function of each part
- compare the structures of insect- and wind-pollinated flowers.

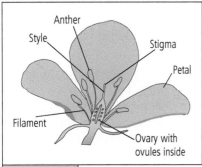

Figure 9.5.1 This drawing has been made by sectioning a flower of *Lignum vitae* in half.

Figure 9.5.2 Flowers of *Lignum vitae* are brightly coloured – an indicator that they are pollinated by insects.

Flowering plant life cycle

Flowering plants grow from seed by **vegetative growth**; at some stage they will begin **reproductive growth** by producing flowers for sexual reproduction. Most plants have flowers with both male and female structures. The **stamens** of the flowers produce **pollen grains** that contain the male gamete, see Table 9.5.1. These are transferred to the female part of the flower where they will deliver the male gamete to the female gamete for internal fertilisation. The zygote grows into an embryo that develops inside the **ovule** which becomes the seed. The embryo remains dormant inside the seed while it is dispersed away from the female parent plant.

The transfer of pollen from the anthers to stigma is **pollination**. Two agents of pollination are insects and the wind. Studying the structure of flowers shows how they are adapted for pollination by insects and by wind.

Insect-pollinated flowers

These flowers are often large and conspicuous to insects, which are attracted by bright colours, scent and the prospect of nectar and pollen (Figures 9.5.1–4). Nectar is a liquid rich in sucrose, and pollen is a good source of protein.

The functions of the different structures in these insect-pollinated flowers are summarised in Table 9.5.1.

Table 9.5.1 Functions of the different structures in insect-pollinated flowers

Structure	Function
Sepal	Protects the flower when it is a bud
Petal	Attracts insects by being large, brightly coloured, and having honey guides (lines that direct the insect towards the source of nectar at the centre)
Stamen (male part of the flower)	**Anther** – produces pollen grains; anthers split when the pollen grains are ripe **Filament** – supports the anther and provides water, ions and sugars through xylem and phloem
Carpel (female part of the flower)	**Stigma** – pollen is deposited **Style** – provides sugars for growth of the pollen tubes **Ovary** – contains ovules which develop into seeds **Ovule** – contains the embryo sac which is the female equivalent of the pollen grain **Embryo sac** – contains the female gamete

Wind-pollinated flowers

These flowers are much smaller and less conspicuous than those of insect-pollinated flowers. They are often green in colour. Often the individual flowers are grouped closely together in an **inflorescence**, which grows above the rest of the plant (Figures 9.5.5 and 9.5.6). This is to ensure that the pollen is blown away from the plant and into the air, so it can be spread far and wide. Anthers are large and lightly attached to the filaments so they shake in the wind to release their pollen. Stigmas are large and feathery to trap pollen grains.

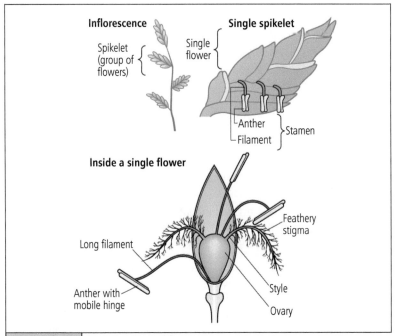

Inflorescence

Spikelet (group of flowers)

Single spikelet

Single flower

Anther
Filament
Stamen

Inside a single flower

Long filament

Feathery stigma

Anther with mobile hinge

Style

Ovary

Figure 9.5.5 A wind-pollinated flower

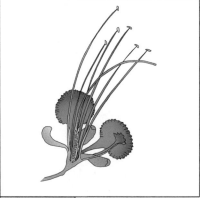

Figure 9.5.3 A half flower drawing of a flower of Pride of Barbados. Use Figure 9.5.1 to identify the parts.

Figure 9.5.4 Flowers of Pride of Barbados are typical of the legume family of flowering plants.

KEY POINTS

1 Pollination is the transfer of pollen from anthers to stigma.

2 The structure of flowers is related to the agent of pollination: insect-pollinated flowers have large, brightly coloured flowers that make nectar and scent; wind-pollinated flowers have small, green flowers that have large anthers to produce much pollen and feathery stigmas to trap pollen in the wind.

DID YOU KNOW?

Lignum vitae wood was used for the locks on Lake Erie. They lasted for over a 100 years.

SUMMARY QUESTIONS

1 Define *vegetative growth*, *reproductive growth* and *pollination*.

2 Draw a flow chart diagram to show the life cycle of flowering plants.

3 a Make a half flower drawing of an insect-pollinated flower.
  b Label the parts and annotate with the functions.

4 Make a table to compare wind- and insect-pollinated flowers.

Figure 9.5.6

Pollination to seed dispersal

At the end of this topic you should be able to:

• compare self- and cross-pollination

• describe how fertilisation occurs in flowering plants

• describe how seeds and fruit develop from ovules and ovaries after fertilisation

• describe how seeds are dispersed.

Figure 9.6.1 Pollen dispersed into the wind from a pendulous sedge

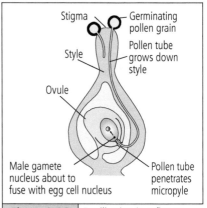

Stigma — Germinating pollen grain

Style — Pollen tube grows down style

Ovule

Male gamete nucleus about to fuse with egg cell nucleus — Pollen tube penetrates micropyle

Figure 9.6.2 Fertilisation in a flower

Self-pollination and cross-pollination

In the examples in this section, pollen is transferred from the anthers of one flower to the stigma of another flower on another plant. This is **cross-pollination**. If any pollen lands on the stigma of the same flower from which it is released then **self-pollination** occurs. In most plants self-pollination does not lead to fertilisation, but there are some plants where self-pollination happens all the time and it leads to fertilisation.

> **STUDY FOCUS**
>
> Remember that pollination comes before fertilisation. The sequence of events is (1) pollen released from anthers, (2) pollination, (3) growth of pollen tube, and (4) fertilisation. Use this sequence for the basis of your revision notes for this topic.

Fertilisation

Fertilisation follows pollination. Pollination is complete when pollen grains land on the female stigma. The male nucleus is now transferred to the female gamete inside the ovule so that fertilisation can occur.

If a pollen grain lands on a ripe stigma of the same species, it produces a pollen tube which grows down the style to the ovary (Figure 9.6.2). As it grows, it gains nutrition from the tissues of the style and carries the male gamete nucleus with it. When it reaches the ovary, the tube grows through the micropyle – the small hole at the entry to the ovule. The tip of the tube breaks down to allow the male gamete nucleus to enter the ovule and fuse with the female gamete nucleus. This is fertilisation in which a zygote is formed by fusion of the two nuclei.

Events after fertilisation

The zygote divides by mitosis and grows into the embryo. The ovule forms the seed with the embryo inside it. After fertilisation, many of the parts of the flower are not needed any more, so the sepals, petals and stamens wither and fall off. They have completed their functions. The ovary swells to form the fruit with seeds inside it. The central part of the ovary is the placenta that contains xylem and phloem to provide water and nutrients to the growing seeds. Fruits develop in ways that are related to the dispersal of their seeds. Some fruits only have one or a few seeds and are dispersed together. Other fruits contain many seeds and split open to release them.

Seed dispersal

Flowering plants have mechanisms for shedding and dispersing their seeds over a wide area. This avoids competition with the parent plant and between the seedlings. The disadvantages are that many seeds will be eaten, or land somewhere not suitable for growth.

Types of seed and fruit dispersal

Wind

The fruits develop hairs or wings that catch the wind and allow the seeds to travel some distance.

Figure 9.6.3 This fruit of the Monarch Amazon vine has two seeds each with a wing to give a structure like a helicopter that spins as it falls from the tree.

Animal

Some fruits have hooks that attach to the fur of mammals that carry them some distance before rubbing or shaking them off.

Figure 9.6.4 Duppy needles have sharp hooks that stick to fur and to clothing.

Fleshy fruits are full of sugars and often brightly coloured to attract animals, such as monkeys and birds, to eat them. The seeds are either scattered on the ground or eaten and egested far from the parent plants.

Figure 9.6.5 A howler monkey is a willing participant in seed dispersal for this forest tree.

Mechanical (self-dispersal)

Fruits dry and split open, often quite suddenly, to project their seeds away from the plant.

Figure 9.6.6 Fruits of legumes dry and crack open into two halves, which twist to eject the seeds.

Water

Some plants that grow along rivers and by the sea produce buoyant fruits that can withstand immersion in water. These are dispersed by water – often thousands of miles away from the parent plant.

Figure 9.6.7 Fruits of manchineel can be dispersed by ocean currents.

KEY POINTS

1 Cross-pollination is the transfer of pollen from the anthers of one flower to the stigma of a flower on a different plant of the same species; self-pollination is the transfer of pollen within the same flower.

2 Pollen tubes grow down the style to deliver the male gamete to the female gamete inside the embryo sac within the ovule.

3 A zygote is produced at fertilisation; this divides to form a multicellular embryo.

4 After fertilisation the ovule becomes the seed, the ovary develops into a fruit, all other flower parts wither and die.

5 Seeds are dispersed to avoid competition and to colonise new areas; seed dispersal occurs by wind, water and by animals.

SUMMARY QUESTIONS

1 Describe what happens between pollination and fertilisation.

2 Describe the changes that occur to the female gamete, ovule and ovary from fertilisation until seed dispersal.

3 List the advantages and disadvantages of seed dispersal.

4 Suggest the advantages of seeds being dispersed by animals that ingest them.

5 Make revision notes comparing fertilisation and development in flowering plants and humans.

SECTION 1: Multiple-choice questions

1 The best definition of growth is

  A a permanent increase in the dry mass of an organism

  B an increase in the size of an organism

  C an increase in the number of cells of an organism

  D an increase in the volume of an organism

2 Which are the features of wind-pollinated flowers?

  A anthers are inside flowers, smooth pollen, no scent

  B coloured petals, sticky pollen, strong scent

  C large flowers, nectaries present, light pollen

  D no petals, anthers are outside flowers, no nectaries

3 What is the function of the ovary in human reproduction?

  A formation of a mature ovum (egg)

  B secretion of FSH

  C secretion of LH

  D site of fertilisation

4 What is cut during a vasectomy?

  A oviduct

  B sperm duct

  C ureter

  D urethra

5 Which features are associated with seeds that are dispersed by animals?

  A light seeds with fruits that are formed into wings

  B fleshy fruits that are brightly coloured

  C fruits that dry to open explosively

  D large seeds that float on water

SECTION 2: Short answer questions

6 Some students investigated the germination and early growth of maize plants. They took 400 seeds and divided them into 10 batches of 40. The seeds were soaked in water and planted in seed compost.

At intervals of time a batch was removed from the compost, washed, dried thoroughly and then weighed. The mean dry mass of each plant was calculated. The results are in Table 1.

Table 1

Stage of growth	Day	Mean dry mass/g per plant	Presence of leaves
Germination	0	0.40	✗
	1	0.33	✗
	15	0.29	✗
Early growth of seedling	30	0.64	✓
	50	4.65	✓
Vegetative growth	64	20.01	✓
	71	34.56	✓
	100	111.65	✓
	113	121.99	✓

  a Explain why the students determined the dry mass of the maize plants. *(2)*

  b **i** Describe the growth of the maize plants as shown in the table. *(3)*

    ii Explain the changes in dry masses of the plants. *(4)*

  c State two disadvantages of using dry mass as a way of recording the growth of plants. *(2)*

  d Figure 1 shows the change in area of a cucumber leaf over 20 days.

Suggest

    i how you would obtain results for the growth in surface area of a leaf *(3)*

    ii the advantages of using leaf area as a way of measuring growth of crop plants, such as cucumbers. *(3)*

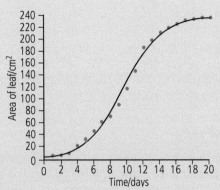

Figure 1

The ovaries of tomato flowers develop into fleshy fruits after fertilisation. Figure 2 shows a vertical section through a tomato fruit.

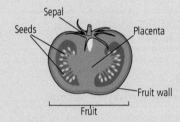

Figure 2

e The placenta provides sugars to support the growth of the seeds. Name

   i   a sugar that is transported to the seeds

   ii the tissue that transports these sugars through the placenta

   iii the source of the sugars. *(3)*

Measurements were taken from many tomato fruits during their growth as shown in Table 2.

Table 2

Features of tomato fruits	Mean size/mm			
	Stage of fruit development			
	early	mid	late	ripe
Seed width	0.2	0.5	1.0	1.1
Placenta width	15.0	21.6	12.2	5.0
Pericarp width	2.6	8.1	10.2	12.2
Fruit diameter	27.0	42.6	79.2	139.2

(OCR March 1999)

f Explain the reasons for the changes shown in the table. *(5)*

Total 25 marks

7 a Describe how the structure of an insect-pollinated flower differs from the structure of a wind- pollinated flower. *(5)*

 b i State the difference between cross-pollination and self-pollination. *(2)*

   ii Explain how plants ensure that their flowers are cross-pollinated and not self-pollinated. *(3)*

 c Describe what happens following pollination to ensure that an embryo is formed. *(5)*

Total 15 marks

8 a Describe the roles of the placenta, amnion and umbilical cord in the development of a foetus. *(6)*

 b Condoms are used for birth control.

   i   What name is used to describe this method of birth control? *(1)*

   ii Explain how a condom acts as a method of birth control. *(2)*

   iii State an added advantage of using condoms. *(1)*

 c Vasectomy is another method of birth control. Explain how this prevents pregnancy. *(2)*

 d Outline *three* social aspects of contraception. *(3)*

Total 15 marks

Further practice questions and examples can be found on the accompanying CD.

10 Disease

10.1

Diseases

Figure 10.1.1 Is poverty a disease? The World Health Organisation (WHO) certainly thinks so, as children like these are at risk of many pathogenic and deficiency diseases.

STUDY FOCUS

The number of cases of some hereditary diseases has decreased. Genetic (DNA) testing has given parents the choice of whether to have children at all or to have assisted reproduction. This involves testing the embryos for inherited conditions before proceeding with pregnancy (see 11.6).

Disease is not an easy word to define; it can be defined as a condition or illness that affects the body. We can describe **symptoms** to medical professionals; they look for certain signs that help to decide which disease we have.

Categories of disease

There are many ways to classify diseases into different categories. One way is to classify them by *cause* as shown in Table 10.1.1. The table gives examples of the four categories of disease that you should know.

Table 10.1.1 Examples of causes of disease

Category and cause	Examples	Cause
Pathogenic (see 10.2): disease-causing organisms or pathogens	HIV, influenza, yellow fever	Virus
	Tetanus, tuberculosis (TB), gonorrhoea	Bacterium
	Ringworm, thrush	Fungus
Deficiency: lack of a nutrient in diet (see 5.7)	Night blindness, total blindness	Lack of vitamin A
	Scurvy	Lack of vitamin C
	(Iron-deficiency) anaemia	Lack of iron
Hereditary: inheritance of a mutant allele	**Sickle cell anaemia** (see 11.6)	Mutant allele of gene for haemoglobin
	Haemophilia (see 11.7)	Mutant allele of gene for blood clotting factor
Physiological: malfunction of organs or organ systems	**Diabetes**	Inability to produce insulin or of tissues to respond to it
	Hypertension	Cause (in most cases) unknown

Treatment and control of disease

Pathogenic diseases are treated with drugs:

• antibiotics, such as penicillin and amoxicillin, are used to treat bacterial infections; they are not suitable for treating viral and fungal diseases

• anti-viral drugs, such as acyclovir for treating herpes and anti-retroviral drugs for treating HIV (see 10.3)

• anti-fungal drugs, such as clotrimazole for treating thrush and ringworm.

Vaccination is an effective control measure for many infectious diseases. It has been used to eradicate smallpox from the world and polio from the western hemisphere. Deficiency diseases are treated by providing dietary supplements. Hereditary and physiological diseases are treated in different ways depending on the cause and its effect.

The concentration of glucose in the blood is maintained within narrow limits. Tissues in the pancreas detect changes in the concentration. This increases when you absorb a meal and decreases in between meals and when you exercise. The tissues in the pancreas secrete the hormone insulin when the concentration increases. Insulin stimulates cells in the liver and muscles to absorb glucose and convert it to the storage compound glycogen. If the concentration of glucose decreases, the pancreas secretes glucagon, which stimulates liver cells to break down glycogen to glucose.

Diabetes mellitus (most often just called diabetes) occurs when the body stops producing insulin or the target cells in the liver and muscles stop responding to it.

Diabetes type I usually starts in childhood or adolescence. The cells that make insulin in the pancreas are often destroyed, so no insulin is produced at all.

Diabetes type II usually starts later in life. There is a very high risk of developing this form of diabetes if there is genetic predisposition, a diet high in fat and refined sugar and not enough fibre. Obesity, high blood pressure and high blood cholesterol concentration are also factors that increase the risk of developing this disease.

Insulin is used to treat diabetes; this has to be injected into the blood at regular intervals to stimulate the storage of glucose as glycogen so that it is not excreted in the urine.

People with hypertension have high blood pressure and are often unaware of the fact as there are few, if any, symptoms. It is one of the best indicators that a person is at risk of heart disease or stroke. Various drugs are prescribed for hypertension, including beta blockers that reduce the effect of stress hormones that increase the heart rate and blood pressure.

The roles of diet and exercise

Rather than pay for expensive drugs, it is better to prevent physiological diseases developing in the first place. Eating a balanced diet, taking exercise, not smoking, and drinking alcohol in moderation (if at all) are simple ways in which people can avoid developing many of these diseases.

A balanced diet provides all the nutrients needed for good health and the prevention of deficiency diseases. It also means that people do not have more energy in their diet than they expend in daily activities. This reduces the risk of storing excess fat and becoming overweight or obese.

STUDY FOCUS

The control of blood glucose is another example of homeostasis. Remember that the glucose concentration fluctuates but stays within narrow limits. People with untreated diabetes are at risk of going into a coma because they do not have insulin to stimulate the storage of glucose as glycogen.

Figure 10.1.2 Exercise benefits people's physical health by reducing the chances of physiological diseases and often improves their mental health as they feel better about themselves.

KEY POINTS

1 Disease can be defined as a condition or illness that affects the body. People can describe their symptoms; medical staff can observe signs to help their diagnosis.

2 Four categories of disease are pathogenic, deficiency, hereditary and physiological diseases.

3 Drugs, such as antibiotics, are used to treat pathogenic diseases; people with physiological diseases often need to take drugs, such as insulin, for much longer – often for their whole lives.

4 The risks of developing physiological diseases can be reduced by taking exercise and eating a balanced diet throughout life.

SUMMARY QUESTIONS

1 Explain how diseases are categorised.

2 Discuss the ways in which diseases can be prevented.

Mosquitoes

At the end of this topic you should be able to:

- identify the different stages in the life cycle of mosquitoes and their habitats
- describe their life cycle explaining the term *complete metamorphosis*
- define the term *vector of disease*
- describe the role of mosquitoes in transmitting malaria, dengue fever and yellow fever
- state the ways mosquitoes are controlled
- discuss the impact on human populations of diseases of crop plants and livestock.

Figure 10.2.1 A female *Aedes aegypti* mosquito taking a blood meal

Figure 10.2.2 Two female *Anopheles* mosquitoes feeding

This section is about two types of mosquito that transmit three serious tropical diseases:

- *Aedes aegypti* which transmits dengue and yellow fever
- *Anopheles* which transmits malaria.

These species have the same life cycle. Female *Anopheles* mosquitoes lay their eggs in bodies of still water, such as ponds, drainage and irrigation channels, water storage tanks, in fact anywhere that fills with water. Female *Aedes* lay eggs that withstand dry conditions and deposit them on the sides of containers of water where they may survive for months until the container fills with water.

The eggs of both types of mosquito hatch to form larvae, which live in water near the surface, feeding on bacteria and small organisms. Larvae of *Aedes* have breathing tubes at their rear end and rest at an angle to the surface; *Anopheles* larvae rest parallel to the surface carrying out gas exchange through their whole body surface.

After moulting several times, each larva changes into a pupa. During the pupal stage the body goes through a change into an adult with a very different appearance. After **complete metamorphosis**, the adults emerge from the pupal case and fly away (Figure 10.2.3).

Both sexes feed on plant juices (nectar and phloem sap), but after mating the females feed on blood to provide the protein that they need to make eggs. Adults of both types live in and around human dwellings using dark, cool places to rest.

Transmission of disease

Female mosquitoes are **vectors of disease**. When the female feeds she may take up parasites from the person she is feeding from. The parasite completes its life cycle inside the gut of the mosquito and then moves to her salivary glands. Transmission is complete when she takes a blood meal from an uninfected person, injecting her saliva to stop the blood clotting as she feeds.

Yellow fever

Yellow fever is caused by the yellow fever virus, which is transmitted by mosquitoes. They feed on infected animals in forests, then pass the infection to humans when they feed on them. The greatest risk of an epidemic occurs when infected humans return to urban areas and are fed on by *Aedes aegypti*, which then transmits the virus to other humans.

Dengue fever

Dengue fever is caused by a virus transmitted by mosquitoes. This disease is increasing across the world, including the Caribbean (Table 10.2.1). Epidemics tend to occur after heavy rains when the population of mosquitoes increases.

Malaria

Malaria is caused by a single-celled parasite that is much more complex than bacteria or viruses. The disease has been eradicated from many countries by breaking the transmission cycle.

Control of mosquitoes

Mosquitoes are controlled by:

- reducing the number of places where they can lay eggs
- covering the surfaces of water with oil or polystyrene beads, so larvae cannot breathe
- stocking larger bodies of water with fish that eat mosquito larvae
- spraying insecticide in houses and on breeding sites.

Plant and animal diseases

By keeping livestock in large numbers and growing crops as monocultures we provide perfect conditions for pathogens to spread and cause epidemics. Almost all of our crop plants are the result of selective breeding and are genetically uniform with little genetic variation. Crops grown over wide areas are at risk of pests and diseases for which they have little resistance. If there is an epidemic of a disease there is a chance that varieties with identical genotypes will be wiped out. This happened with the Gros Michel variety of banana that was attacked by a fungal disease known as Panama disease in the 1950s. This may happen again as Cavendish, the most commonly grown variety, is at risk of a new strain of this disease.

The screw-worm fly attacks cattle and other livestock. The adults lay their eggs in the flesh of animals. The eggs hatch and the maggots use their sharp jaws to burrow into the animals. If untreated the animals die.

The consequences of plant and animal diseases are:

- death of livestock and loss of crops so farmers lose money
- expenditure on control measures, such as drugs for livestock and pesticides and fungicides for crops
- less food for human and animal consumption
- possible famine if main staple foods, such as wheat, rice and maize, are destroyed by widespread disease.

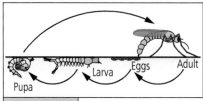

Figure 10.2.3 The life cycle of *Anopheles* mosquitoes

Table 10.2.1 Distribution of vector-transmitted diseases in the Caribbean

Disease	Countries where there is a risk of the disease
Dengue fever	Throughout the Caribbean region
Malaria	Haiti, Guyana, Belize, Suriname and the Dominican Republic
Yellow fever	Trinidad and Tobago, Guyana, Suriname

SUMMARY QUESTIONS

1 Define the term *vector*.

2 Describe the roles of mosquitoes as vectors.

3 Redraw the life cycle diagram of mosquitoes as a flow chart diagram (without pictures).

4 State the habitats of the larvae, pupae and adults of mosquitoes.

5 Summarise the impact of plant and animal diseases on human populations.

KEY POINTS

1 A vector is an animal that transmits an infectious disease to humans.

2 Two types of mosquito transmit the pathogens of human diseases: *Aedes aegypti* is the vector of dengue fever and yellow fever and *Anopheles* is the vector of malaria.

3 Adult mosquitoes are controlled by spraying insecticides; other stages in the life cycle are controlled by draining likely habitats and covering bodies of water so they cannot breathe.

4 Growing crops with limited genetic variation puts them at risk of disease that may wipe them out and lead to reduction of food supplies, loss of income for farmers and possible famine.

Sexually transmitted infections (STIs)

DID YOU KNOW?

The gonorrhoea bacterium has become resistant to many antibiotics, which are now useless for treating some cases. Experts have warned that soon the bacterium will be resistant to all suitable antibiotics and cases will go untreated.

Figure 10.3.1 Across the world there are many children like these who have been orphaned by HIV/AIDS.

Sexually transmitted infections (STIs) are transmitted from infected people to uninfected people during intimate sexual activity. Some STIs may be transmitted in other ways, but most transmission occurs during heterosexual or homosexual activity.

Gonorrhoea

Gonorrhoea is caused by a bacterium that can only survive inside the moist lining of the male or female reproductive tract. If present in either the vagina of a woman or the urethra of a man, the infection can be transmitted from one to the other during sexual intercourse.

The first symptoms of the disease appear in men between two to seven days after infection. Sores develop on the penis and the bacteria multiply within the urethra, producing an unpleasant discharge and pain when urinating.

Bacteria multiply in the cervix and, to a lesser extent, inside the vagina. Women may notice a discharge but often there may be no pain or other symptoms as in men. Most infected men will know that they have gonorrhoea from their early symptoms, whereas many women will not realise that they have the infection and may pass on the disease to other sexual partners. If not treated, there may be long-term damage to the urinary and reproductive systems of both men and women resulting in sterility.

Gonorrhoea can be treated effectively by antibiotics. However, as with many diseases, prevention is better than cure. The following steps can be taken to prevent infection:

- Have only one partner; if both partners are disease-free, then infection is not possible.
- If the man uses a condom the bacteria cannot pass through it to another person and he is unlikely to be infected.
- If a person is diagnosed with gonorrhoea, then all sexual contacts should be traced, warned and treated with antibiotics to stop the spread of the disease.

HIV/AIDS

In 1982, doctors in North America and in Africa began to see patients with rare conditions especially a rare cancer and a rare form of pneumonia. Scientists discovered that these conditions were the result of immune systems that did not function efficiently. This condition was called **acquired immunodeficiency syndrome** or AIDS. The causative agent of this collapse in the immune system is a virus – **human immunodeficiency virus** or HIV. AIDS is a collection of different diseases, some cancers and some infectious diseases. People who have AIDS do not always have the same collection of diseases. The condition is now generally known as HIV/AIDS.

Transmission of HIV

HIV does not survive for long outside the human body. It is passed from an infected person to an uninfected person in body fluids:

- in semen and vaginal fluids during unprotected (unsafe) sexual intercourse
- in blood if there is blood-to-blood contact between two people, for example intravenous drug users sharing needles to inject drugs such as heroin, and by 'needle stick' accidents in hospitals if surgical instruments are not sterilised thoroughly
- in blood that is used in transfusion if it is not heat-treated to kill HIV
- from mother to baby during birth and in breast milk.

Treatment of HIV/AIDS

Anti-viral drugs control the spread of HIV in the body and other drugs, such as antibiotics and anti-fungal drugs control opportunistic infections caused by bacteria and fungi. The life expectancy for people living with HIV/AIDS is now very much higher than it used to be. Some doctors think that people newly infected now will live a normal life span. However, there is still no cure for the condition and no vaccine (as of 2013).

Since the early 1980s it is estimated that about 30 million people have died of AIDS.

When HIV enters the body it infects a certain type of lymphocyte. It enters the DNA in the nucleus and uses it to make many copies of its genetic material. The result is that the lymphocyte fills up with new virus particles. These 'bud' off from the surface to infect other cells (Figure 10.3.2).

Anti-retroviral drugs used to treat HIV disrupt the way the genetic material of the virus is copied. These drugs have side effects, such as nausea, fever, diarrhoea, skin rashes and mood swings.

Treatment of mothers who have HIV has reduced the transmission of the virus to babies. If this is not done, babies are often born with the infection and need a lifetime of treatment.

Controlling the spread of HIV

One effective way to control the spread of HIV is the use of condoms during sex. Other barrier methods of contraception, such as the diaphragm or cap, are not effective as there is still contact between semen and vaginal fluids.

SUMMARY QUESTIONS

1 Describe the transmission, treatment and control of gonorrhoea.

2 Distinguish between HIV and AIDS.

3 Describe three different ways in which HIV is transmitted.

4 Explain the steps that can be taken to reduce the number of new cases of HIV infection.

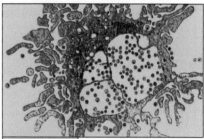

Figure 10.3.2 This lymphocyte is full of HIV particles which are released to infect many other lymphocytes.

KEY POINTS

1 Gonorrhoea is caused by a bacterium; the causative agent of HIV/AIDS is the human immunodeficiency virus (HIV). They are examples of sexually transmitted infections (STIs).

2 Gonorrhoea may cause sterility; it is treated with a course of antibiotics.

3 HIV causes a decrease in the number of lymphocytes making those infected at high risk of opportunistic infections, such as TB, and cancers.

4 HIV is transmitted during unprotected sex, blood-to-blood contact, breast feeding and at birth.

5 Anti-retroviral drugs are used to treat HIV.

6 Preventing the spread of HIV is by health awareness campaigns, especially encouraging men to use condoms.

Much of the information you will find about disease is in the form of tables and charts. You need to know how to make these and how to use them by analysing and interpreting the information that they present. Try drawing all of the graphs in this section, and then check your answers with those on the CD. There you will find advice on selecting and drawing the correct graphs for presentation of data – not only on disease but other topics as well. You may need to refer to other units in this book for help with some of the answers to these questions.

1 *Aedes aegypti* is the vector of several diseases including dengue fever.

   a   Explain what is meant by the term *vector* in the context of pathogenic diseases.   *(2)*

   Figure 1 shows two stages, A and B, in the life cycle of *Aedes aegypti*.

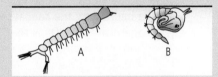

Figure 1

   b   i   Name the stages and state their habitat.   *(2)*

      ii   Outline what happens in the life cycle between stages A and B.   *(3)*

      iii   Explain how these two stages are controlled.   *(4)*

Figure 2 shows the number of new cases of dengue fever reported in the city of Ribeirão Preto, São Paulo State, Brazil between 2000 and 2009.

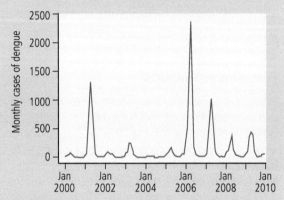

Figure 2

   c   i   Describe the pattern of outbreaks of dengue fever shown in Figure 2.   *(4)*

      ii   Suggest an explanation for the pattern you have described.   *(3)*

   d   i   Explain why data on pathogenic diseases, such as that shown in Figure 2, may not be accurate.   *(2)*

      ii   Suggest steps that health authorities should take to reduce the number of people infected during an outbreak of dengue.   *(4)*

   e   Name another disease that is transmitted by *Aedes aegypti*.   *(1)*

Total 25 marks

2 a State *three* ways in which HIV is transmitted. (3)

Table 1 shows the number of new reported cases of HIV infection in the Caribbean region between 1982 and 2010.

b Present the data for the total number of cases in Table 1 as a line graph. (5)

c Use Table 1 and your line graph to describe the progress of the HIV/AIDS epidemic in the Caribbean. (4)

d Scientists state that the data for the HIV/AIDS epidemic in the Caribbean shows that transmission in the region is mainly between males and females rather than between males. How does the data in Table 1 support this? (2)

Sub-Saharan Africa has the highest proportion of the population living with HIV infection. The Caribbean region has the second highest percentage of the population living with HIV.

Table 2 shows data on HIV/AIDS for seven Caribbean countries. All data are estimates.

e **i** Calculate the percentage of people in each country that live with HIV. (1)

ii Present the results of your calculations as a bar chart. (5)

iii Explain why it is important to show the percentage of the population rather than the numbers. (2)

The number of new cases of HIV infection and the number of deaths from AIDS in many part of the world may be decreasing.

f Suggest why this may be happening. (3)

Total 25 marks

Table 1

Year	Gender			
	male	female	not known	Total
1982	0	0	0	0
1984	0	2	0	2
1986	238	84	0	322
1988	370	161	34	565
1990	755	469	76	1300
1992	1020	661	134	1815
1994	1095	735	220	2050
1996	1198	866	274	2338
1998	1219	966	305	2490
2000	1572	1205	309	3086
2002	1817	1484	96	3397
2004	1670	1495	66	3231
2006	1865	1779	479	4123
2008	1815	1789	26	3630
2010	507	570	45	1122

Table 2

Country	Population (2012)	Number of people living with HIV/AIDS (2009)	Number of reported new HIV infections (for 2009 unless indicated)	Number of deaths from HIV/AIDS (for 2009 unless indicated)
Barbados	280 000	3360	400 (2010)	30 (2010)
Belize	330 000	7590	150	250
Cuba	11 000 000	11 000	600	< 100
Haiti	9 800 000	186 200	10 000	7100
Guyana	740 000	8880	300	200
Jamaica	2 900 000	52 200	2000	1200
Suriname	550 000	5500	200	< 200
Trinidad and Tobago	1 200 000	18 000	1077 (2011)	500

Data from Indexmundi.com

Further practice questions and examples can be found on the accompanying CD.

Nucleus and chromosomes

The nucleus controls the activities of cells. Contained within the nucleus are **chromosomes.** These are thread-like structures made from **deoxyribonucleic acid** (DNA) and proteins, known as **histones**. Each chromosome has one very long molecule of DNA wound around the histones as you can see in Figure 11.1.1. Each molecule of DNA can be up to 50 mm long.

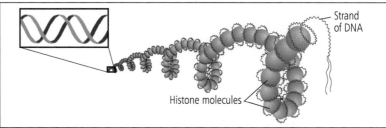

Strand of DNA

Histone molecules

| **Figure 11.1.1** | DNA in each chromosome is packed around histone molecules. The DNA is the genetic material; the histones provide structural support. |

Each organism has a certain number of chromosomes in each nucleus. The number is not associated with the complexity of the organism. Humans have 46 in each nucleus of body cells; the record is held by a fern, which has over a thousand chromosomes in each nucleus.

Figure 11.1.2 shows that the chromosomes can be sorted into pairs based on their size and shape. In the photograph a man's chromosomes have been sorted into 22 **homologous pairs** and the sex chromosomes, X and Y. A pair of chromosomes is homologous because the two chromosomes are the same size and shape and have the same genes. Chromosomes X and Y are not homologous as they are different sizes and shapes. The chromosomes are copies of those that were in the zygote when he was conceived. One chromosome in each pair was inherited from his father and the other from his mother.

Life cycles

Chromosome numbers do not remain constant throughout the life cycle of sexually reproducing organisms (Figure 11.1.3). The number of chromosomes in the gametes is called the **haploid number** (*n* for short). The number in a zygote and in cells derived from the zygote is the **diploid number** *(2n)*. In humans, $n = 23$ and $2n = 46$.

| **Figure 11.1.2** | A research worker studies images of human chromosomes, arranging them into homologous pairs. |

DID YOU KNOW?

Not all the DNA is in the nucleus. There are small loops of DNA in mitochondria and chloroplasts that have genes for these cell structures. Scientists are using this DNA to identify species – a process known as 'barcoding'.

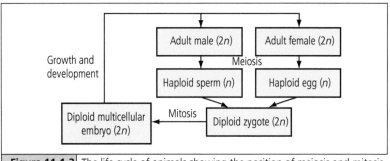

Figure 11.1.3 The life cycle of animals showing the position of meiosis and mitosis

Genes and alleles

The length of DNA in a chromosome is divided into segments known as **genes**. Each gene is an instruction for assembling amino acids to make a specific protein, such as catalase or amylase (see 5.4). DNA is composed of four bases: adenine, thymine, guanine and cytosine, usually abbreviated to A, T, G and C. A sequence of these bases codes for a sequence of amino acids. There are 20 different amino acids that are used to make proteins. Cells 'read' the four bases in groups of three. Each group of three bases (e.g. ATC) codes for one of the types of amino acid (Figure 11.1.4).

The sequence of bases in DNA can change. Such a change to DNA is a **gene mutation** and this can affect the sequence of amino acids in a protein. Sometimes the changes are very significant and change the protein so it does not function, or functions in a different way. This change to the protein may be life-threatening, as you will see in 11.6. In other cases the changes are beneficial, as you will see in Unit 12. The different forms of a gene are known as **alleles**. In some cases there are two alleles for a gene; some genes within a species have many alleles, but each diploid organism can only have two of them.

LINK

Question 7 on page 168 shows the chromosomes of a female muntjac deer. Make sure that you know what to look for when identifying pairs of homologous chromosomes. Also see 11.7 for more about the sex chromosomes.

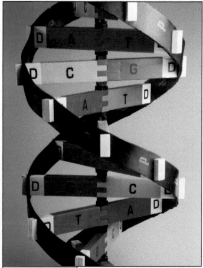

Figure 11.1.4 This model shows a very small part of DNA. Note the double helix and the four bases, A, T, C and G, which together make up the genetic code. The letter D stands for the sugar that is part of the DNA molecule.

KEY POINTS

1 Chromosomes are made of the nucleic acid DNA and histone proteins; they are located in cell nuclei. DNA is the genetic material that codes for the synthesis of proteins from amino acids.

2 DNA is passed from generation to generation in gametes and is the material of inheritance.

3 Homologous chromosomes are the same size and shape and have the same genes.

4 Diploid cells have two of each type of chromosome; haploid cells have one of each type.

5 A gene is a length of DNA that codes for a specific protein; an allele is a different form of a gene that codes for the same protein, but in a different way.

6 A mutation is a change to the sequence of bases in DNA that code for the sequence of amino acids in proteins.

SUMMARY QUESTIONS

1 Arrange these structures by size, smallest to largest: histone, nucleus, gene, chromosome and cell.

2 Explain the difference between each of the following pairs: chromosome and gene; gene and allele; haploid and diploid; amino acid and protein.

3 State the number of chromosomes in the haploid nuclei of all humans.

4 Explain what happens to DNA when there is a mutation.

Mitosis

At the end of this topic you should be able to:

- define the following terms: *cell division*, *nuclear division* and *mitosis*
- outline the events that occur during mitosis
- state that mitosis maintains the number of chromosomes
- state the role of mitosis in growth, replacement of cells, tissue repair and asexual reproduction.

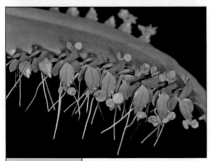

Figure 11.2.1 An example of asexual reproduction: the Mexican hat plant produces large numbers of plantlets from its leaves.

Figure 11.2.2 These sugar cane cuttings are all genetically identical and will give a uniform crop when harvested. Fields of sugar cane are a monoculture, which are at risk of all being wiped out by the same disease.

A cell, such as a zygote, cannot grow by getting larger because its surface area to volume ratio would *decrease* and it would not get enough oxygen to sustain itself. Therefore for an organism to grow larger, **cell division** occurs and each cell divides into two. Before this can happen, there is a **nuclear division.** The nucleus divides by **mitosis**, so that each new cell has the genetic information it needs to function.

Before mitosis

Before a cell divides, new copies of the genetic information in the DNA of each chromosome must be made. This happens before the nucleus divides. During copying, the DNA in the chromosomes is uncoiled and arranged very loosely in the nucleus. After copying, each chromosome consists of two copies of all DNA material. As mitosis begins, the DNA coils up tightly. Each chromosome appears as a double-stranded structure. The two genetically identical strands are **chromatids**. The process of copying DNA is **replication**.

During mitosis

Figure 11.2.3 shows what happens to four chromosomes as the nucleus divides during mitosis. Human cells have 46 chromosomes, so what you see in the diagram happens to all 46 chromosomes each time a human cell divides like this.

As a result of mitosis each daughter cell has the same number of chromosomes as the original parent cell. As the DNA in the chromosomes is copied by a reliable system they are genetically identical to one another and to the parent cell.

Mitosis occurs in:

- Growth – this starts with the first division of the zygote and then throughout the body of a plant or animal embryo; later it is restricted to certain places, such as meristems in plants and the growth regions in long bones (see 7.4 and 9.1).
- Tissue and wound repair – for example, stem cells at the base of the epidermis divide to repair wounds in the skin (see 8.8).
- Replacement of cells – cells wear out and die, such as red blood cells, which only live for a short time as they do not have a nucleus and cannot divide (see Table 7.4.1).
- Asexual reproduction – occurs in fungi and in plants, but is rare in the animal kingdom. All the organisms produced by asexual reproduction from one individual are genetically identical and form a clone. Identical twins are a clone as they are formed from the same embryo that splits into two. The plantlets that are produced on the leaves of the Mexican hat plant, *Bryophyllum*, by **vegetative reproduction** are a clone (see Figure 11.2.1).

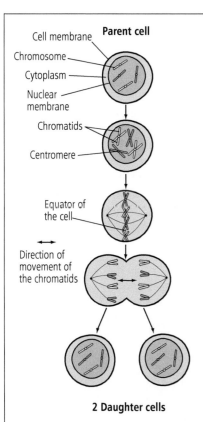

Parent cell

- Cell membrane
- Chromosome
- Cytoplasm
- Nuclear membrane

- Chromatids
- Centromere

- Equator of the cell

← → Direction of movement of the chromatids

2 Daughter cells

1 The chromosomes shorten and thicken; they can be seen under a light microscope.

2 Due to replication, each chromosome is double stranded with two genetically identical chromatids.

3 The double-stranded chromosomes line-up in the middle (equator) of the cell. The membrane around the nucleus has disintegrated.

4 The chromatids separate to form single-stranded chromosomes. These move to opposite poles of the cell.

5 The single-stranded chromosomes are now in the daughter nuclei and the cytoplasm of the original cell has divided to form two daughter cells.

Figure 11.2.3 | Mitosis in an animal cell

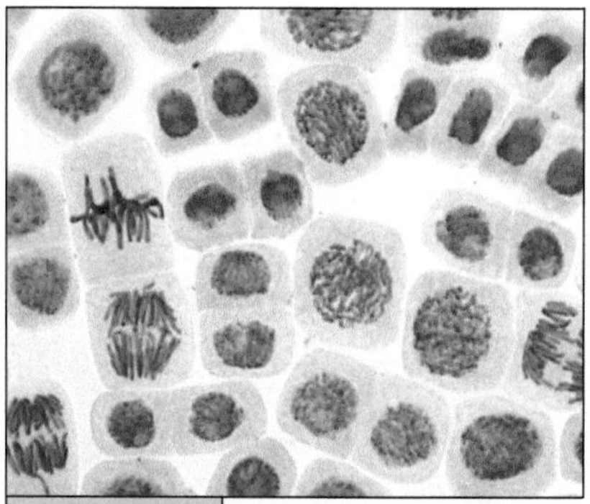

Figure 11.2.4 In this photograph of a growing region of a root tip, you can see the different stages of mitosis that are drawn in Figure 11.2.3 (× 170).

LINK

See 10.2 and 12.4 for the consequences of having crops, such as sugar cane and bananas, which are genetically uniform with little variation.

KEY POINTS

1 When a cell reaches a certain size it divides into two by cell division; nuclear division by mitosis occurs before the cytoplasm divides.

2 Mitosis is a type of nuclear division, which forms two genetically identical nuclei.

3 The daughter nuclei always have the same number of chromosomes as the parent nucleus.

4 Mitosis occurs in growth, asexual reproduction, repair of tissues and replacement of cells.

5 Crops that are produced by vegetative reproduction are genetically identical and at risk of being wiped out by disease.

SUMMARY QUESTIONS

1 Explain what is meant by: *chromosome*, *chromatid*, *mitosis* and *cell division*.

2 a Describe what happens inside a cell *before* it can divide by mitosis.

  b Describe what happens to a chromosome *during* mitosis.

  c Describe what happens to a cell *after* mitosis is complete.

3 Make models of chromosomes using modelling clay, pipe cleaners or lengths of wool or string. Use your models to show what happens to chromosomes when cells divide by mitosis.

4 Explain why:

  a Human red blood cells do not live very long and why they cannot divide.

  b The cells in Figure 11.2.4 must be plant cells.

5 Suggest why all the individuals in a clone are genetically identical but may not look alike.

Meiosis – the process

At the end of this topic you should be able to:

- define the term *meiosis*
- explain the importance of meiosis in halving the chromosome number and generating variation
- describe the movement of homologous chromosomes and chromatids during meiosis
- explain the role of meiosis in sexual reproduction
- state when meiosis occurs in flowering plant and animal life cycles.

If human gametes were produced by mitosis it would mean that in every generation the number of chromosomes would double when fertilisation occurs. Since the number of chromosomes in humans remains the same (at 46), in every generation there must be a different type of nuclear division involved in the production of gametes, which halves the number of chromosomes. **Meiosis** does this and also generates variation among the gametes, so the nuclei in the daughter cells are genetically different from the parent cell and from each other.

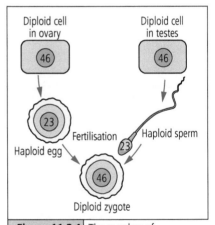

Figure 11.3.1 The number of chromosomes halves during the formation of gametes in humans and is restored to the diploid number at fertilisation.

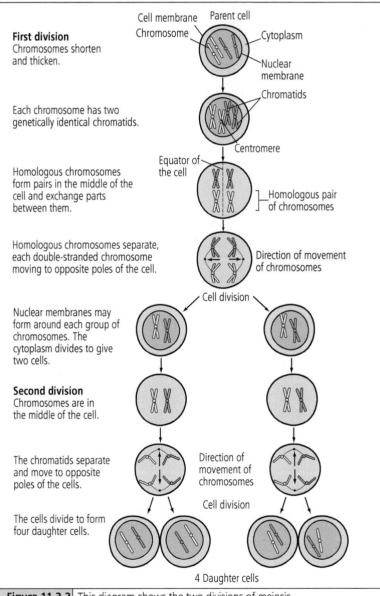

First division
Chromosomes shorten and thicken.

Each chromosome has two genetically identical chromatids.

Homologous chromosomes form pairs in the middle of the cell and exchange parts between them.

Homologous chromosomes separate, each double-stranded chromosome moving to opposite poles of the cell.

Nuclear membranes may form around each group of chromosomes. The cytoplasm divides to give two cells.

Second division
Chromosomes are in the middle of the cell.

The chromatids separate and move to opposite poles of the cells.

The cells divide to form four daughter cells.

Figure 11.3.2 This diagram shows the two divisions of meiosis

Figure 11.3.2 shows what happens to two pairs of chromosomes during meiosis. There are two divisions of the cell to give four cells. In the diagram, each of these has two chromosomes so the number has been halved. Imagine this happening within a cell with 46 chromosomes to give four haploid cells, each containing 23 chromosomes. In the testis each will develop into a sperm cell. In the ovary, three of the cells die to leave one large haploid cell – the egg cell.

In meiosis the daughter cells are not identical. They are genetically different and this contributes to genetic variation which allows organisms to evolve in response to changing environments.

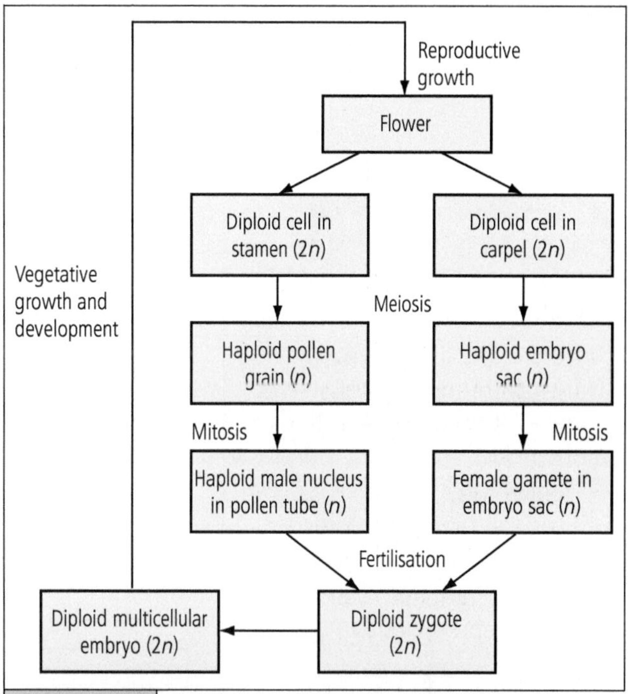

Life cycle of flowering plants

This differs from that of animals. In animals, meiosis occurs in the production of gametes (see Figure 11.1.3). In flowering plants, meiosis results in pollen grains and embryo sacs. These both divide further by mitosis to give the male and female gametes, respectively. Anthers contain many diploid cells that divide by meiosis to produce pollen grains, which are haploid. In the developing ovule one diploid cell divides by meiosis to produce four haploid cells. One of these develops to form a haploid embryo sac. The other three cells die. The embryo sac then divides by mitosis to form several cells, one of which is the female gamete. At fertilisation a haploid nucleus from the pollen tube fuses with a haploid female gamete in the embryo sac within the ovule (Figure 11.3.3).

Figure 11.3.3 Meiosis occurs in flowering plants in the production of pollen grains and embryo sacs. Pollen grains are released, embryo sacs remain in the ovule inside the ovary.

SUMMARY QUESTIONS

1 How many chromosomes are there in the following human cells:

    a a cell from the lining of an alveolus, **b** an egg cell, **c** a sperm cell, **d** a zygote, **e** a red blood cell?

2 a State the products of meiosis in animals and flowering plants.

    b Each leaf cell of an onion has 16 chromosomes; what are the chromosome numbers in:

       i a pollen grain, **ii** a root tip cell, **iii** a nucleus in an embryo sac, **iv** a xylem vessel?

3 a State *three* ways in which meiosis differs from mitosis.

    b Explain the advantages of genetic variation among gametes.

4 Use models of chromosomes to show what happens during the two divisions of meiosis.

KEY POINTS

1 Meiosis produces nuclei that have half the number of chromosomes as the parent nucleus. The number of chromosomes in daughter nuclei is the haploid number.

2 Haploid gametes fuse together to form a zygote that has the diploid number.

3 There are two divisions in meiosis. Homologous chromosomes pair in the first division and then separate. In the second division the chromatids of each chromosome separate.

4 In animals, meiosis produces haploid gametes; in flowering plants, pollen grains and embryo sacs are the products.

STUDY FOCUS

Make some models of homologous chromosomes to understand what happens during meiosis to introduce variation. Start with one pair to show what happens to them during meiosis (see 11.3) and crossing over (Figure 11.4.2) and then use two pairs to model random assortment (Figure 11.4.1).

Random assortment of chromosomes

One way in which meiosis generates the variation between gametes is to 'shuffle' the pairs of chromosomes. Figure 11.4.1 shows two ways in which two pairs of homologous chromosomes are arranged during the first division of meiosis. The different pairs are arranged randomly across the middle of the cell. Now imagine this happening with 23 pairs of chromosomes. There are many possible random arrangements of the 23 pairs, giving many mixtures of chromosomes to pass on to the next generation. The random arrangement is known as **random assortment** – think about sorting out the homologous chromosomes in a random fashion on either side of an imaginary plate across the middle of the cell. It is a good idea to model this as suggested in Summary question 2.

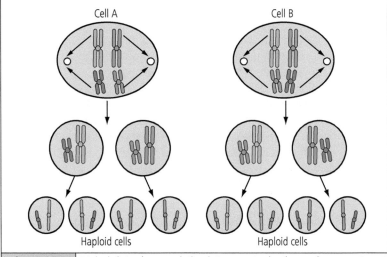

Figure 11.4.1 Meiosis introduces variation into gametes by the random assortment of homologous chromosomes – see how the nuclei produced from parent cell A differ from those from parent cell B.

For any cell about to divide by meiosis there is a 50% chance that the chromosome will be arranged as in cell A and 50% as in cell B. The advantage of random assortment is that gametes from one adult organism contain different combinations of chromosomes. This means that gametes produced by that organism have different combinations of alleles of all the genes.

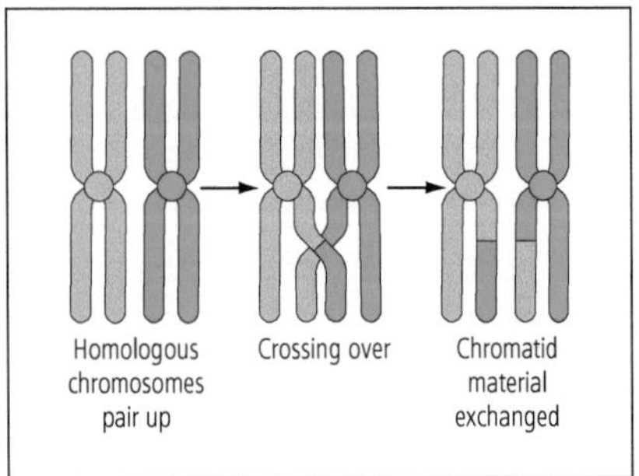

Crossing over

During meiosis, homologous chromosomes exchange parts between them as you can see in Figure 11.4.2. This process, known as **crossing over**, also introduces variation.

Variation in the genetic material in the gametes results from these two processes that occur in meiosis. Few, if any, gametes produced

Homologous chromosomes pair up | Crossing over | Chromatid material exchanged

Figure 11.4.2 Crossing over occurs when homologous chromosomes are paired together during the first division of meiosis.

during an organism's lifetime are genetically exactly the same. Further variation is caused at fertilisation. The choice of mate is often random and the gametes fuse at random. These other two factors introduce the opportunity for even more variation. The advantage of all this variation is to increase chances of survival of the next generation in a changing environment. See 12.2 and 12.3 for more about this.

Some species of flowering plant reproduce by self-pollination, which leads to self-fertilisation. Even though the male and female gametes have come from the same individual, meiosis introduces some limited variation so that the next generation of a self-pollinating plant are not exactly the same genetically. Remember that in asexual reproduction there is *no* meiosis and *no* fusion of gametes, so all the offspring are genetically identical, forming a clone (see 9.2 and 11.2).

Comparison of mitosis and meiosis

Table 11.4.1 summarises the differences between mitosis and meiosis.

Table 11.4.1 The differences between mitosis and meiosis

Feature	Mitosis	Meiosis
Number of divisions of the nucleus	1	2
Pairing of homologous chromosomes	No	Yes
Crossing over	No	Yes
Number of daughter nuclei produced	2	4
Genotypes of daughter nuclei	Identical to the parent nucleus and to each other	All are different from each other and to the parent nucleus
Roles in organisms	Growth, replacement of cells and tissues, wound repair, asexual reproduction	Production of gametes in animals; production of pollen grains and embryo sacs in flowering plants
Chromosome numbers of daughter nuclei	Same as the parent nucleus	Half the number as the parent nucleus

KEY POINTS

1 Gametes differ from each other as they have different combinations of chromosomes as a result of the random assortment of homologous pairs in the first division of meiosis.

2 Crossing over occurs in meiosis and involves the swapping of DNA between chromosomes in a homologous pair.

3 Mitosis and meiosis are the two different types of nuclear division; meiosis halves the chromosome number and generates variation; nuclei produced by mitosis are genetically identical.

SUMMARY QUESTIONS

1 a State *three* ways in which meiosis differs from mitosis.

b Explain the advantages of genetic variation among gametes.

2 Use models of chromosomes to show how variation can be generated in meiosis by the random arrangements of homologous chromosomes in the first division of meiosis.

3 a Use Figure 11.3.2 to make a drawing of the stages of meiosis, but include crossing over between a homologous pair.

b Explain the advantage of crossing over.

Figure 11.5.1 Fruit flies are small, easy to keep, mate easily, produce many offspring and have short life spans. The only disadvantage for researchers is that they fly!

EXAM TIP

Notice that we always show the dominant allele as a capital letter and the recessive allele as a small letter. Never use different letters for the alleles of the same gene.

Genetics is the study of inheritance of genes. Each gene controls a characteristic of an organism. We have learnt a lot about genetics from studying the fruit fly. **Monohybrid inheritance** concerns the inheritance of a single characteristic, such as the wing length of fruit flies which determines their ability to fly.

The **phenotype** is the appearance of an individual. It refers to all the aspects of an organism's biology except its genes. It includes features we can see, such as wings, and features that we cannot see, such as blood groups in humans. We often use the term to apply to one feature of an organism, for example wing length in fruit flies (Figure 11.5.1).

Figure 11.5.2 shows the inheritance of wing length in fruit flies. Almost all flies have long wings, but there are some that have very short wings and are unable to fly. The gene for wings therefore has two alleles (see 11.1 to make sure you know the difference between a gene and an allele).

A male with long wings is crossed with a female with short wings and then males and females of the next generation are crossed amongst themselves.

Parental generation	**First generation (F₁)** – large numbers of males and females all with long wings	**Second generation (F₂)** – large numbers of flies of both sexes with long wings and smaller number of flies with short wings
Male Female	F₁ flies were allowed to interbreed	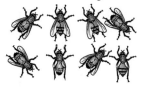

Figure 11.5.2 The recessive feature does not appear in the first generation.

You can see that all the fruit flies in the first generation have long wings. This shows that long wing is the **dominant trait** and short wing is the **recessive trait**. From the results in the second generation, we can see that the recessive trait reappears so the allele for short wing has been passed on, but did not affect the wings of the flies in the first generation.

The **genotype** is the genetic composition of an organism. The term is usually used to refer to the alleles of the genes being investigated. In fruit flies, there is a gene that controls wing length. There are two alleles of this gene and they are represented in a genotype by letters: **W** for the allele for long wings, and **w** for the allele for short wings.

The parental generation in this investigation are pure breeding flies as they come from a stock of fruit flies that had either long wings or short wings for many generations. As a result we know the long-winged flies only have the allele, **W**, and short-winged flies only have the allele, **w**. Genetic diagrams are drawn to explain how the alleles are inherited.

Parental phenotypes	Male long wing	$\times$	Female short wing
Parental genotypes	WW		ww
Parental gametes	(W)	+	(w)
F_1 genotype		Ww	
F_1 phenotype		All long wing	
F_1 phenotypes	Long wing	$\times$	Long wing
F_1 genotypes	Ww		Ww
F_1 gametes	(W),(w)	+	(W),(w)

		Male gametes	
		(W)	(w)
Female gametes	(W)	WW	Ww
	(w)	Ww	ww

F_2 genotypes and phenotypes	WW long wing	2Ww long wing	ww short wing

F_2 phenotypic ratio: 3 long wing : 1 short wing

EXAM TIP

When you write out genetic diagrams like this one, make them simple – homozygous organisms only make gametes of one genotype so only write this once in the diagram. Always use a grid, called a Punnett square, to show all the possible genotypes. When you have read this section, try question 7c on page 169.

If an organism has two identical alleles it is **homozygous** for the gene concerned. If the alleles are both dominant, then it is homozygous dominant, if they are recessive then it is homozygous recessive. If the two alleles are different then it is **heterozygous**. If the males and females in the first generation are homozygous, then the first generation is known as the F_1 **generation**, and the second generation is the F_2 **generation**.

Amongst the F_2 generation ¼ (or 25%) are homozygous dominant; ½ (or 50%) are heterozygous; ¼ (or 25%) are homozygous recessive. Since the phenotypes of **WW** and **Ww** are the same, ¾ of the F_2 flies have long wings and ¼ have short wings. This can also be written as a ratio, 3 long wing: 1 short wing.

KEY POINTS

Follow these points when writing genetic diagrams.

1 Genotypes of organisms have two alleles as they are diploid (have two sets of chromosomes).

2 Genotypes of gametes (sperm and eggs) have one allele as they are haploid (have one set of chromosomes). This is because they are produced by meiosis which halves the chromosome number.

3 Always use a grid to show all the possible combinations of alleles that can occur at fertilisation.

4 Write out the genotypes and make sure that you show clearly the phenotypes that they will have.

5 If the males and females in the first generation are homozygous, then the first generation is known as the F_1 generation, and the second generation is the F_2 generation.

SUMMARY QUESTIONS

1 Fruit flies with grey bodies are crossed with fruit flies with ebony bodies. All the offspring had grey bodies. When these offspring were crossed among themselves, ¼ of the flies in the next generation had ebony bodies and the rest were grey. Using the symbols **G** for the allele for grey body and **g** for the allele for ebony body, draw a genetic diagram to explain this result.

2 A fruit fly with a grey body was crossed with a fruit fly with a black body; 50% of the offspring had grey bodies and 50% had black bodies.

3 Define the terms *homozygous*, *heterozygous*, F_1 and F_2.

4 Suggest why fruit flies make good animals for studying genetics.

Inheritance

At the end of this topic you should be able to:

- describe the effects of mutations
- define *codominance*
- interpret pedigree charts
- state the causes and explain the inheritance of albinism and sickle cell anaemia

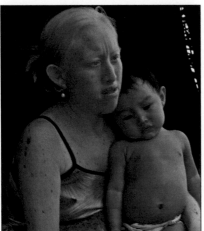

Figure 11.6.1 An albino Kuna Indian woman and her normally pigmented child. The Kuna Indians live along the eastern Caribbean coast of Panama. They have the highest percentage of people with albinism in the world.

STUDY FOCUS

Look very carefully at the pedigree chart and work out the genotypes of as many people as you can. If you cannot be absolutely sure whether someone's genotype is homozygous dominant or heterozygous, then you can write A- where the dash stands for a dominant allele *or* a recessive allele.

Mutations affect the ways genes work. In some cases, there is so much change to the gene that it does not code for any protein at all. In others, the change to the DNA is quite small and a protein is produced but it functions in a different way.

Albinism

People with albinism cannot make the pigment, melanin, which is in the skin and the iris of the eye. Several enzymes are needed to make this pigment and it is a mutation in a gene that codes for one of these enzymes that is the cause of the condition. People who are albino are homozygous recessive, **aa**. People who are homozygous dominant, **AA**, or heterozygous, **Aa**, have the allele that codes for the functioning enzyme and so melanin is produced. This means that they have normal pigmentation. People with albinism are at greater risk of sunburn, skin cancer and damage to the eyes than people with normal pigmentation.

A family with albinism is shown in this pedigree chart.

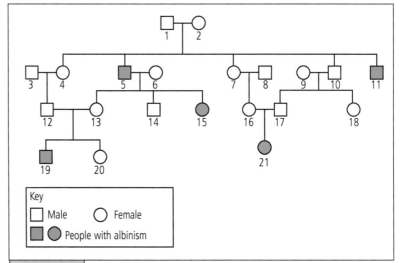

Figure 11.6.2 Several people in this family have albinism. Look carefully at the key.

Codominance

The examples that we have looked at involve alleles that are recessive. The recessive allele is not expressed in the phenotype of individuals with the heterozygous genotype. Sometimes, genetic diseases can be caused by dominant alleles, an example is **Huntington's disease** (see question 10 on the CD). Other examples arise when neither allele is dominant, and *both* alleles are expressed, so that the phenotype is a mixture of the effects of each allele.

This condition is known as **codominance** and the alleles are called **codominant alleles**. The Four o'clock plant can have red flowers or white flowers. Flower colour is determined by one gene. However, if you cross homozygous red-flowered plants with homozygous white-flowered plants, the offspring are all pink. Both alleles are expressed to give pink – an intermediate colour. Codominant alleles are not written as capital and lower case letters – instead they are usually written as superscripts of the letter chosen to represent the gene, e.g. C^R for red and C^W for white (see question 7di on page 169 for an example).

The ABO blood group system is a human example of codominance. There is more about codominance in 12.1.

Figure 11.6.3 Codominance is visible in these flowers of the Four o'clock plant.

Sickle cell anaemia (SCA)

People with **sickle cell anaemia** have red blood cells in the shape of a sickle. The abnormal haemoglobin makes it difficult for the red blood cells to carry oxygen. SCA is common in West and East Africa, and is found in parts of Asia and in North and South America, including the Caribbean. People who have the genotype **ss** have the symptoms of the disorder. People who are heterozygous, **Ss**, have both the normal and abnormal forms of haemoglobin. They rarely have a problem with transport of oxygen, but they are resistant to malaria. The allele is common among people from areas where malaria is common or used to be common, such as parts of the Caribbean and the USA. As both forms of haemoglobin are made by people with the genotype **Ss,** the two alleles are codominant.

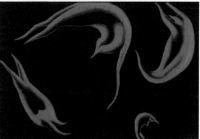

Figure 11.6.4 Red blood cells from a person with sickle cell anaemia

LINK

You can find out about the inheritance of SCA by writing a genetic diagram in answer to question 8 on the CD. Genetic (DNA) tests exist for the three human conditions described in this section. This means that it is possible for people to know if they carry the mutant allele or not.

KEY POINTS

1 Genes determine the sequence of amino acids in each protein. If the sequence changes as a result of mutation then the protein functions in a different way, or not at all.

2 Albinism is the result of a mutation in one of the genes for the production of skin pigment. Albinism is a recessive trait and is present from birth.

3 Codominance occurs where two alleles of a gene are both expressed with neither being dominant or recessive. The phenotype of heterozygous organisms is intermediate between organisms with the homozygous genotypes.

4 Sickle cell anaemia is caused by a mutation in the gene that codes for haemoglobin. Both the normal allele and the mutant allele are active in people who are heterozygous to give the sickle cell trait, which gives a resistance to malaria.

SUMMARY QUESTIONS

1 State the health risks of being very fair skinned or an albino.

2 Use the examples described here to distinguish between the following pairs of terms *gene* and *allele*, *genotype* and *phenotype*, *homozygous* and *heterozygous*, *dominant* and *recessive*.

3 State the genotype of the Kuna woman and her child in Figure 11.6.1. Suggest the two possible genotypes of the child's father.

4 a State the genotypes of the people in the family tree in Figure 11.6.2.

  b What is the probability that the next child of 16 and 17 will have albinism? Draw a genetic diagram to explain your answer.

Sex determination and sex linkage

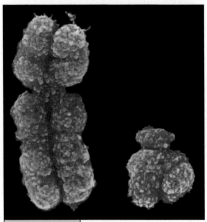

Figure 11.7.1 An X and a Y chromosome viewed in an electron microscope (× 12 000)

EXAM TIP

Figure 11.7.2 shows only the inheritance of the sex chromosomes, X and Y. Do not forget that each of the gametes (egg and sperm) contain 22 other chromosomes to give the haploid number of 23.

Sex determination

Your chromosomes determine which sex you are. In humans there are 46 chromosomes and these occur in 23 pairs. In females all 46 chromosomes can be matched together into pairs. Males have two chromosomes that are not alike. They are known as the X and Y chromosomes. Females have two X chromosomes and males have an X chromosome and a Y chromosome. The diagram shows how **sex chromosomes** in the gametes determine the sex of individuals.

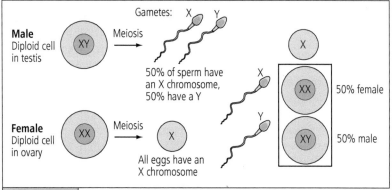

Figure 11.7.2 The inheritance of X and Y chromosomes determines whether we are male or female.

All egg cells contain an X chromosome. Half of the sperm contain an X chromosome and half of the sperm contain a Y chromosome. At fertilisation, an egg may fuse with either an X-bearing sperm or a Y-bearing sperm. There is an equal chance of the zygote inheriting XX or XY and the child being female or male because there are equal numbers of X-bearing sperm and Y-bearing sperm (Figure 11.7.2).

The Y chromosome has far fewer genes than the other chromosomes and far fewer than the X. One gene on the Y chromosome stimulates the development of testes in the embryo. If it is not present, or if it has mutated, then the body that develops is female.

Sex linkage

Genes located on the X chromosome are **sex-linked**. The X chromosome is a large chromosome with many genes. Most have nothing to do with the determining features associated with gender. There are genes involved with controlling vision and blood clotting. Males only have one copy of the genes that are on X chromosomes; if any of them are recessive, then the effect will be seen. Because women have two X chromosomes they are less affected by sex-linked recessive alleles and this is why sex-linked conditions are more common in boys than in girls. Women who are heterozygous and have a mutant allele of a gene on the X chromosome are **carriers**. Two examples are colour blindness and haemophilia.

Colour blindness

One of the genes on the X chromosome controls the ability to see red and green colours. There is a mutant allele of this gene which does not produce a protein necessary for colour vision. The allele is recessive, so any girl or woman who is heterozygous, **Rr**, has normal colour vision. Males only have one X chromosome so if they have inherited the allele **r** they will be colour-blind.

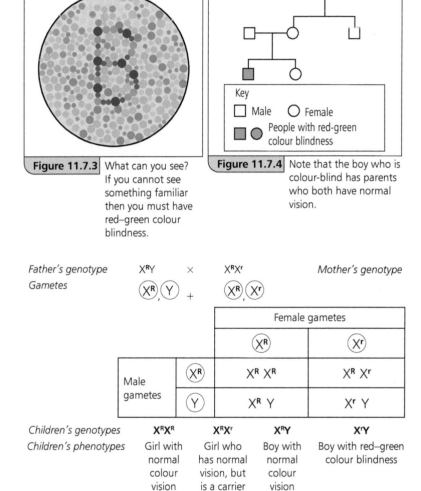

Figure 11.7.3 What can you see? If you cannot see something familiar then you must have red–green colour blindness.

Figure 11.7.4 Note that the boy who is colour-blind has parents who both have normal vision.

Key
☐ Male ○ Female
■ ● People with red-green colour blindness

		Female gametes	
		X^R	X^r
Male gametes	X^R	X^R X^R	X^R X^r
	Y	X^R Y	X^r Y

Father's genotype X^RY × X^RX^r *Mother's genotype*
Gametes (X^R),(Y) + (X^R),(X^r)

Children's genotypes **X^RX^R** **X^RX^r** **X^RY** **X^rY**
Children's phenotypes Girl with normal colour vision | Girl who has normal vision, but is a carrier | Boy with normal colour vision | Boy with red–green colour blindness

Haemophilia

Haemophilia is a disease in which the blood clots very slowly. It is a result of a mutation of the gene that codes for a blood clotting protein that is on the X chromosome. The mutant allele is recessive. A carrier of haemophilia is a woman who has the recessive allele, **h**. Her blood clots normally because she also has the dominant allele, **H**. It is rare for a woman to have haemophilia. This is because she would have to inherit the mutant allele from her father as well as from her mother. Historically, many haemophiliac men did not live long enough to have children. Successful treatment is now available, so a haemophiliac man may have a daughter with the genotype **HH**.

SUMMARY QUESTIONS

1 The ratio of males to females is about 1:1 with slightly more females than males in the population. Draw a genetic diagram to show why the ratio is 1:1 and suggest why there are slightly more females.

2 What is the probability of a woman who is a carrier of haemophilia having a child with the disease if her husband has normal blood clotting time? Draw a genetic diagram to explain your answer.

3 None of the conditions described in 11.6 are sex-linked. How can you tell the difference between a genetic condition that is sex-linked and one that is not?

LINK

Now try question 9, on the CD, to test your understanding of sex-linkage.

SECTION 1: Multiple-choice questions

1 Which of the following describes the cells formed by meiosis in humans?

  A They are genetically identical and they become gametes.

  B They are genetically identical and they become tissues.

  C They are not genetically identical and they become gametes.

  D They are not genetically identical and they become tissues.

2 In a species of plant, the allele for blue flowers (**B**) is dominant over the allele for white flowers (**b**). Two blue-flowered plants were crossed. There were 86 blue-flowered and 30 white-flowered offspring. What are the genotypes of the parents?

  A **BB** and **bb**

  B **BB** and **Bb**

  C **Bb** and **Bb**

  D **Bb** and **bb**

3 How does a haploid nucleus differ from a diploid nucleus of the same species?

  A It has different genes.

  B It has twice as many chromosomes.

  C It has half as many chromosomes.

  D It has twice as much DNA.

4 A short-haired cat was crossed with a long-haired cat. All the offspring had short hair. One of these offspring was crossed with another long-haired cat.

Which ratio of short-haired to long-haired cats would be expected?

  A 1 : 1

  B 1 : 2 : 1

  C 2 : 1

  D 3 : 1

5 One of the genes for blood clotting is on the X chromosome. People who do not have the dominant allele, **H**, have haemophilia in which blood is slow to clot.

Which of the following is the genotype of a carrier of haemophilia?

  A $X^H X^H$

  B $X^H X^h$

  C $X^h X^h$

  D $X^h Y$

6 What is an allele?

  A a length of DNA that codes for a gene

  B an alternative version of a gene

  C a thread of DNA made up of a string of genes

  D the genetic make-up of an organism

SECTION 2: Short answer questions

7 Each female Indian muntjac deer has a diploid number (2*n*) of 6. Figure 1 shows all the chromosomes of this species, labelled A to F, in a cell dividing by mitosis.

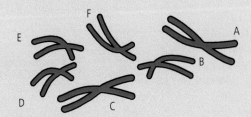

Figure 1

  a **i** Use the letters to identify the homologous pairs of chromosomes. *(1)*

     ii Describe in outline what will happen to the chromosomes after the stage visible in Figure 1. *(3)*

     iii State the number of chromosomes in the gametes of female Indian muntjac deer. *(1)*

b Figure 2 shows a diploid cell with four chromosomes. Copy and complete the diagram in Figure 2 to show the possible combinations of chromosomes in the gametes of this organism. *(3)*

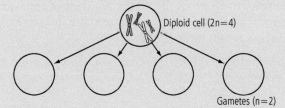

Figure 2

c A gene in fruit flies controls eye colour. The allele **R** gives red eyes and the allele **r** gives purple eyes. A researcher crossed homozygous red-eyed flies with homozygous purple-eyed flies (Cross **1**).

The offspring of Cross **1** were allowed to interbreed (Cross **2**). Further Crosses (**3** and **4**) were carried out with the offspring of Cross **1**.

Cross red eyes		Phenotype of the fruit flies		Ratio of red-eyed flies to purple-eyed flies
			purple eyes	
1	red-eyed × purple-eyed	✓	✗	1:0
2	red-eyed × red-eyed			
3	red-eyed × purple-eyed	✓	✓	
4	purple-eyed × purple-eyed			

i State the genotypes of the fruit flies used in Cross **1**. *(1)*

ii Copy and complete the table by indicating:
- the type of flies present in the offspring with a tick (✓) or a cross (✗)
- the ratio of red-eyed to purple-eyed flies. *(5)*

d The Four o'clock plant can have flowers of three different colours, red, white and pink (see Figure 11.6.3).

A student crossed some red-flowered plants with some white-flowered plants (Cross **1**). She collected the seeds and grew them. All of the plants that grew from these seeds had pink flowers.

i Using the symbols C^R for red and C^W for white, make a genetic diagram to explain this result. *(4)*

ii Explain how the result of Cross **1** shows that the alleles are codominant. *(1)*

The student then carried out three further crosses as follows:

Cross **2**: offspring of Cross **1** × offspring of Cross **1**

Cross **3**: offspring of Cross **1** × red-flowered plants

Cross **4**: offspring of Cross **1** × white-flowered plants

iii State the genotypes and phenotypes of the offspring of Crosses **2**, **3** and **4**, using the same symbols as in the genetic diagram in **d i**. *(3)*

e Explain the importance of meiosis in the life cycles of plants and animals. *(3)*

Total 25 marks

Further practice questions and examples can be found on the accompanying CD.

12 Variation and selection

12.1   Variation

LEARNING OUTCOMES

At the end of this topic you should be able to:

• define the terms *variation*, *continuous variation*, *discontinuous variation* and *species*

• distinguish between variation within a species and variation between species

• distinguish between continuous and discontinuous variation

• describe the causes of variation.

Look around at your friends and family and you will see how different we can be from each other. These differences are the variation that exists in our species. Domesticated animals and plants also show variation; for example, think about the different breeds of cats, dogs, cattle and chickens. If you look closely at wild animals and plants, you will also find variation within these species too.

Variation refers both to the differences that exist *within* species and to the differences *between* species. Here we will deal with variation within species.

Types of variation

The most widely known blood group system is the ABO system, which has four blood types: A, B, AB and O. The gene that controls the ABO system has three alleles, I^A, I^B and I^O. Alleles I^A and I^B are codominant, so people with the genotype $I^A I^B$ have the AB blood group. Allele I^O is recessive to the other two alleles.

Blood group is an example of **discontinuous variation**. People have a distinct blood group: there are no intermediates. Data on this type of variation is presented as bar charts as you can see in Figure 12.1.2.

Height and body mass are features that show **continuous variation**. If you measure heights, widths and masses you will find a range of measurements. The data do not fit into distinct groups; there are many intermediates between the two extremes at either end of the range. To present this data as a histogram you first have to divide the data into groups (Figure 12.1.3).

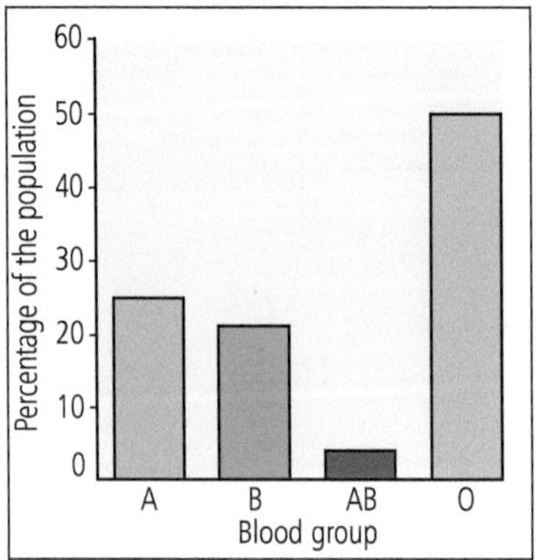

Figure 12.1.1 What differences can you see between these people?

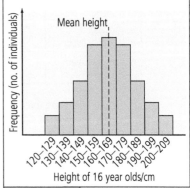

Figure 12.1.2 Blood groups in the Jamaican population

Figure 12.1.3 A histogram showing the normal variation in heights of 16 year olds. The mode is 160–169 cm.

STUDY FOCUS

We used the term *species* in Unit 1. This means a group of closely related organisms that are able to interbreed and produce fertile offspring. See 12.3 for more about this.

Both genes and the environment influence variation. Genes determine blood groups. Your blood group does not change during your lifetime as a result of where you live or your way of life. Features that show continuous variation, such as height, are influenced both by genes and by the environment. Your final height is determined both by the genes you inherited and by environmental factors, such as your food, exercise and illness. There are some long-term features that are the result of environmental influences alone, such as scars and the effects of diseases, such as polio (see Unit 10).

There are several causes of genetic variation:

- random arrangement of homologous chromosomes during meiosis (see Figure 11.4.1)
- exchange between homologous chromosomes when they cross over during meiosis (see Figure 11.4.2)
- alleles of all the genes that are inherited from genetically different parents
- random fusion of gametes at fertilisation
- gene mutation – when new genetic material is formed.

Mutation

There are two forms of mutation:

- **Chromosome mutation** is a change in the number or structure of chromosomes.
- **Gene mutations** occur by a copying error during the replication of DNA. This is the only way in which new alleles are formed.

Gene mutation occurs at random, but the rate at which mutations occur is increased by exposure to radiation and some chemicals, such as some in tobacco smoke. Ultraviolet radiation, X-rays and gamma rays are the most damaging. Mutations in body cells may affect the individual, for example they may lead to cancers. This happened after the atomic bombs were dropped in Japan in 1945 and the nuclear power station at Chernobyl in the Soviet Union exploded in 1986. Mutations that occur in gamete-forming cells, or in gametes themselves, are important in the long term as they can be inherited and provide new forms of variation.

Many gene mutations are harmful, but sometimes they can be useful and help organisms to survive in certain environments, as is the case with a mutation in the gene for haemoglobin (see 11.6 for information about the sickle cell trait).

Genetic variation is the raw material for natural selection.

KEY POINTS

1. Variation refers to the differences between species and to the differences between individuals within a species.
2. Discontinuous variation has distinct groups without any intermediates; in continuous variation there are many intermediates within a range between two extremes.
3. A gene mutation is a change in the DNA.
4. Genetic variation is important for the survival of species in changing environments.

LINK

Work through question 12 on page 181 to learn more about the inheritance of the ABO blood group. If you know your blood group, you probably know that it is also positive or negative. This is the Rhesus system, named after rhesus monkeys in which it was discovered.

STUDY FOCUS

Make a list of the environmental factors that influence the way children develop. Think of all the factors that affect the way people behave as well as how they grow.

SUMMARY QUESTIONS

1. The mean of the group of students is indicated in the histogram. What term is given to the most commonly occurring group?

2. Measure the height, foot length, length of index finger, or body mass of as many people as you can (at least 20). Present your results as a histogram.

3. Use examples to explain the difference between continuous and discontinuous variation.

4. a Explain the term *mutation*.
   b State two examples of mutation in humans.
   c Explain why genetic variation is important.
   d State three factors that increase the chances of mutation occurring.

Natural selection

At the end of this topic you should be able to:

- define the terms *natural selection*, *struggle for existence* and *adaptation*
- explain the importance of genetic variation
- use examples to describe how natural selection occurs.

STUDY FOCUS

The term *struggle for existence* does not mean that organisms fight each other to survive. The phrase refers to the difficulties that organisms have in obtaining food, water, shelter, evading predators and defending themselves against disease.

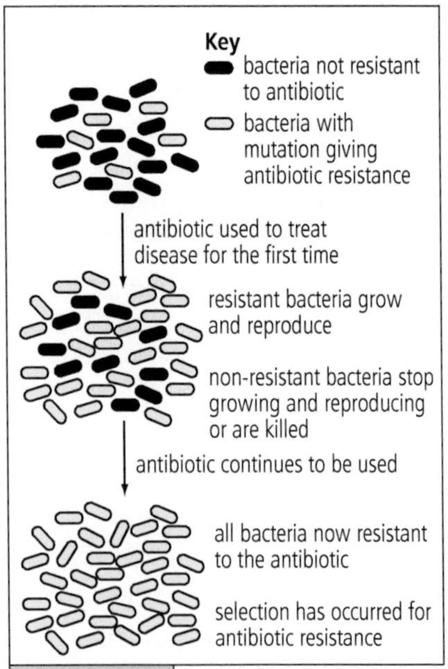

Key
- bacteria not resistant to antibiotic
- bacteria with mutation giving antibiotic resistance

antibiotic used to treat disease for the first time

resistant bacteria grow and reproduce

non-resistant bacteria stop growing and reproducing or are killed

antibiotic continues to be used

all bacteria now resistant to the antibiotic

selection has occurred for antibiotic resistance

Figure 12.2.1 Antibiotic resistance arises by mutation and is selected by our use of antibiotics.

Natural selection occurs when organisms are well adapted to their environment, have a greater chance to breed and pass on their alleles to the next generation than those that are less well adapted. Natural selection involves the following.

- Overproduction – each generation produces large numbers of offspring, far more than can survive in the environment. Populations of most organisms remain fairly stable from generation to generation because they are limited by environmental factors, such as:
  - Competition, where individual organisms compete for resources, such as food, water and space. Some will have better ways to obtain these resources than others.
  - Predation, where many individuals are eaten by predators. Grazing animals eat seedlings (primary consumers); tertiary consumers eat herbivores.
  - Disease, where many individuals are infected by pathogens and are killed or weakened by the diseases that they cause.
- Differential survival – the individuals that survive long enough to breed are good at obtaining resources from their environment, evading predation and withstanding disease. Less successful individuals die before reproducing, or only have small numbers of offspring.
- Reproduction and inheritance – organisms that are successful in the struggle for existence have a higher chance to breed and pass on the alleles for the features that have made them successful.
- Adaptation – organisms that survive are those suited best to the environment at that particular time.

If the environment does not change, natural selection maintains populations of organisms so they do not change much over time. Individuals at the extremes of the range of variation do not survive as they are not well adapted. For example, female sparrows with very long or very short wings do not survive to breed as they are often killed during stormy weather. However, when the environment changes, individuals with features that help them survive the changed conditions are at an advantage. They then compete successfully, survive, breed and pass on their alleles which become more common in the population. **Selective agents** are those aspects of the environment, such as predators, disease and competitors, that have these profound effects.

Genetic variation is described as the raw material for natural selection because it is responsible for all the different phenotypes in each generation. Environmental factors select for the most favourable phenotype in a particular situation. Mutation, meiosis and sexual reproduction ensure that there is genetic variation among individuals in each generation for natural selection to act on.

Human impact on natural selection

In these examples, humans are responsible for changing the environment by introducing antibiotics, pesticides or pollution, but have not consciously chosen which organisms will breed.

Antibiotic resistance – Antibiotics are chemicals that kill bacteria or inhibit their growth. Soon after the introduction of antibiotics in the 1940s, some bacteria developed resistance and were unaffected. Fortunately, other antibiotics were soon discovered.

When bacteria are exposed to an antibiotic, such as penicillin, most are killed. However, some bacteria have a mutation that gives them the ability to survive the antibiotic. They are able to produce an enzyme that breaks down penicillin. The resistant bacteria reproduce and pass on the gene for resistance to their offspring. This is an example of natural selection.

Pesticide resistance – Selection has also happened to insect pests that have been sprayed with insecticides. Insects susceptible to insecticides die, while resistant forms survive and increase in number. The same happens to weeds that are resistant to herbicides and fungal pathogens resistant to the fungicides used to control them.

Industrial melanism – Found in temperate regions of the northern hemisphere, there are two forms of the peppered moth – a speckled variety and a melanic (black) variety. Before the industrial revolution (19th century), populations of this species were nearly all speckled. A few melanic individuals appeared by mutation but because they were easily spotted and eaten by predatory birds, never survived to breed. Industrialisation led to an increase in the burning of coal with an increase in sulfur dioxide and soot in the environment. Lichens died and trees became covered in soot. Now the speckled variety was most conspicuous and the melanic best camouflaged. The proportion of the melanic form increased in populations around the big cities, such as Manchester in Britain. In rural areas it still remained rare. With Clean Air Acts and less industry, the speckled forms are again at a selective advantage and the numbers of melanics has decreased.

These examples of selection occur to change some aspect of a species; no new species have evolved.

Figure 12.2.2 Your view of these moths is very similar to that of the predatory birds that act as selective agents.

SUMMARY QUESTIONS

1 Define the term *natural selection*.

2 Explain the following terms: *overproduction*, *variation*, *competition*, *struggle for existence*, *differential survival* and *reproductive success*.

3 List the factors that limit the growth of populations of animals and plants.

4 a Explain the roles of humans in the three examples of natural selection in this topic.

  b State the agent of selection in each case.

KEY POINTS

1 There is variation between individuals of the same species.

2 There is a 'struggle for existence' due to competition, predation and disease.

3 Only well-adapted individuals survive to breed and pass on their genes to their offspring.

4 Antibiotic resistance in bacteria, industrial melanism and pesticide resistance among insect pests, plant pathogens and weeds, are examples of natural selection.

Species and their formation

At the end of this topic you should be able to:

• define the terms *species* and *speciation*

• use examples to describe how speciation occurs with and without physical separation by geographical barriers

• use Caribbean examples to discuss the extinction of species.

Figure 12.3.1 A mule is the result of a cross between a male donkey and a female horse. It cannot produce fertile offspring.

DID YOU KNOW?

The idea that small terrestrial animals can cross large bodies of ocean seems far fetched. But in the late 1990s a group of green iguanas was found washed up on a raft of trees on a beach in Anguilla. Scientists reckon that they came from Guadeloupe, following a severe storm, which had thrown the trees and iguanas into the sea.

The Caribbean is a biodiversity 'hot spot'. This means that there are many different habitats occupied by many different species. A **species** is a group of related organisms that are able to breed together and produce fertile offspring. In some species there appears to be very little variation, while in others, individuals may look as if they belong to different species. Sometimes two species look very alike and it takes an expert eye to tell them apart.

Species remain distinct because individuals from different species cannot breed together successfully. Some individuals of different species do attempt to breed together; some mate but produce embryos that do not develop; some produce sterile offspring like the mule (Figure 12.3.1). Mules have donkey and horse chromosomes, which cannot pair together during meiosis, so no gametes are produced.

DNA testing allows scientists to look at the genes of organisms and decide whether they are similar enough to be classed as the same species or not. It is extremely difficult to test whether different species of organisms can breed, as they can be rare, difficult or impossible to keep in captivity, or do not breed in captivity.

Formation of new species

Speciation is the formation of new species. There are two ways in which new species may arise: from geographical separation or from ecological or behavioural separation.

Geographical separation

Populations of the same species may become separated by geographical barriers, such as bodies of water or mountain ranges. Environmental conditions either side of the barrier are likely to be different, so over a period of time the populations become significantly different from each other through natural selection. They are not able to interbreed and produce fertile offspring; this means that they no longer belong to the same species.

Anolis lizards have colonised islands in the Caribbean from the mainland. They have adapted to conditions on different islands and diversified into different species. This **adaptive radiation** is a result of natural selection on different islands operating in different ways.

Ecological and behavioural separation

Speciation can occur within a population without there being any physical barriers. This may happen because some individuals occupy part of a habitat that the others do not and become adapted to the conditions there (Figure 12.3.2). It may also result from a change in behaviour. Female cichlid fish in Lake Victoria in Africa select males of a certain colour and this has resulted in the formation of new species. (See question 15 on the CD.)

Extinction

Organisms become extinct for a variety of reasons, for example:

• Habitat destruction – deforestation led to the extinction of the Cuban macaw during the 19th century; lack of water for breeding led to the extinction of the golden toad in Costa Rica in the 1980s.

• Hunting – hunting contributed to the extinction of the Caribbean monk seal in the mid 20th century; fishermen considered seals to be competitors and so killed large numbers of them from the time of Columbus onwards. The last reported sighting of a Caribbean monk seal was in 1952 on the Scranilla Bank between Jamaica and Honduras. It was officially declared extinct in 1996. Other species of monk seal are endangered (Figure 12.3.3).

• Predation – by introduced species, for example, the mongoose which probably ate the Antiguan owl to extinction; goats introduced to St Helena in the Atlantic destroyed about half the native species found nowhere else.

• Disease – a fungal infection is causing significant decreases in populations of many amphibian species; disease is affecting the mountain chicken in Dominica and Montserrat; the Christmas Island rat has become extinct as a result of disease.

• Competition – between indigenous and introduced species, this has wiped out many island species.

Extinction leads to a loss in biodiversity. But extinction is not all bad. When species become extinct, habitats become available for new species to fill.

Figure 12.3.2 The St Lucian parrot and the Dominican parrot are two Caribbean species that evolved from a mainland species that migrated to these islands.

KEY POINTS

1 A species is group of related organisms that are able to breed together and produce fertile offspring.

2 Speciation is the formation of new species.

3 Speciation can occur when populations are separated by a geographical barrier; speciation also occurs when there are ecological or behavioural differences between populations living in the same place at the same time.

4 Habitat loss, hunting, disease and competition are three reasons why species become extinct.

STUDY FOCUS

Extinction is a fact of life. There have been seven great extinctions over the history of the Earth; the mass extinction of the dinosaurs 65 million years ago being the most well-known.

SUMMARY QUESTIONS

1 Make revision notes on speciation using local examples. For example, find out which species of Anolis lizards live near you.

2 Mules are not fertile because meiosis cannot occur to produce gametes. Explain why meiosis does not occur in female or male mules (see 11.3 for help with this question).

3 Suggest an explanation for the evolution of different species of parrot in the Caribbean.

4 Make a list of the factors that can cause species to become extinct.

Figure 12.3.3 Two species of monk seal are endangered: the Mediterranean and this one – the Hawaiian monk seal.

Artificial selection

People have grown crops and kept animals for at least ten thousand years. Over that time farmers have kept seed from one year to another and have bred livestock. Across the world there are many **land races** – varieties of livestock and crop plants adapted to local conditions. **Artificial selection** is responsible for the considerable changes that have occurred to species, such as sheep, goats, cattle, wheat, rice and maize.

In artificial selection:

- humans choose a feature (or trait) to improve
- animals or plants showing this trait are chosen for breeding
- the offspring that show improvement in this trait are used to breed the next generation; the rest are culled, eaten or not used for breeding.

This process of **selective breeding** may continue for many generations. This is called *artificial* selection as it is humans who are the selective agent, not the environment as it is with *natural* selection. Humans decide which features to improve and which individuals survive to breed and pass on their alleles.

Land races have been replaced in many places by commercial varieties, such as modern high-yielding varieties of maize, wheat and rice. Scientists in research institutes have developed these.

Breeds of cattle adapted to local conditions

Figure 12.4.1 **a** East African Zebu cattle are resistant to ticks (parasitic animals) and eye diseases. They can survive on very small amounts of water.

b Nguni cattle from southern Africa (South Africa, Swaziland, Zululand and Mozambique) are tolerant of the heat, have thick pigmented skins and are less prone to ticks and diseases than other breeds. They have high calf production.

c Ankole cattle from Uganda can survive on poor quality food and limited quantities of water.

Crossing existing varieties to combine features produces many new varieties (Figure 12.4.1). Hope cattle in Jamaica were bred from high yielding Jersey cattle, Holsteins and Zebu cattle. This is known as **hybridisation** and is followed by a programme of selective breeding. For some features, the males do not show the feature but contribute important genes. Males are chosen by checking the performance of their daughters. Sperm is collected from superior males so that they can go on siring daughters long after they are dead.

Inbreeding can be a danger of selective breeding between closely related individuals. This may result in harmful recessive alleles being passed on to the descendants and a reduction in variation. Many breeds of dog suffer from the effects of inbreeding, e.g. failure of the hip joint to develop properly leading to lameness.

Many of our crop plants are genetically uniform, which is a big risk to food security. Varieties of wheat, for example, differ from each other by very few genes. This makes them susceptible to infection by plant pathogens with the possibility of wide scale famine (see 10.2).

Differences between natural and artificial selection

Artificial selection is similar to some forms of natural selection in that there is a change in one or more aspects of the species over time. Table 12.4.1 summarises the differences between them.

Table 12.4.1 Natural and artificial selection

Feature	Natural selection	Artificial selection
Selective agent	The total environment although one factor may be very important, e.g. predation	Humans, e.g. farmers, plant and animal breeders
Type of traits selected	Adaptations to the conditions in the environment at a particular time	Useful characteristics for humans, e.g. fast growth, high yield, docile temperament
Number of traits selected	All traits	One, or a few traits, e.g. disease resistance
Speed	Generally slower	Faster – improvement can occur in several generations

KEY POINTS

1 Artificial selection is carried out by humans to improve the performance of livestock and crop plants.

2 Humans choose features to improve, such as yield, and select individuals that show the feature as parents. The offspring are tested for improvement and those that exhibit the desired feature are used for breeding the next generation. Others are not used for breeding. This continues for many generations.

EXAM TIP

Do not confuse artificial selection with genetic engineering. Artificial selection involves selecting individuals and breeding them together; genetic engineering involves using laboratory procedures to transfer one (or a few) genes from one organism into the cells of another (see 12.5).

SUMMARY QUESTIONS

1 Define the term *artificial selection*.

2 State four features of livestock that breeders have improved.

3 Most of the cattle in a herd have horns. Some of the herd are hornless. The farmer decides to breed more hornless cattle. Explain how this could be achieved by selective breeding.

4 A plant breeder wants to improve the yield of pinto beans.

   a State three features of these bean plants that could be improved by selective breeding.

   b Describe the steps the breeder would follow to improve one of these features.

12.5 Genetic technology

LEARNING OUTCOMES

At the end of this topic you should be able to:

- define the terms *genetic engineering*, *gene therapy* and *genetic (DNA) testing*
- describe how genetic engineering is used to introduce new traits to organisms
- use examples to discuss the advantages and disadvantages of genetic engineering.

DNA is the genetic material of all organisms. We have exploited our knowledge of DNA to develop ways to modify species genetically, develop tests for genetic conditions, treat and cure genetic disorders, analyse evidence in forensics and compare the genes of different species to examine the relationships between them.

Genetic engineering involves moving genes from one organism to another. Genes can be transferred from one species to a completely different species, such as bacteria to plants, and from an individual of one species to another individual of the same species. This can be done by simply firing a gene into a cell, or the gene can be placed into a **vector** that 'carries' it into a cell. Examples of vectors are viruses and small loops of DNA known as **plasmids**. DNA produced by joining up DNA from two or more different organisms is called **recombinant DNA**. Organisms containing recombinant DNA have been **genetically modified** (GM).

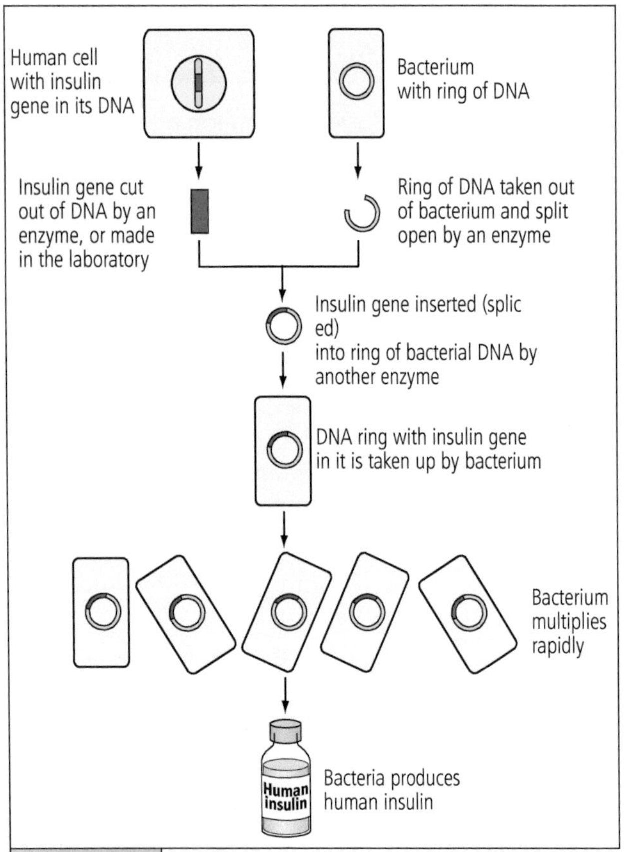

Figure 12.5.1 This process was carried out in the 1970s to make genetically-modified bacteria that could produce human insulin.

Insulin and other medicines

All diabetics used to be treated with insulin obtained from pigs and cattle, which were slaughtered for the meat trade. People were worried that people with diabetes were at risk of getting diseases from animals and that the demand for insulin would exceed supply. In the 1970s, scientists identified the gene that codes for insulin in humans. They transferred the piece of DNA responsible for coding insulin (gene) to bacteria. Figure 12.5.1 shows how this is done. Bacteria with recombinant DNA divide to produce many more bacteria. The insulin-producing bacteria are given the nutrients and conditions they need to produce human insulin. Human insulin, produced like this, became available in 1982.

Many other medicines and chemicals for research into human diseases are made using genetically modified bacteria. However, bacteria are not always very good at producing human proteins, so yeasts and certain mammalian cells are also modified in similar ways for industrial production of medicines and other substances.

Examples of these medicines are:

- a protein that prevents thrombin from forming blood clots (see 6.4)
- vaccines for influenza and for protection from cervical cancer
- factor 8 to treat haemophiliacs (see 11.7).

Gene therapy – genetic engineering is also used in **gene therapy**. This involves putting a dominant allele into human cells. Gene therapy has been used to treat forms of leukaemia and a disorder of the retina. There are medical trials in progress to use gene therapy to treat or cure other genetic disorders, such as cystic fibrosis.

Genetic modification – many crops are genetically modified. Examples of features that have been put into crops, such as soya, cotton, maize and tobacco, are:

- herbicide resistance, so weed killers can be used while the crop is growing
- pest resistance, so insect pests are killed when they eat the crop
- drought resistance, so crops will grow where there is little rainfall
- improved nutritional qualities, such as increasing the vitamin A content of rice to reduce the number of children with blindness.

Domesticated animals have also been genetically modified, for example sheep and goats that produce human proteins in their milk and a type of fish that grows very quickly.

Genetic testing – **gene (DNA) tests** can be carried out to identify mutations in people who think they might be carriers of genetic diseases. This can help reduce the number of children born with these diseases. Tests are also used to ensure that breeding between captive animals in zoos and wildlife parks does not lead to inbreeding. Cheetahs are an endangered species. About 10 000 years ago, cheetahs nearly became extinct. They went through a 'genetic bottleneck' as few survived to give rise to the cheetahs alive today. In zoos the DNA of a breeding pair of cheetahs is tested to ensure that they are not too genetically similar.

Social, ethical and ecological implications

Here are some of the implications of genetic technology:

- Chemicals available in tiny quantities can be produced in much larger quantities, for example, a GM goat can produce the same quantity of a human plasma protein in its milk in a year as can be collected from 90 000 blood donations.
- Medicines, e.g. insulin, can be produced in large quantities to meet the growing demand.
- Food crops have better resistance to pests, so not as many pesticides are used.
- Herbicide resistance could pass from crops to weeds so that they become 'superweeds' that farmers cannot control.
- GM microbes could escape from laboratories and factories and become dangerous.
- GM technology gives huge advantage to the companies that develop and market GM crops; this discriminates against small farmers who cannot afford them.
- Knowledge from genetic tests helps people make decisions about their life and their children's lives. It could also affect people's ability to have life or health insurance, if that information was disclosed.

KEY POINTS

1 Genetic engineering is the process of moving genetic material from one organism and putting it in another.

2 GM bacteria, yeasts and mammalian cells produce useful chemicals such as insulin.

3 GM crops and livestock with different features are available or in development.

4 There are social, ethical and ecological implications of genetic engineering.

5 Genetic (DNA) testing is used for identifying the mutant alleles for genetic disorders that run in families.

SUMMARY QUESTIONS

1 Define the following terms: *genetic engineering*, *vector* and *plasmid*.

2 Describe the roles of enzymes in genetic engineering.

3 Discuss the advantages and disadvantages of genetic engineering.

4 a What is the danger of breeding cheetahs from closely related individuals?

b Discuss the advantages and disadvantages of DNA testing for human genetic disorders such as sickle cell anaemia and Huntington's disorder.

SECTION 1: Multiple-choice questions

1 The best definition of a *species* is

  A   a group of closely related organisms

  B   organisms that interbreed to give fertile offspring

  C   organisms that live in the same habitat

  D   organisms that look alike

2 Which is *not* an example of continuous variation in humans?

  A   body mass

  B   foot length

  C   height

  D   blood group

3 Jamaican Hope cattle were developed by

  A   artificial selection

  B   environmental variation

  C   natural selection

  D   reproductive isolation

4 Transferring genes from bacteria into rice to improve its nutritional content is an example of

  A   gene mutation

  B   gene therapy

  C   genetic engineering

  D   genetic variation

5 In captive breeding programmes for endangered species, genetic variation is maintained by

  A   breeding between distantly related individuals

  B   hybridisation between species

  C   inbreeding between closely related individuals

  D   storing frozen embryos

6 Humans have changed the environment of many organisms. Which of the following is *not* an example of natural selection influenced by human activities?

  A   adaptive radiation of Anolis lizards

  B   antibiotic resistance of tuberculosis bacteria

  C   melanism in peppered moths

  D   insecticide resistance in mosquitoes

7 Which of the following may result in speciation?

  A   inbreeding

  B   codominance

  C   discontinuous variation

  D   geographical isolation

8 Human genetic disorders are often expressed in specific cells and tissues. Which of the following would *not* make a suitable target for gene therapy?

  A   epithelial cells in the airways

  B   muscle cells

  C   red blood cells

  D   liver cells

9 A species of bird feeds on seeds. A scientist measures the diameter of a large number of seeds eaten by this species. Over ten years the mean diameter of the seeds has increased. The beaks of these birds have also increased in size. Which of the following is responsible for this?

  A   artificial selection

  B   ecological isolation

  C   geographical isolation

  D   natural selection

10 Which of the following is a correct statement about gene mutation?

  A   It is the only form of new genetic variation

  B   It is always harmful

  C   It is very common

  D   It changes the number of chromosomes

11 A student was investigating variation in a species of *Ilex*. He measured the lengths of 30 leaves from one plant and recorded the results in millimetres:

60	60	64	65	65
82	82	83	83	84
65	67	71	73	75
87	88	89	90	93
75	77	77	77	79
93	93	95	100	108

a i Calculate the range of lengths by subtracting the shortest length from the longest length. *(1)*

ii Divide the range into classes, e.g. 60–69 mm, 70–79 mm, etc. Record how many leaves there are in each class. Use the results to draw a histogram to show the variation in the leaves. *(6)*

iii Explain why variation in length of leaves is an example of *continuous variation*. *(3)*

One variety of the peppered moth has pale, speckled wings. A second variety has black wings and is known as the melanic variety.

b A student crossed moths of the two varieties and all the offspring had speckled wings. When these moths were crossed with black-winged moths the offspring were of both varieties.

Use genetic diagrams to explain why:

i All the offspring of the first cross had speckled wings. *(4)*

ii Moths of both varieties were present in the offspring of the second cross. *(4)*

Equal numbers of both varieties were released into woodland made up of trees with bark covered in lichens making a pale coloured mottled background. After two weeks a moth trap was used to catch as many of these moths as possible.

The results are shown in the table.

Colour of moths	Number released	Number recaught
pale, speckled	100	82
black	100	36

c i Suggest an explanation for the results. *(3)*

ii Suggest the likely results if the same number of moths of the two varieties had been released in an area of woodland with high atmospheric concentrations of sulfur dioxide and soot. *(2)*

iii Explain why the melanic moth is not a different species from the speckled moth. *(2)*

Total 25 marks

12 There are four blood groups in the ABO system; they are A, B, AB and O.

a A couple who have blood groups A and B have four children. Each child has a different blood group.

Using the symbols, I^A, I^B and I^O, for the alleles of the blood group gene, draw a genetic diagram to show how this is possible. *(5)*

b The ABO blood group system is an example of dominance and codominance. Use the genotypes of the children to explain why this is so. *(5)*

c Explain why the ABO blood group system is an example of *discontinuous variation*. *(2)*

d State *three* ways in which genetic variation is produced among offspring. *(3)*

Total 15 marks

Further practice questions and examples can be found on the accompanying CD.

13.1 Paper 1

At the end of this topic, you should know how to:

• analyse multiple-choice questions looking for key words and key ideas.

STUDY FOCUS

Flowering plant reproduction is in Unit 9. It is quite difficult to remember the sequence of events that occur after pollination leading up to seed dispersal. Writing out the sequence as part of your revision notes helps with questions like this.

EXAM TIP

When you have decided which answer is the right one, ask yourself why the others are incorrect. In question 3, what would be the genotypes of the parents if each of the other answers was correct?

STUDY FOCUS

In question 3, write out the genetic diagram starting with the phenotypes of the parents and ending with the phenotypes of the children. If you draw a Punnett square to show all the possible genotypes of any children, you will see the probabilities.

Paper 1 consists of 60 multiple-choice questions. The Paper lasts for 75 minutes, which means you have 75 seconds to answer each question. That's not long if you need thinking time.

There is some advice in this section on how to answer multiple-choice questions using five topics from across the syllabus. There are many more multiple-choice questions in the Test yourself sections on the CD.

Multiple-choice questions (MCQs)

The MCQs in Paper 1 test your recall of knowledge and your skill at comprehension. Each question has four possible answers and you must choose one. In the examination you put your answers on a special answer sheet.

1 The following four processes occur within a carpel after pollination is complete.
   1 The zygote divides by mitosis.
   2 The male nucleus is released from the pollen tube and fuses with the female gamete.
   3 A pollen tube grows down the style to reach the micropyle.
   4 The male nucleus travels down the pollen tube.

In which sequence do these events occur?

	first → last			
A	1	2	3	4
B	2	4	1	3
C	3	4	2	1
D	2	1	3	4

Read the question very carefully and then look at the four answers. Before you make your choice, read the question again to be sure you have chosen the right answer. If you are not sure of the answer, put an asterisk (*) by the side of the question and come back to it later. When you are sure of the answer shade the appropriate space on the answer sheet. Do not shade more than one. If you change your mind make sure that you erase your first answer thoroughly.

2 Which of the following changes cause expiration (breathing out) to occur?

	Diaphragm muscle	Internal intercostal muscles	Volume of thorax	Pressure in thorax
A	contracts	contracts	decreases	increases
B	contracts	relaxes	increases	decreases
C	relaxes	relaxes	increases	decreases
D	relaxes	contracts	decreases	increases

Questions like this can be confusing because there is so much information to sift through. It is best to read the question first. The key word here is *expiration*. Next look at the column headings and try to remember what happens to these four items when you breathe out. Then look for the row that matches your answer.

3 Figure 13.1.1 shows the inheritance of albinism in a family.

The family is expecting their third child. What is the probability that this child will inherit albinism?

A 0 % (none)

B 25 % (1 in 4)

C 50 % (1 in 2)

D 100 % (all)

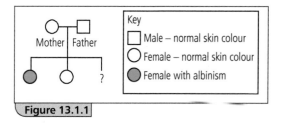

Figure 13.1.1

This question requires you to work out the genotypes of the parents. Do not guess; work it out logically by writing out a genetic diagram on the exam paper so you can be sure of the answer.

4 State the name of the blood vessel that transports oxygenated blood to the liver.

A coronary artery

B hepatic artery

C hepatic portal vein

D pulmonary artery

This is a straightforward question that tests your recall of the names of blood vessels. You do not have to work anything out here, but you do have to read very carefully. Three of these vessels are arteries, but only two carry oxygenated blood. Two of them have *hepatic* in their names. Only one is a vein. Two of them carry blood to the liver. All of these are clues to the right answer, if you do not know it immediately read the question again.

5 Which of the following is *not* a consequence of deforestation?

A Less transpiration may decrease rainfall.

B More rainwater runs off the land causing flooding.

C More nutrients are lost from the soil.

D There are more habitats for animals and plants.

Look very carefully for MCQs with 'not' in the question. Also look out for questions that have 'best' and 'most' in them. These are quite common and require careful reading.

If you are not 100% certain of an answer, then find what you think is the best answer based on what you can remember. After making your choice, you could look at the other answers and decide why you think that they are not correct.

EXAM TIP

This question shows how important it is to know the names of the blood vessels. See Unit 6 to revise these if you have forgotten them.

EXAM TIP

Do not look at the pattern of the answers on the answer sheet to predict an answer. Do not expect an equal number of each answer (A, B, C and D) and they do not follow a sequence (e.g. ABBA, ABCABC, etc.).

STUDY FOCUS

The answers to the questions here are:

1 C, 2 D, 3 B, 4 B, 5 D

183

Paper 2 lasts for 2 hours 10 minutes. Section A in Paper 2 consists of one structured data analysis question with a total of 25 marks and two structured questions for 15 marks each. The total mark for this section is 55. You should spend about 60–70 minutes on this section.

First of all read the whole of each question before you start writing any answers.

Bean seeds store starch and protein. During germination, enzymes are produced in the seeds to break down these stores.

Some students investigated the activity of amylase in the bean seeds by taking 120 seeds and dividing them into six batches, **A** to **F**. The seeds were soaked in water for 24 hours.

After 24 hours, the batches of seeds were placed on damp paper and kept warm.

After a further 24 hours, the seeds in batch **A** were ground up with a pestle and mortar and $45\,cm^3$ of distilled water. The water was filtered to make an extract containing enzymes in solution. $40\,cm^3$ of the extract was added to $40\,cm^3$ of a 1% starch solution. The mixture was placed in a water bath at $30\,°C$. Samples of $0.5\,cm^3$ were taken from this mixture at 30 second intervals and tested with $2\,cm^3$ iodine solution in test tubes.

This procedure was repeated with the other batches (**B** to **F**) at 24 hour intervals.

The students recorded how long it took for iodine solution to give a negative result. They calculated the relative enzyme activity as $1000/t$; t = time in seconds.

The students' results are in the table.

Germination time/days	Batch	Time taken for a negative result with iodine solution/seconds	Relative enzyme activity
1	A	870	1.15
2	B	210	4.76
3	C	240	4.17
4	D	420	2.38
5	E	930	
6	F	960	1.04

a State **two** variables that the students have kept constant.
(2 marks)

b i Calculate the relative enzyme activity for Batch **E**.
(1 mark)

   ii Draw a graph to show how enzyme activity varies with germination time. *(5 marks)*

c Name

   i the enzyme responsible for the breakdown of starch *(1 mark)*

   ii the product of the reaction. *(1 mark)*

d Describe what happens to the product of the reaction during germination of the seeds. *(3 marks)*

e Explain the changes in the activity of the enzyme during germination. *(4 marks)*

Next, the students took seeds that had soaked for two days and investigated the effect of temperature on the activity of the enzyme using the same procedure. The results are shown in the graph.

EXAM TIP

Tables of data can be difficult to understand. Read the column headings first. Then read what is in the left-hand column to find the independent variable, which in this case is germination time.

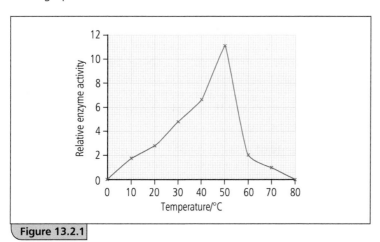

Figure 13.2.1

f Suggest why the students chose to make their enzyme extract using seeds that had been germinating for two days. *(1 mark)*

g i Describe the effect of temperature on the activity of the enzyme extract. *(3 marks)*

   ii Explain the results. *(4 marks)*

2 a Copy and complete the chemical equation for respiration.

$$C_6H_{12}O_6 + \_\_\_\_ \longrightarrow \_\_\_\_ + \_\_\_\_ + \text{energy released}$$
(3 marks)

b List the products of anaerobic respiration in plants and humans. *(3 marks)*

c Describe the structure of the gaseous exchange surface of a fish. *(2 marks)*

d Describe the features of gaseous exchange surfaces shown by the alveoli of the human lung. *(4 marks)*

e Describe briefly **three** effects of smoking on the body. *(3 marks)*

Answers to these questions are on the CD.

EXAM TIP

All the questions in this structured question are on the topic of respiration. There are two of this type of question on the paper and no choice – so you cannot neglect any topic in the syllabus during your revision.

Paper 2 Section B – essay questions

Section B in Paper 2 consists of three compulsory structured questions. Each question has a total of 15 marks. You should spend about 25–30 minutes on each question.

It is a good idea to look at the essay titles in Section B of Paper 2 before you start answering Section A. If you read through these questions you will start to think about what you want to include. You may need time to recall the information. Often your subconscious will work on a problem while you are doing something else. When you think of appropriate things to include, write them down.

When you are ready to start Section B, read through the questions again, highlighting the command word that usually starts each question and any key words in the rest of the question. Write a brief plan. This could be in the form of a spider diagram (see page 8) or a list of bullet points. When you have decided what you are going to write, begin writing in continuous prose. You may want to include a diagram in your answer, if so, make sure it is labelled and annotate it if that helps to convey your ideas.

There are plenty of essay questions in the book, but here are three more annotated with comments that show you the sort of things to write as you think about and plan your answers.

Essays

1 A girl touches a hot object and withdraws her hand very quickly.
   a   Describe how this action is coordinated.   *(6 marks)*
   b   Explain how the structure of the elbow joint allows the movement of the hand to occur easily.   *(5 marks)*
   c   Discuss the importance of locomotion for animals. *(4 marks)*

Remember the simple reflex from 8.4? You could make a simple flow chart diagram and use it in your answer to show how the response to the hot object is coordinated by the nervous system. You could also use a diagram in answering part 1b. You cannot answer the questions with diagrams alone, you should write prose as well.

2 a   Describe the changes that occur in the ovary and the uterus during the menstrual cycle.   *(6 marks)*
   b   Explain the roles of hormones in controlling the menstrual cycle.   *(5 marks)*
   c   Discuss the ways in which the spread of sexually transmitted infections (STIs) is controlled.   *(4 marks)*

Before you start writing part b make a list of the hormones that you know control the menstrual cycle. Now you have a plan for writing the answer since you can write about the roles of each hormone in turn.

3 The element carbon is in all biologically important compounds. Plants absorb carbon in the form of carbon dioxide and use it as a raw material in photosynthesis.

   a Outline the process of photosynthesis.   *(6 marks)*

   b Discuss how humans are dependent on the activities of plants.   *(5 marks)*

   c Explain how decomposers are involved in the recycling of carbon dioxide.   *(4 marks)*

4 a Explain why large multicellular animals need a transport system.   *(5 marks)*

   b Describe, in outline, the circulatory system of a human.
                                                                   (6 marks)

   c Explain the principles involved in controlling the spread of communicable diseases using vaccines.   *(4 marks)*

Here is some advice on writing your answers in Paper 2:

- Make sure that you write legibly so the examiner can read what you have written.

- Look at the mark allocation and the space available and write enough to answer the question and gain the marks available but not too much.

- While you are writing, keep looking back at the question and *stick to the point.*

- Use short sentences.

- Do not repeat yourself: do not say the same idea in two or more different ways.

- Always use the correct scientific terms; remember the words in your revision glossary.

- When you have finished, read your answer and *check it answers the question*.

Answers to these questions are on the CD.

Index

Index

Acknowledgements

The authors and publishers would like to thank the following for permission to reproduce photographs:

0.1.1 Jacques Langevin/Sygma/Corbis; **1.1.1** Richard Fosbery; **1.2.1** Stuart LaPlace; **1.2.2** Philippe Psaila/ Science Photo Library; **1.2.3** Richard Fosbery; **1.3.2** Laurence Wesson and John Luttick, James Allen's Girls' School; **1.5.2** iStockphoto; **1.5.4** Nigel Cattlin/Alamy; **1.6.1** Vilainecrevette/Alamy; **1.6.2** iStockphoto; **1.6.3** Richard Fosbery; **1.6.4** Dr Morley Read/Science Photo Library; **1.6.5** Merlin Tuttle/Science Photo Library; **1.6.6a** Dr Jeremy Burgess/Science Photo Library; **1.6.6b** Dr Jeremy Burgess/Science Photo Library; **1.6.6c** Power and Syred/Science Photo Library; **2.1.1** iStockphoto; **2.1.2** iStockphoto; **2.2.2** Getty Images/Kim Steele; **2.3.1** iStockphoto; **2.4.2** Getty Images/Bernhard Limberger; **2.5.1** iStockphoto; **2.5.2** iStockphoto; **2.6.1** iStockphoto; **2.6.2** Nigel Cattlin/Alamy; **2.6.3** iStockphoto; **3.1.1** Herve Conge, ISM/Science Photo Library; **3.1.4** Dr George Chapman/Visuals Unlimited, Inc.; **3.1.5** Dr Donald Fawcett/Visuals Unlimited, Inc.; **3.2.4** iStockphoto; **3.2.5** Wim van Egmond/Visuals Unlimited, Inc.; **3.3.2** Richard Fosbery; **3.3.5** Richard Fosbery; **3.4.1** Michael Abbey/Science Photo Library; **4.1.1** Richard Fosbery; **4.1.2** FLPA/Alamy; **4.1.3** Richard Fosbery; **4.1.4** BSIP SA/Alamy; **4.1.5** Gregory Dimijian/Science Photo Library; **4.2.1** Getty Images/Nigel Cattlin/Visuals Unlimited, Inc.; **4.3.1** iStockphoto; **4.3.2** Steve Gschmeissner/Science Photo Library; **4.3.3** Richard Fosbery; **4.3.5** Eye of Science/Science Photo Library; **4.4.2** iStockphoto; **4.5.1** Richard Fosbery; **4.5.3** iStockphoto; **4.5.4** Nigel Cattlin/Visuals Unlimited/Corbis; **4.5.5** Nigel Cattlin/Visuals Unlimited/Corbis; **4.5.6** Science Photo Library/Alamy; **5.1.1** Andrew Lambert Photography/Science Photo Library; **5.1.2** Richard Fosbery; **5.3.1** Carol & Mike Werner/Visuals Unlimited, Inc.; **5.5.1** Dr Richard Kessel & Dr Gene Shih, Visuals Unlimited/Science Photo Library; **5.6.1** Bob Krist/ Corbis; **5.7.1** Amit Bhargava/Corbis; **5.7.2** BSIP SA/Alamy; **5.7.3** Biophoto Associates/Science Photo Library; **5.8.1** Shutterstock; **5.8.2** Shutterstock; **5.8.3** Martyn F. Chillmaid/Science Photo Library; **5.8.4** Edward Kinsman/Science Photo Library; **5.8.5** Prof. David Hall/Science Photo Library; **5.9.1** Dr Jeremy Burgess/ Science Photo Library; **5.9.3** iStockphoto; **5.9.4** Dr Fred Hossler, Visuals Unlimited/Science Photo Library; **5.10.2** iStockphoto; **5.11.3** iStockphoto; **5.11.4** Medimage/Science Photo Library; **6.3.1** Richard Fosbery; **6.3.3** Richard Fosbery; **6.4.2** Biophoto Associates/Science Photo Library; **6.4.4** Science Photo Library/Alamy; **6.5.2** Caro/Alamy; **6.6.1** Ian Couchman, Cambridge International Examinations; **6.6.2** Getty/Ed Reschke; **6.6.3** Getty/Visuals Unlimited, Inc./Scientifica; **6.6.4** Power and Syred/Science Photo Library; **6.7.1** Science Photo Library; **6.7.3** Richard Fosbery; **6.7.4** Richard Fosbery; **6.8.2** Randy Moore, Visuals Unlimited/ Science Photo Library; **6.8.3** Dr Ken Wagner/Visuals Unlimited, Inc.; **6.8.4** Power And Syred/Science Photo Library; **6.8.5** Getty/Martin Harvey; **7.1.3** Eye of Science/Science Photo Library; **7.2.2** Richard Fosbery; **7.2.3** Richard Fosbery; **7.3.2** MedicImage/Alamy; **7.4.1** Nigel Cattlin/Science Photo Library; **7.4.2** Getty/ Mitsuaki Iwago; **7.5.1** Shutterstock; **8.1.3** iStockphoto; **8.1.5** Daniel Lamborn/Alamy; **8.1.6** Clouds Hill Imaging Ltd/Corbis; **8.1.7** Thierry Berrod, Mona Lisa Production/ Science Photo Library; **8.3.3** iStockphoto; **8.6.3** Shutterstock; **8.6.4** Richard Fosbery; **8.7.1** Wellcome Library, London; **8.8.4** AFP/Getty Images; **9.5.2** Richard Fosbery; **9.5.4** iStockphoto; **9.5.6** Jim W. Grace/Science Photo Library; **9.6.1** Tim Gainey/ Alamy; **9.6.3** EAG, Environmental Awareness Group (website: www.eagantigua.org); **9.6.4** Fotolia; **9.6.5** Fotolia; **9.6.6** Claude Nuridsany & Marie Perennou/Science Photo Library; **9.6.7** EAG, Environmental Awareness Group (website: www.eagantigua.org); **10.1.1** Fotolia; **10.1.2** iStockphoto; **10.2.1** Fotolia; **10.2.2** Fotolia; **10.3.1** Amanda Koster/Corbis; **10.3.2** Dr Hans Gelderblom, Visuals Unlimited/Science Photo Library; **11.1.2** James King-Holmes/ICRF/Science Photo Library; **11.1.4** iStockphoto; **11.2.1** Adrian Davies/Alamy; **11.2.2** Bill Barksdale/AGSTOCKUSA/Science Photo Library; **11.2.4** Shutterstock; **11.5.1** Solvin Zankl/Visuals Unlimited, Inc./Science Photo Library; **11.6.1** Visual & Written SL/Alamy; **11.6.3** Dr Robert Calentine/Visuals Unlimited, Inc.; **11.6.4** Francis Leroy, Biocosmos/Science Photo Library; **11.7.1** Science Photo Library; **12.1.1** Ian Shaw/Alamy; **12.2.2a** Bill Coster/Alamy; **12.2.2b** Bill Coster IN/ Alamy; **12.3.1** iStockphoto; **12.3.2a** Dave Watts/Alamy; **12.3.2b** Petra Wegner/Alamy; **12.3.3** Fotolia; **12.4.1a** iStockphoto; **12.4.1b** Shutterstock; **12.4.1c** iStockphoto. CD: Further questions, Unit 8, question 13 Laurence Wesson and John Luttick, James Allen's Girls' School.

Figure 7.3.1 has been adapted from *Heinemann Coordinated Science: Higher Biology* by R. Fosbery and J. McLean (Pearson 1996).

Every effort has been made to trace the copyright holders but if any have been inadvertently overlooked the publisher will be pleased to make the necessary arrangements at the first opportunity.

Thanks are also due to Clare van der Willigen for reviewing the answers for the CD.